Praise for Deep Reality

"This remarkable book is a fresh look at the connections between science and spirituality. Written in an easy-flowing conversational style, it dives deep into what authors Matzke and Tiller call 'Source Science.' Fully grasping the implications of their expansive view of reality will make your head spin. *Deep Reality* is not for the faint of heart or those with rigid heads, but it is heartily recommended for everyone else."

—Dean Radin, PhD

Chief Scientist, Institute of Noetic Sciences, and Distinguished Professor, California Institute of Integral Studies.

"Powerful, paradigm changing information that all scientists and those interested in the evolution of thought must read."

—Dr. Ervin Laszlo

author of Science and the Akashic Field

"*Deep Reality* is a fascinating and thought-provoking exploration of the nature of reality. The authors weave together science from a diverse array of disciplines to challenge many commonly held assumptions about consciousness, life/death, artificial intelligence, the power of thoughts, and beyond. It is this sort of open-minded discussion that will usher in a more comprehensive scientific framework than the reigning (and deeply flawed) materialist paradigm."

—Mark Gober

Author of *An End to Upside Down Thinking* and Board member at the Institute of Noetic Sciences

"Fascinating... Matzke and Tiller's *Deep Reality* is like a rich and splendid conversation with two learned friends probing quantum science and hyperdimensional space. Their sharing is like a devotional exercise weaving timeless truths with what we know about the science of quantum mechanics. It engages the mind and the heart, to the ultimate benefit of both."

—Nisha J. Manek, MD

Author, *Bridging Science and Spirit: The Genius of William A. Tiller's Physics and the Promise of Information Medicine*

"This book is an amazing, dynamic piece of work. Two inspired and unique minds came together to achieve something that transcends their individual work. Doug Matzke and William Tiller are both brilliant producers of information on science and human consciousness. In this book, they bring together the science behind how we, as individuals and collectively, live, love, and exist with each other in the Universe, emotionally, mentally, and spiritually.

Perhaps we are ready for this information and answers that might help us to be more responsible for ourselves and more forgiving of others; to begin healing ourselves and our world in a new way, and recognize the miracle that we already are!"

—Deborah Singleton

President, A Healing Place Enterprises

"*Deep Reality* takes readers on a highly educated and insightful exploration of the intersection between physics and metaphysics. The connections made in the conversations between Dr. William Tiller and Dr. Doug Matzke effortlessly ground metaphysics, while simultaneously expanding physics. The two become one, and expand beyond both. As someone who has lived my life trying to negotiate these realities, it is nice to be introduced to an integrated option!"

—Suzy Miller

Visionary speaker, author, telepathic communicator, multidimensional seer, and embodiment facilitator. Founder of the groundbreaking Awesomism Practitioner Process, the Journey Back to Love Series and Avatar Energetics.

Deep Reality

Deep Reality

Why Source Science May Be the Key to Understanding Human Potential

Doug Matzke, PhD and William A. Tiller, PhD

Waterside Productions

www.DeepRealityBook.com

Disclaimer: The contents of this book, such as text, graphics, images, and other material contained in the "Content" are for informational purposes only; the content is not intended to be a substitute for professional medical advice, diagnosis, or treatment. Always seek the guidance of your doctor or other qualified health professional with questions you may have regarding your health or a medical condition. Never disregard the advice of a medical professional, or delay in seeking it because of something you have read in this book. If you choose to rely on any information provided in *Deep Reality*, you do so solely at your own risk. Under no circumstances are the authors or the Tiller Institute responsible for the claims of third-party websites or educational providers.

Structural Editing by Eye Comb Editors (www.eyecombeditors.com)
Line Editing by Kenneth Kales (www.waterside.com)
Copy Editing by Ann Aubrey (www.annaubrey.com)
Illustrations and cover design by Ken Fraser (www.impactbookdesigns.com)

Printed in the United States of America

First Printing, 2020

ISBN-13: 978-1-949001-73-0 print edition
ISBN-13: 978-1-949001-74-7 ebook edition

Waterside Productions
2055 Oxford Ave
Cardiff, CA 92007
www.waterside.com

Dedication

This book is written in recognition and support of all the people who experience their divine gifts every day as part of their spiritual existence. You are not alone and are true leaders.

"I am more than my physical body.

Because I am more than my physical body, I deeply desire to experience that which is greater than the physical world.

Therefore, I deeply desire to expand, experience, know, use, control, and to understand such greater energies as will be beneficial to me and to those who follow me.

I also deeply desire the help, cooperation, assistance, and understanding of those individuals whose wisdom, development, and experience is greater than or equal to my own. I ask for their guidance, and their protection from any outside influence that might keep me from my stated desires."

— The Gateway Affirmation from The Monroe Institute

Table of Contents

List of Illustrations and Tables

Figures

Tables

Introduction

We live in a special time in history when scientists and physicists are learning more than ever before about the structure of the universe. This understanding can be broken into three domains: (1) the nature of the very small, using quantum laws; (2) the very large, using gravitational laws; and (3) the very intelligent, using informational laws. The convergence of these three big areas helps us to understand our universe and how we humans fit in. This is ultimately coming full circle to the ancient understanding of the shamans, sages, kahunas, and monks.

The goal of this book is to link the deep layer of reality to the sacredness of life. The book is written in a dialog style as a way to make this information more accessible. However, the conversations are not verbatim transcripts but rather are based on my recollections, materials shared, and other writings. Dr. Matzke is the primary author, having incorporated some contributions and perspectives of Dr. Tiller. We hope to give as close to a commonsense understanding of this complex topic as reasonably possible.

Many people have personal experiences and abilities not decipherable by traditional Western science, which we refer to as "psychoenergetic phenomena." Examples include precognitive dreams, telepathy, near-death experiences, spontaneous healing, and out-of-body journeys. Many researchers state that no scientific evidence supports the existence of these psychoenergetic phenomena, and some skeptics even resort to insulting those who lay claim to such evidence. Plenty of occurrences support the existence of such phenomena, especially for those who have experienced them, but a model is missing to describe these phenomena that are consistent with known physics. However, the field of physics has drastically changed over the past hundred years due to discoveries in information theory, quantum entanglement, quantum gravity, black holes, dark energy, and dark matter—discoveries that do actually support these phenomena—leading us to propose that physics and psychoenergetic phenomena do, in fact, share a common framework. We shall present specific research that connects the two.

Psychoenergetic phenomena and physics are connected by this simple guiding principle found on some t-shirts: "There is a reason for everything, and that reason is usually physics." Another related t-shirt slogan is: "Quantum Mechanics: The dreams stuff is made of." This story presents neither proof nor a how-to on these matters, but rather weaves elements of critical research into a cohesive "source science" model of how life fits into the universe. The primary purpose of source science is to explain the ordinary, though with some flexibility the unordinary can also be explained using advanced and widespread information physics concepts. Anyone, even a skeptic, who is intelligent, curious, and willing to learn about the latest intersection of this research with commonly accepted modern physics can find this book thought provoking and worthwhile.

Our joint collaboration is significant because we both have significant traditional credentials, plus Dr. Tiller brings decades of laboratory research in psi phenomena and Dr. Matzke brings the latest in information sciences, neural computing, and quantum computing. Together, we have something unique and interesting to say about models that could account for observed metaphysical behaviors documented in the laboratory and experienced in real life.

Part I: The Source Science Model

There are many names for the topics covered in this book, including consciousness studies,[1] psychoenergetics,[2] spirited science, and New Age physics.[3] We have chosen the name "source science" to emphasize the information connection between quantum physics and metaphysics.[4] It is virtually impossible to talk about this subject without including protophysics concepts ("proto" means "primitive" or "more fundamental than") because that is the primitive hyperdimensional domain beyond familiar time and space, which is occupied by quantum physics. The modern consciousness studies research has been around for more than twenty-five years and we extend that idea with "thoughts must be informational"—meaning that we believe that thoughts with attention and intention can be discussed more scientifically by using information science than merely as part of consciousness studies.[5]

Chapter 1: What Is Source Science?

The term "source" has a dual meaning that we believe intersects with:

1. All physical things (e.g., fields, matter, energy, spacetime, gravity, and the Big Bang)
2. All nonphysical things (e.g., quantum mechanics, thoughts, life force, prana, and chi)

Modern physics has concluded that even physical things such as particles are also quantum waves, so when we put quotes around "physical" it is to emphasize that interactions of physics dominate over things. For example, electrons and photons are both wave-like things that can interact. Thus, the distinction between physical and nonphysical is really not useful anymore, since all particles are really fundamentally quantum waves, which is the basis of all quantum physics. These quantum waves are the mathematical "dreams" that the universe is constructed from and is described in detail in this book.

Even "observable versus unobservable" is not useful, since much of modern physics tries to measure things that are extremely difficult to observe, such as neutrinos, the Higgs boson, dark matter, dark energy, and even spacetime perturbations (see the extensive Glossary for unfamiliar terms). Some particles, such as individual quarks, will never be directly observed, yet we know that quarks must exist. There are many other as-of-yet directly unobservable things, such as the actual quantum states, love, thoughts, and mind. Well-documented quantum behaviors suggest that certain nonphysical things, such as the mathematical formalism of quantum mechanics (i.e., quantum probability amplitudes and quantum bits), must exist as much as physical things exist. These quantum states cannot be directly observed and may only show up in the statistics of some measurement, so physicists tend to label such things as mathematical constructs, even though this neglects their physical existence and their effect on the physical world. In summary, modern understanding of quantum physics now realizes that the categories of physical and nonphysical are indistinguishable, as are the categories of observable and unobservable.

Source science is a theory of everything—whether physical, nonphysical, observable, or unobservable—based on the idea that everything is made of bits,[6] including physics, thoughts, and mind. Bits, the binary one or zero values used in computers, are not just mathematical or used only in computers, but are now also a part of traditional physics: One bit represents the smallest discrete increment of a black hole surface area. We propose that bits are actually quantum dimensions that form a universal quantum computer supporting all phenomena in the universe, both in physics and in metaphysics.[7] "Source science" is our name for this comprehensive model of the universe. It integrates the latest collective understanding about information and computing sciences, entropy, quantum computing, quantum physics, high-energy physics, black hole mechanics, neural networks, high-dimensional math, Law of Attraction, prana, chakras, and metaphysics.

Most of these deep topics are highly technical, with significant advances having been made in the past and current centuries. Unless they are a science channel junkie, the average person is unaware of these results or knowledgeable about what they mean to our collective understanding of the universe and our place in it. Our source science approach is a quantum bit physics-centric view versus the traditional energy-centric physics perspective. We present these ideas in an orderly fashion and describe how they are related.

Reductionists succeeded in understanding the rules of physics by dividing things into parts until they reached the quantum physics domain, where the rules completely changed. The traditionalists, including Einstein, did not like the results of quantum theory, so they ignored its profound existential meaning by thinking about it mostly mathematically (an attitude colloquially known as "shut up and compute"). The following three topics are the cornerstones of source science, and are discussed in detail in subsequent chapters: (1) Information is physical, not just mathematical; (2) Reality is hyperdimensional, beyond time and space; and (3) Thoughts are quantum things beyond the brain.

Information Is Physical, Not Just Mathematical

In 1961, the pioneer in thermodynamics of information processing and IBM Fellow Rolf Landauer first proposed that "information is physical," because any time information is erased or created there is a minimum energy per bit associated with that process.[8] For example, it takes energy to set a bit to a known value of one or zero, and subsequent erasure of that bit must be accounted for in order to satisfy the law of entropy (law of increasing disorder). Landauer's principle of this minimum energy was measured in 2012 and matched the theoretical value predicted in 1961.[9] This limit is so low compared to normal computer technology that it primarily influences computational theoreticians' thinking, more than anything else. Landauer's principle also sparked a revolution in computing and helped create fields such as reversible computing, which is directly related to quantum computing because, theoretically, computation can occur with minimal or no energy.

Similarly, black hole physicists now understand that quantum physics, information theory, entropy, and gravity must be unified to consistently define black holes. They have identified a "bit" as the smallest discrete change to a black hole, which leads to a change in the surface area of the black hole by approximately a Planck area.[10]

Max Planck is considered the father of quantum mechanics because he invented the Planck constant *h* to connect the energy *E* of a photon to its wavelength *v*, where $E=hv$. A "quantum" is the minimum discrete amount of any physical entity involved in an interaction. This means that the physical property can take on only certain discrete and countable values. The "quantum physics" name is derived from this discreteness property and the Planck constant shows up as the quantization constant in almost all aspects of quantum theory.

As all photons and particles approach a black hole event horizon, they are stretched and pulverized into their equivalent bits. In 1989, physicist John Wheeler described this phenomenon as "it from bit,"[11] since everything is derived from bits.[12] Just as matter is equivalent to energy (from Einstein's $E = mc^2$),[13] so bits also are equivalent to energy (from Landauer's $E = kT \ln 2$ per bit),[14] meaning bits have an effective mass. This unifies information theory (bits and data) with the rest of physics (physical "things"). The high-level takeaway of this is Landauer's principle: Information is physical.

Reality Is Hyperdimensional, Beyond Space and Time

Researchers have demonstrated that bits are physical, while quantum bits (qubits) and entangled bits (ebits) are also real and produce behaviors that no system of regular classical bits can exhibit.[15] Each qubit represents a discrete unit where the fundamental representation is a phase angle called "superposition of states," which forms a built-in probability that arises in quantum measurements. When two qubits are specially prepared, they form an ebit (entangled bit), which represents a discrete unit of "nonlocal" relationship called "entanglement." For example, when two qubits are connected in this manner, a change on one qubit instantly affects the other, no matter how far apart they are. Entanglement has been repeatedly demonstrated in the laboratory and is now considered a verified part of quantum theory. Both superposition and entanglement make the foundations of quantum mechanics fundamentally different than the foundations of classical physics.

In 1935, Einstein named this nonlocal behavior "spooky action at a distance"[16] because he believed it violated what he understood about relativity. Any math describing ebits requires a minimum of *four orthogonal dimensions for each ebit.* "Orthogonal dimensions" means all dimensions are oriented at ninety degrees with respect to the other dimensions, just like the X, Y, and Z dimensions are in our conventional 3D space. The concept of orthogonal dimensions is important since they define the dimensionality (D) of the space, which cannot be compressed or removed. And just like it is impossible to embed a 3D cube inside a 2D plane, so it is also impossible to embed a 4D ebit inside a 3D space—this is the root of the apparent ebit nonlocality. Any ebit is constructed of four tiny quantum dimensions, and based on my geometric algebra research,[17] these primitive building block dimensions (also known as "protodimensions") are actually bits that can combine to form more-complex structures. Later, we explore in more detail how these quantum dimensions that support entanglement are also real and not just mathematical abstractions.

For most people who think about a 3D world, imagining a one-gigabyte disk storage is relatively easy, since even most flash thumb drives have much larger capacity than that. For most of us, thinking of this virtual infinity of bits as tiny mutually orthogonal protodimensions is extremely difficult or nearly impossible. They do not fit in our 3D spacetime but rather form the substrate[18] and quantum operating system from which our spacetime is built. If our daily reality is a quilt made of square patches of the familiar four dimensions (length, width, height, and time), then quantum dimensions are the threads that make up those patches. These quantum dimensions also make up unexplained parts of our quilt, like empty space, black holes, and even the quantum mind. These protodimensions can be described using hyperdimensional mathematics, which leads to the unintuitive geometric properties of content-addressable spaces and space-like computational mechanisms. We discuss these topics in more detail in later chapters.

These protodimensional bits are a powerful concept because they form the basis of empty space, black holes, quantum computing speeds faster than current computing limits,[19] and the infrastructure of the quantum mind, to be explained in the next chapter. The term "bit physics"[20] refers to the protophysics layer defined by the mathematical intersection of these topics of bits, protodimensions, hyperdimensional math/physics, protospace, and prototime.[21]

Thoughts Are Quantum Things beyond the Brain

Thoughts are primarily information things, and given that information is physical, research shows that people's intentions can directly interact with and affect the physical world at the quantum level (see examples in next chapter).[22] Because many humans exhibit a variety of metaphysical phenomena that violate classical physics, some nonclassical mechanism must exist to explain them. The Law of Attraction (LOA) movement states that "thoughts are things,"[23] and this can be expanded to the idea that "thoughts are quantum things."[24] Just as quantum states are not directly observable,[25] so ebits and thoughts are not directly observable either. Still, we discuss how both quantum states and mental states can and do affect the physical world through information changes in probabilities, which show up as a changes in the order or disorder of the system (see examples in next chapter). Also, since research shows that thoughts can directly affect quantum states, they must be interconnected.[26] Just like many unintuitive quantum properties, many of the properties of mind are emergent, such as learning, meaning, insight, awareness, and consciousness.

Commentary Regarding Skeptics

Skeptics deem metaphysical phenomena to be impossible because those phenomena violate the critics' assumed classical Western physics electromagnetic energy model. Yet quantum information, entanglement, and quantum gravity mechanisms also violate those same electromagnetic assumptions, so they too represent known nonclassical solutions for these phenomena. The term "scientism"[27] can be assigned to strict orthodox researchers who insist that the scientific method can only be applied to classically measurable phenomena, which automatically excludes novel areas of scientific enquiry as de facto impossibilities. Although quantum science studies only phenomena that are statistically observable, those same inventive and carefully designed experiments can be, and have been, applied to source science phenomena, directly observable or not. The scientific method represents the "techniques for investigating phenomena, acquiring new knowledge, or correcting and integrating previous knowledge,"[28] and can be applied to source science topics, as long as these techniques are inventively expanded to include hard-to-measure and indeterminate phenomena, like many other areas of modern physics and psychology.

Chapter Summary

Modern physics has revealed a lack of true distinction between two aspects of science previously thought to be separate: physical and nonphysical. Source science is a theory that all things—including material, nonmaterial, and mental phenomena—are made of the bits of physics. People's thoughts are informational and can affect reality—source science explains how this is possible. Since information has an effective energy, it also has an effective mass, meaning "thoughts are things" or, more accurately, "thoughts are quantum things" since they appear to transcend space and time. Both metaphysical phenomena and quantum physics seem unobservable or in violation of classical physics, yet quantum physics is accepted while metaphysics is regarded as impossible, despite the fact that research supports the reality of metaphysics phenomena. This underscores why a source science model is long overdue.

Chapter 2: Thoughts on Thoughts

Thoughts and mind represent a big mystery in the fields of computer science and physics because generalized learning and even normal intelligence have not truly been reproduced by computer scientists or through use of physics principles.[1] Genius, savant intelligence, awareness, and metaphysics behaviors are even more baffling from a classical physics and computational perspective. These supernormal behaviors happen everywhere and are obviously real,[2] but no accepted classical scientific model exists that can account for them, so they are often dismissed out of hand. This chapter contains our list of requirements for a complete model of mind, which includes thoughts, thinking, attention, intention, knowing, and meaning. Later, we discuss these topics from an information perspective and also as topics distinct from the idea of consciousness.

Descartes Disproven: Thoughts Affect Reality

Dr. Tiller: René Descartes helped advance the scientific method in the early 1600s by proposing that science laws are a mechanistic framework that can be discerned using the experimental methods of observation and reason.[3] The Descartes assumption can be paraphrased as: "No human qualities of consciousness, intention, emotion, mind, or spirit can significantly influence a well-designed target experiment in physical reality."[4] This was a useful assumption in those early days to help distinguish the scientific method from old prejudices, teleological thinking, and theological beliefs.

Fast-forward now to modern times, where this underlying assumption is proven no longer to be true, due to the discovery of quantum principles and research results by me and many others. The Descartes assumption was just that—an *assumption*—and most of the classically minded people believed it to be fact.[5] But as you will see in my earlier work and in this book, we can still use the scientific method of observation and reason to study the effect of thought on the physical world and, thereby, effectively discard the Descartes assumption.

Dr. Matzke: To that point, I have always been intrigued by the class of mental behaviors that includes telepathy, remote reviewing, precognition, and psychokinesis, and why they are not explainable by standard classical physics mechanisms, especially the research by Robert Jahn.[6] I reviewed Jahn's work back in 1985.[7] Physics can be divided into two main areas: classical and quantum. "Classical physics" is the familiar, orthodox, traditional Newtonian physics we witness in our everyday lives, which has been expanded and revolutionized by relativity. "Quantum physics" deals with a new frontier of both accepted and baffling, unfamiliar science. It is clear from your research that certain behaviors of mind and thoughts cannot be comprehended by classical physics. Since thoughts can be classified as informational and perhaps computational,[8] any modern theory of physics that includes information and quantum computation then would be directly related to these topics.[9] Bill, can you describe your key research results regarding how thoughts can affect the physical world?

Dr. Tiller: You and I have the same long-term curiosity about these subjects. My research has focused on the key areas related to psychokinesis (PK), the ability of the mind to affect the physical world. My team uses a device to store intention, which we call an intention host device (IHD). My team meditated to imprint the IHD with an intention, and then I placed it in the experimental area where it continually broadcast that intention to the targets. It was a small, simple electronic device, no more complex than a garage door opener (Figure 1).

Figure 1. Intention Host Device (IHD)

My research used either direct intention or intention broadcasted from an imprinted IHD to influence inorganic, organic, living, and nonliving experimental targets. For more details on this experimental protocol, see later in this book and also see my previous papers, online whitepapers, and books.[10] Here is the classifications and summary of these four research areas:

- Inorganic, via IHD: change the pH of water up or down by one unit
- Organic, via IHD: significantly increase the reaction rate in a beaker of the liver enzyme alkaline phosphatase (ALP)
- Living, via IHD: significantly increase reproductive rate of living fruit fly larvae and, subsequently, the adult fly development time
- Nonliving, via direction intention: increase ion avalanche rate for sandwich-like gas discharge device

The main conclusion to be drawn from this research, and that of others, is that the Descartes assumption accepted in today's world—that thoughts do not affect physical reality—is *no longer valid* for both traditional science and medicine. Human intention *can* alter the properties of materials in our world, even if intricate research design is required to prove that fact. For example, my experiments to change the pH of water with intention (using the IHD) have produced results where the pH of water has changed by more than 1 pH unit either up or down, as shown in Figure 2 and Figure 3.

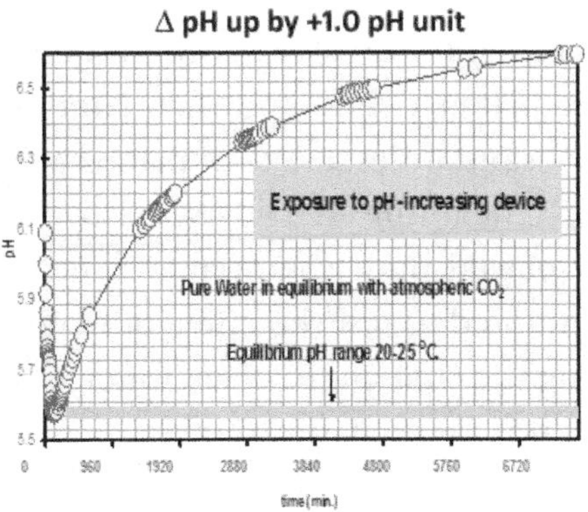

Figure 2. pH changes increasing

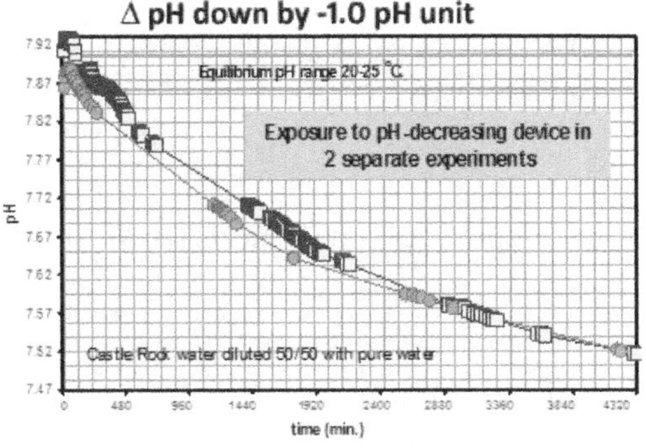

Figure 3. pH changes decreasing

My research suggests that the space around the IHD becomes conditioned or ordered due to intention, similar to how healers and deep meditators affect the space around their body. Reducing the disorder, or entropy, of the target space is an information effect having an effective energy. Our experiments have defined protocols to measure these effects. For these effects to occur, there must be some other mechanism at play besides the brain, since we showed that thought and intention directly affect the physical world via the IHD.

In a series of three replication experiments for the water pH research, we established control sites two to twenty miles away from each of the three primary sites, and then later established control sites up to six thousand miles away. All primary sites used the same equipment setup, including IHDs. We also used a disk-shaped ceramic magnet placed under the water reservoir at the primary sites because we wanted to test the effect of magnetism on the process of modulating the changes in pH of water. Our research design allowed us to test several related variables:

1) The effect of an imprinted IHD on the pH of water
2) The nonlocal effect of a primary site's IHD on a distant control site
3) The role, if any, of electromagnetic (EM) fields in nonlocal effects on pH
4) The role, if any, of the orientation of magnets in local effects on pH

Here are the results we reported from these experiments (Figure 4):

1) Demonstrated there was an effect at the main site using IHD compared to no IHD
2) The remote sites, which did not have IHDs, had the same pH tracking as the primary sites
3) With the south pole of the magnet pointing upward, pH changed with IHD present
4) With the north pole of the magnet pointing upward, no pH changes occurred with IHD present

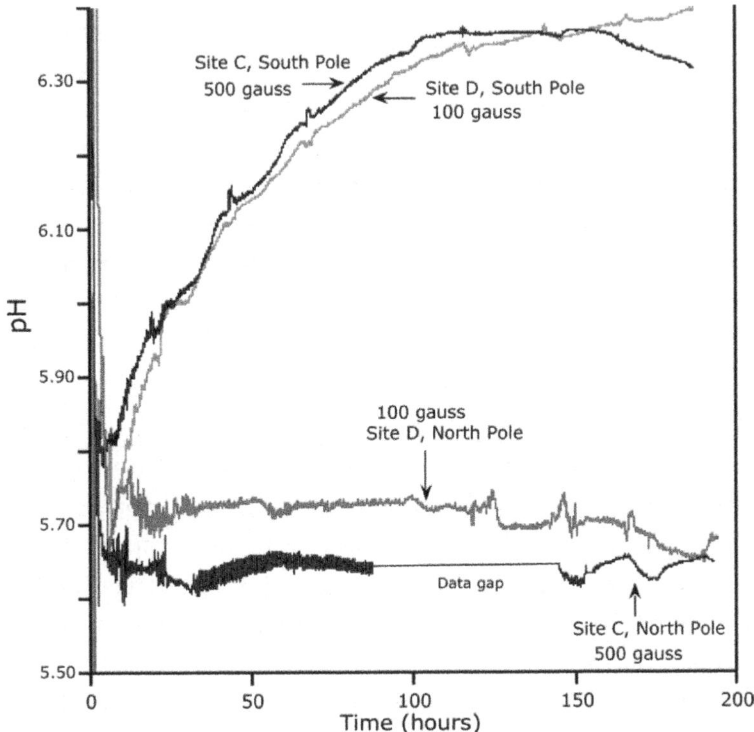

Figure 4. Changes in pH vs magnet orientation

Our results demonstrate that intention, broadcast via IHDs, can reach up to six thousand miles away, and that local magnetic fields can influence the effect of IHDs. We feel assured that intention effects do not utilize EM fields, because all of our experiments used Faraday cage shielding and yet demonstrated nonlocal affects. At least in the case of pH water experiments, my prediction is the IHD increases the conditioning of the space to be more ordered by tapping into supersymmetry properties. These ideas are supported by the differences we observed when magnetic fields were applied.

"Supersymmetry string theory" is an advanced physics theory that uses higher-dimensional math to unify forces and particles. Electromagnetic waves exist because of the symmetry between charge movement and magnetic flux movement, except that no magnetic particles (the monopole) exists equivalent to electrons.

From this theoretical perspective, gauge symmetry states of space, denoted as "SU(2)," can be formulated wherein both electric and magnetic monopoles—normally considered impossible—do coexist and function. From my theoretical perspective, the only way one could expect any change in pH to occur is if a laboratory space, conditioned by intention, accessed a gauge symmetry state of nature wherein magnetic monopoles exist and could be aligned to give the observed effect. This conditioning, or reduction in entropy, provides thermodynamic free energy to the space so that physical effects can be manifest.

Our research team now has an experimental procedure for quantitatively measuring the degree of elevation of this thermodynamic free-energy level above the normal state of space, denoted by "U(1)." We have also found that humans' acupuncture and meridian system can access the higher EM gauge SU(2) level. This is why bioelectromagnetism is very different than conventional electromagnetism.

The raises the real question: Is there a larger model that connects all varieties of PK experiments? This is an important question, since PK effects can influence so many different types of targets with apparently many different underlying mechanisms. Doug, you said you see a common pattern in these devices where thoughts affect the physical world?

Dr. Matzke: Historically, many of the researched PK devices were variations of random event generators (REGs). It is well understood that entropy, information theory, and quantum systems are directly related to probabilities, so changes in probabilities due to intention strongly suggests a connection between these topics. Here is an expanded list of some REG and PK devices reported over the years, including references:

1) Hardware REG: random event generators (pseudo random and truly random) used in casinos and cryptography[11]
2) REG PK using radioactive decay: Helmut Schmidt using electronic REG coin flips[12]

3) Random mechanical cascade: PEAR Labs Princeton University using mechanical random devices[13]
4) Electronic REG PK: PEAR Labs Princeton University using electronic random devices[14]
5) Global Consciousness Project REGs PK: electronic REGs distributed around the world[15]
6) Commercial REGs PK: Psyleron commercial company with standalone, online REG PKs[16]
7) Group meditation study: Dean Radin summary of group PK work[17]
8) Double-slit REG: Dean Radin of IONS created the first quantum double-slit PK device target[18]
9) Gas discharge device: created by Dr. Tiller where mind affects cascade rate of gas discharge[19]
10) IHD thought capture: created by Dr. Tiller's team to capture and rebroadcast intent to affect the world[20]
11) DNA folding and unfolding: HeartMath Institute showed DNA folding rate can be influenced[21]
12) Remote staring experiments: where people know attention is focused on them[22]
13) Copper wall experiment: Dr. Elmer Green of Menninger Institute showed how meditators could generate several hundred volts on isolated copper plates lining the walls in a room. This shows the mind can directly influence EM waves, as well as probabilities, but does not mean that thoughts are actually EM waves[23]
14) Psychoneuroimmunology: effect of the mind on the healing properties of the body (placebo, anchoring, reframing, biofeedback, hypnosis, etc.)[24]
15) Intercessory prayer: using double-blind control groups shows that prayer can affect people[25]
16) Maharishi Effect: Transcendental Meditation (TM) group to reduce crime rates in many cities over many years[26]
17) Humans affecting electronics: mental noise affecting or destroying electronic devices[27]

Since humans are intelligent, thoughts with intention represent an information system, but not necessarily from the brain. It is expected that injection of information as "order" would change the probabilities and subsequent entropy of the target system, thus acting like a net entropy change. For example, a change in the probabilities of a REG or PK device suggests that information was injected, representing a net change in the entropy of the system a la Landauer's principle. I believe this is the general mechanism by which the mind affects the physical world directly at the level of quantum probabilities, which generally shows up as either more order[28] or more noise, an increase in entropy. By definition, the entropy of a system is normally defined for a closed system, but due to quantum states the system appears to be open. If this is true, then the mind can affect the world without directly manipulating any of the standard four forces of classical physics (from weakest to strongest: gravity, weak nuclear force, electromagnetic force, and strong nuclear force). We also propose that qubits, ebits, and thought are related and can influence these four standard forces using quantum field theory ideas.

In addition to your PK research, Bill, interesting PK research was recently reported by PhD parapsychologist Dean Radin.[29] Radin built a PK target using a standard double-slit quantum interferometer device in which a photon can interfere with itself to form an interference wave pattern of peaks and valleys. This double-slit experiment is a standard physics experiment originally performed in 1801 that demonstrates the wave nature of particles.[30] In Radin's experiment, the measured interference pattern changed in a shielded device using intention compared to the baseline, as with your gas discharge device. Specifically, the wave amplitude interference varied with intention due to focus on the device during the trials. This research demonstrates a fundamental connection between mind, intention, and quantum mechanics. An interesting related experiment we propose would be to show that the mind can affect the entangled states by changing the Bell's statistics (the unexpected statistical correlation between entangled systems).

The mind's ability to directly affect quantum probability amplitudes means that change is possible to almost any physical system using quantum fields, which is the basis for quantum field theory (QFT), one of the most successful theories of all time and the basis of the Standard Model of physics where all primitive particles are excitations in their own particle-specific field (see more on QFT later in this chapter). This is an intriguing line of research, since if the mind appears to directly affect quantum probability amplitudes, then we could likely build an electronic equivalent to the brain using standard semiconductors designed to be a high-bit-rate PK device.[31] We would need to achieve a higher bit rate because most conventional PK devices have relatively low bit rates, and the human brain would have to support a high bit rate to control all its motor neurons.

I believe this high-bit-rate PK phenomenon is happening in the brain at some or all of the proposed neural interfaces:

- Tunneling affecting synapse firing[32]
- At the microtubule level[33]
- At the pyramidal cell motor neuron level[34]

Conventional artificial intelligence (AI) theory believes that the brain is a computer, but perhaps the brain is an antenna where the mind controls the probabilities of synapse firings. If this is true, then PK of the mind on the brain must be extremely robust and of a relatively high bit rate. Brain–mind models are not new, but with source science we are proposing a physics-compatible model of how this effect is possible without relying on the conventional four forces.[35]

A quantum computing-based model of the mind would be much smarter than any model using a classical computer brain and would have significant evolutionary survival benefits. This prediction might shed light on the long-term dilemma called "the myth of AI,"[36] in which each generation of scientists developing artificial intelligence (AI) predicts we will have intelligent machines within ten years or so.[37] Unfortunately, this prediction has been made repeatedly over the past sixty years[38] and still no general solution to machine intelligence and machine learning has emerged, despite an enormous performance lift thanks to semiconductor scaling during these sixty years, in which more than two billion times smaller and faster computing performance has been achieved.[39] Many false assumptions about mind and intelligence have been made, leading to mythical thinking that *Wired* author Kevin Kelly labels as "thinkism."[40] We believe real intelligence (RI) exhibited by humans is fundamentally different than AI, due to the reasons we discuss in this chapter.

Thoughts Are Quantum and Source-Complete

Artificial intelligence appears to have made significant progress in specific areas, such as playing chess,[41] playing Go,[42] translating languages,[43] and playing Jeopardy.[44] Some of these successes are built with neural network software using deep learning and big data sets.[45] In spite of these useful results, critics report that engineers are not sure how deep-learning neural networks really work and cannot understand or build true unbounded generalized intelligence, such as exhibited by any typical one – or two-year-old infant. For example, philosopher Hubert Dreyfus has led the criticism of AI for the past fifty years.[46] Based on our current level of understanding, we do not have to worry about "the singularity"[47] producing Skynet, from the *Terminator* movies, to take over the world.

As predicted by Moore's law, semiconductor scaling is already slowing down and will stop in the next ten years[48] due to the physical limits of computing (e.g., wires, high-κ dielectrics, and heat dissipation), quantum limits (tunneling), lithographic limits (extreme ultraviolet), and even price per transistor.[49] Even one of the Intel co-founders, Gordon Moore, who proposed "Moore's Law," has said, "No exponential is forever." In addition to the end of semiconductor scaling, there is still no clear algorithmic solution in hand for meaning, generalized learning, machine intelligence, and AI.

Deep-learning-based neural networks are all the rage right now and are useful in categorizing business problems. The applications of these technologies are useful, but the applications are quite narrow and specific, and require massive amounts of data to train the AI network.[50] This deep-learning process results in trained systems still without any real meaning—even human babies demonstrate this. The AI might recognize the image of a dog but does not know what a dog is. Also, the current capabilities of quantum computers will not replace the classical computers that run our corporate or commercial infrastructure any time in the foreseeable future, if at all, because current quantum computers have no long-term memory.[51] We believe that the failure of generalized AI is due to the assumption that the mind is a classical computation based on the brain, while source science assumes that our mind is most likely based on hyperdimensional quantum mechanisms.[52] We distinguish the real intelligence (RI) and meaning exhibited by humans as fundamentally different than artificial intelligence (AI) and its classical assumptions. What are your thoughts on this, Bill?

Dr. Tiller: People sleep, dream, share dreams, meditate, intuit, exhibit genius, report out-of-body trips, channel, and experience near-death phenomena, all of which are processes in which the mind significantly changes its connection with the brain. I know telepathic people who can reliably read other people's minds and apply this ability in business settings.[53] Remote viewers can access information at remote distances with no traditional communication except thoughts.[54] This remote-viewing ability was heavily used during the Cold War by the US government to spy on the Russians.[55] Using only classical information processes, these mental phenomena are as mysterious to explain as PK, so a more fundamental and powerful information technology is at work here. Many of these experiences are apparently nonlocal or faster-than-light, just like entangled quantum systems.

Aside from the brain not being a computer, the other major requirement for any new model of the mind is the ability to perform out-of-time behaviors. For example, precognitive remote viewing experiments were successfully performed where the targets were selected the day following the experiment. Here is a list of the key precognitive research studies:

1. Precognitive dreams: people dream about events before they happen[56]
2. Precognitive remote viewing: target is selected more than twenty-four hours after the experiment and result is performed[57]
3. Presentiment: Galvanic skin response (GSR) and electromyography (EMG) measure changes in the body before selection of highly emotional pictures[58]
4. Global Consciousness Project: REG PK devices change statistics before significant world events[59]
5. Retrocausation: ability to tap into future knowing to change your current decisions[60]

Psychokinesis and precognitive research results require some information mechanism that works outside of normal spacetime. We both know that any classical spacetime-based solution just will not meet these requirements. Doug, do you believe that ebits formed from bit dimensions can support these behaviors?

Dr. Matzke: As we reasoned earlier—"information is physical" and "it from bit"—the tiny bit dimensions of quantum computing must exist and must be physical. Let me invoke Occam's razor—that the simplest solution is the most likely[61]—and state that nothing new need be invented to explain thoughts and metaphysical phenomena; just apply the powerful bit dimensions to describe mind and thoughts. These bit dimensions are more fundamental than are our classical, metrics-dominated space, time, matter, energy fields, and gravity-based universe that likely gave rise to the Big Bang that created it. I refer to this event as the "Bit Bang"[62] because of the required low entropy state of this event. These quantum bit dimensions are not only outside of space and time, but we propose they form the topological and computational building blocks that create space, time, and all quantum states.[63]

Modern computability theory includes the concept of a Universal Turing Machine, which uses a system of rules, states, and transitions to form an automaton rather than a real machine. Alan Turing defined this abstract device in 1936, which became a benchmark for computational completeness, dubbed "Turing-complete." There is also an equivalent Quantum Turing Machine (QTM) that captures all of the power of quantum computations. In a like manner, I have established four computational completeness properties for our source science model in order for a system to be source-complete:

1. Turing-complete: must be universal for computations
2. Quantum computing-complete: the quantum version of von Neumann architecture that includes the Quantum Turing Machine
3. Shor-complete: must be able to provide the computational speed-up of Shor's algorithm
4. Ebit-complete: must be able to provide entangled states as ebits, typically by producing Bell's statistics

From a quantum computing perspective, bit dimensions form a Turing-complete classical computational system[64] (see my quantum computing dissertation from 2002).[65] In addition, Shor's algorithm proves that marshalling this virtual infinity of orthogonal bit dimensions gives significant computational leverage over classical computers.[66] My label for this Shor quantum computational speed-up requirement is "Shor-complete." Likewise, the topological nature of orthogonal bit dimensions is both *space-like* distributed concurrency of states, referred to as entanglement, that exceed the *time-like* causal behaviors of classical computation. My label for supporting the space-like entanglement properties is "ebit-complete."[67]

Turing-complete solutions are an important computational requirement for any model of the mind, and other models fall short here. For example, purely holographic models of information used in 3D imaging are not necessarily Turing-complete or Shor-complete. Holographic models of the universe or the mind are just metaphors for the actual entity. The mathematics of holograms is simply a way to represent higher-dimensional spaces by mapping them into fewer dimensions.[68] It is not possible to actually reduce the dimensionality of the universe, because hyperdimensional spaces with orthogonal dimensions must exist to support bits, qubits, and ebits—their dimensionality cannot be arbitrarily reduced or even simulated efficiently (due to anisotropic behaviors) in fewer dimensions.[69]

Another important requirement for computational systems is representing both: (1) Data states: "The wall is white," and (2) Changes of state: "The wall is being painted from white to red." A person, place, or thing can be thought of as data, while an action can be thought of as a program that changes state. John von Neumann helped to develop early computers by creating his von Neumann architecture, wherein both data and programs could be stored in the same memory, thus allowing the central processing unit (CPU) to run programs that could modify themselves.[70] This class of machine is Turing-complete and requires that any computational model of mind must support a high-dimensional quantum version of the von Neumann architecture, where thoughts can act as a state, an operator, or both.

This idea can be stated simply as, "All mental states are programs." Since data are space dominant and programs are change dominant, I call this "unified quantum state space quantum computing-complete" when all states are enmeshed in balance as "verbnouns." We show later that in geometric algebra, all states are also operators, meaning geometric algebra (GALG) is naturally verbnoun balanced, just as relativity represents a perfect fusion of proto-spacetime concepts. It is easy to prove there exist GALG expressions where $\mathbf{X} * \mathbf{X} = \mathbf{X} + \mathbf{X} = -\mathbf{X}$, which means they can act on themselves the same as either an operator (*) or as concurrency (+).

In summary, "source-complete" is defined as the aggregate of these four types of informational completeness: Turing, quantum computing, Shor, and ebit. From this hyperdimensional perspective, bit dimensions represent a fundamental information framework that supports all of physics, and their power is such that they exist outside of, and form the fabric of, spacetime and black holes.

Our choice of words is critical when discussing source science ideas. In 2002, author Lynne McTaggart wrote her great book *The Field,* in which she talks about many source science concepts.[71] Though her writing is excellent, the term "field," used both in her book and even by quantum physicists, is misleading since it assumes the representation is automatically embedded in spacetime. However, the ideas of fields, waves, frequencies, and vibratory modes appear to be important in many metrics of physics. Bill, there are many unconscious meanings and uses of the term "field" present in both classical and quantum physics, so would you talk about them and how they are related to frequency?

Dr. Tiller: The history of physics includes our development of theories for particles and waves, as well as how fields exert action at a distance. Early physicists in the nineteenth century struggled with understanding how gravity and electromagnetism could exert action at a distance, until they invented the concept of fields.[72]

Here are some of the known uses of the terms "waves" and "fields." We are being very specific here because, as you mentioned, Doug, many of these uses assume an embedding in spacetime. But that assumption is a slippery slope to go down because we first need to disentangle those ideas and talk about representations of quantum states outside of spacetime. As we progress down this list, the representation becomes less like a field and more like pure mathematical quantum states, which are not fields or waves at all, since they exist without energy, space, time, gravity, or electromagnetism. For example, the following definitions can help debunk assumptions about fields and waves:

- Classical waves: propagation of energy through matter at a speed that varies with the carrying medium and drops off with distance.

- Electromagnetic waves: classical EM waves that have a value at all points in spacetime, traveling at speeds that vary with the index of refraction of the carrying medium and amplitude that drops off with distance.
- Photons: smallest discrete quanta of EM energy that act as both particle and wave. Since photons are bosons that have no rest mass, they travel at the speed of light.
- Matter waves: particles with mass that also act like waves. Electrons are the smallest discrete quanta of electric charge. Electrons are fermions, which mean they have a mass when at rest (rest mass) and thus travel slower than the speed of light.
- Gravity waves: ripples in spacetime itself traveling at the speed of light with amplitude that drops off with distance.
- Quantum probability amplitude: the likelihood of a given quantum state at each point in spacetime, responsible for superposition and tunneling and all quantum phenomena, which does not drop off with distance and is not directly observable like other fields.
- Ebit locality: despite sometimes being labeled as a field or wave, it is neither and exists outside of spacetime, supporting instantaneous entanglement constraint between two items, independent of their distance or measurement timing.[73] Ebits states are probability amplitudes, so are also neither fields nor waves.
- Prana or aura: sometimes called a biofield despite being neither biological nor a field, the life force that either intersects with a physical body "suit"[74] (even when the body moves)[75] or exists on its own.[76] Prana itself is also neither a field nor a wave.
- Thought or intention: sometimes called fields despite existing outside of spacetime, access information near, far, past, present, and future[77] and affect the physical world. Thoughts themselves are also neither fields nor waves.

This list illustrates that "waves" come in many forms, sometimes even as fields. Fields also come in many forms, sometimes even as waves.[78] Finally, quantum probability amplitudes are not fields or waves at all, since there is no energy, space, time, gravity, or electromagnetism. The most telling reason why quantum states are not a field is that quantum states do not drop off with distance, because they are not embedded in spacetime.

The essence of quantum systems is quantum states, which are pure probability amplitudes, where its value squared is a probability. Einstein did not like these probabilistic underpinnings of QM and he stated, "God does not play dice with the universe." In 1925, Erwin Schrodinger defined the Schrodinger wave equation that describes how probability amplitude values change at spacetime coordinates, but these mathematical states are not directly observable fields. Likewise, QFT models successfully predict how perturbations of quantum fields translate to quantum particles and forces.[79] Yet any attempt to observe the quantum probabilities acts like a measurement[80] and changes the quantum state due to decoherence.[81] Ebits cannot be mapped using the Schrodinger wave equation, because entangled ebit states do not have localized spacetime properties. Prana and thoughts are more like quantum states than like any classical fields. Now that we have clarified the various uses and misuses of the term "field," could you explain your thoughts about frequencies and metrics?

Dr. Matzke: Physicists know that spacetime is the dominant coordinate system for classical metrics. Most physicists assume that all disciplines of physics, including quantum computing and quantum field theory, are embedded in relativistic spacetime. But this cannot be true for entangled quantum systems that operate outside of spacetime. Each ebit is constructed from its own private four dimensions, which intersect with our three dimensions and thus appear nonlocal. The term "nonlocal"[82] is really a language mistake, since it is applying a term in the wrong context—applying a spacetime word for a process *outside* of spacetime. Describing entanglement as faster-than-light[83] or instantaneous is a similar semantic error.

The highly successful "quantum field theory" name requires a comment since it combines both the terms "quantum" and "field." QFT assumes that all of spacetime is constructed of twenty-five (depending how you count) overlapping quantum fields, one to support each of the primitive particles, including quarks, electrons, neutrinos, antiparticles, and bosons. These fields are described as a grid of little, coupled spring oscillators, where simple quantized excitations of each field cause a wave to propagate in that field. For example, a photon is a quantized excitation of the quantum electromagnetic field. But the current QFT model does not account for ebits, gravity, dark matter, and dark energy, which most physicists conjecture may ultimately be additional parts of a hypothetical "unified field." We propose later that these unaccounted primitives are four dimensional and do not map into a 3D spacetime field model. The field-like property assumes they can be embedded in spacetime, but higher and hyperdimensional states do not fit inside a 3D construct and so cannot really be labeled as fields.

R-Space, Deltrons, and Monopoles to H-Space, Bits, and Spinors

Dr. Matzke: Let us look at different kinds of metrics in order to differentiate between metric and nonmetric environments. Under relativity conditions, such as velocities approaching the speed of light, time slows down and distance becomes shorter by the same relative amount. This means that the velocity of light would appear the same in all local inertial frames, which is the formal mathematical language used with regard to relativity. Wavelength (calculated by distance between successive crests of a wave, or one wave) and frequency (calculated by cycles per unit time) are both dependent on space and time measures. These metrics are only defined inside a spacetime, a metric environment, and therefore any hyperdimensional space composed of bit dimensions might not contain normal metrics of distance, time, velocity, frequency, wavelength, or any other quantity derived from these metrics. This represents a nonmetric space.

Another important linguistic matter is that I prefer the term "prana" (the Hindu term for life force) over the Western term "subtle energy." In physics, we do not call energy as subtle mass, so likewise we should not call prana as subtle energy.[84] Quantum states and prana are sophisticated information systems, and in the correct context, represent an effective energy, though they should not be labeled as quasi-energy themselves. Since language affects our thinking, we must clean up our language and think more clearly.

Qubits and ebits are both formed from bit dimensions. As topological structures outside of spacetime, they do not vibrate in the sense of moving through space over a time period but, rather, switch back and forth between states or modes of being. A rope with a loop, knot, or coil is an example of an object having complexity modes without using frequency—this idea is used heavily in string theory and knot theory. Therefore, although "amplitude" is often a term related to waves, quantum probability amplitudes do not have a frequency, although the corresponding states can be mapped into a frequency. Again, to help clean up our language, when I discuss mind and prana, I use the term "vibratory modes," since no frequencies exist in the nonmetric environment. Law of Attraction literature also prefers the term "vibrations."

This difference between a metric space and a nonmetric one is an important concept, since the language we use impacts our thought processes and vice versa. The concepts of *distance* and *time* and any derived metrics do not apply to nonmetric spaces.

Bill, you have used the term "reciprocal space (R-space)"[85] (with reciprocal coordinates: 1/x, 1/y, 1/z, 1/t) to distinguish your nonmetric, frequency-based space from normal metric spacetime. My analogous nonmetric model, which I call "hyperdimensional space (H-space)," is the bit dimensional model that supports the informational source-complete properties of being Turing-complete (computationally complete), quantum computing-complete (verbnoun balanced enmeshment), Shor-complete (quantum algorithmic speedup), and ebit-complete (entanglement).

As we gather requirements for nonmetric spaces, it appears that you and I have a difference of opinion about R-space versus H-space. My biggest concern with R-space is that it is based on frequency domain: I believe a space primarily based on any type of frequency cannot be informationally source – complete—not Turing-, Shor-, quantum computing-, or ebit-complete—for the same reasons that holograms are not computationally complete, because they represent a transformation but not an arbitrary Turing computation. I approach nonmetric H-space requirements as informational and computational, from my perspective as an engineer working on quantum computations, whereas your nonmetric R-Space requirements are based on your experiences and perspective as a material scientist. Can you please share more about your ideas?

Dr. Tiller: My proposed reciprocal space (R-space) model was designed to solve the problem of nonlocality and magnetic anomalies in our IHD experiments, as demonstrated by coupled systems and states in all our experiments. I intuited the same need as you did for a nonmetric space, where distance is not an obstacle and thought can directly affect the physical world. When I developed this model more than thirty years ago, scientists did not understand quantum computing, black hole mechanics, or entanglement, as they do today. With that said, here is a summary of my model, with more details available out in my previous publications.[86]

During the IHD pH experiments, I proposed that very tiny magnetic monopoles (a hypothetical elementary particle that is an isolated magnet with only one magnetic pole) were oriented in an organized fashion that could affect and link aspects of the experiments, specifically applicable to the water pH experiments. I proposed that R-space is the medium through which nonlocal interactions (demonstrated in our experiments) exist between the intention captured in IHDs and remote targets. I also proposed a new particle, the deltron,[87] that connects direct-space with reciprocal-space.

Most of our experiments in the laboratory used electromagnetic-insulating Faraday cages to isolate the target from stray electromagnetic (EM) effects. We observed that while the space inside the Faraday cage was apparently isolated from EM effects, intention still had an effect, suggesting that the space inside the Faraday cage was not isolated from an entangled bit dimension effect, captured in the IHD. In other words, intention effects or bit dimension effects are not electromagnetic. When I refer to a "new physics" in my publications, I am identifying the requirements of a model for this kind of coupling. These are the requirements needed to show how the mind can affect quantum-based psychokinesis (PK) apparatuses, including Dean Radin's quantum double-slit interferometer changes and quantum tunneling threshold changes in my gas discharge device.

Thoughts must be able to affect physics at a very fundamental level to directly affect quantum probabilities, support the magnetic interaction we detected for an IHD targeting water pH, orient the electromagnetic properties of space (monopole orientation), and accelerate growth of a life form (in fruit fly experiments)—increasing the order of a system at a fundamental quantum level is the common theme between these all. I have focused on magnetic monopoles and deltrons in R-space as the possible solution, yet you have proposed a quantum model that could also directly solve this.

Dr. Matzke: Right. You and I are trying to define similar models that incorporate explanations for these experimental results in multiple domains, based on physics principles. But we are using slightly different language to discuss the same requirements and solutions. My approach assumes that quantum states are the universal fundamental mechanism and, thus, nothing new has to be invented. These quantum states are built on bit dimensions, which is the mathematical foundation of all physics. When I see your descriptions and images of your deltrons, they appear to portray the same nonlocal properties as entangled bits—they appear to be analogs in our respective models (see Figure 5 and Figure 6). We are using different terms to describe the same phenomenon.

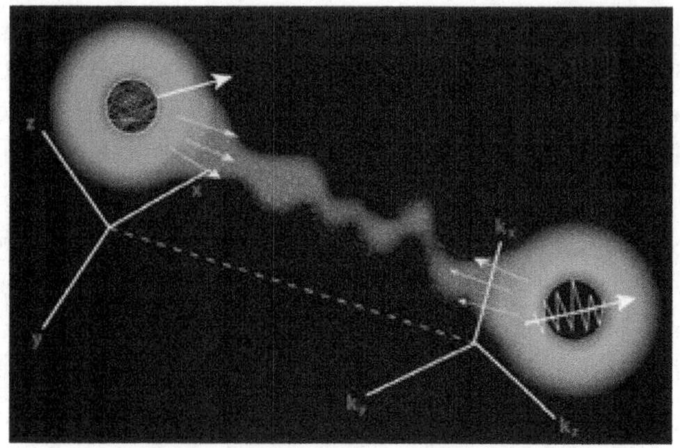

Figure 5. Deltron agency

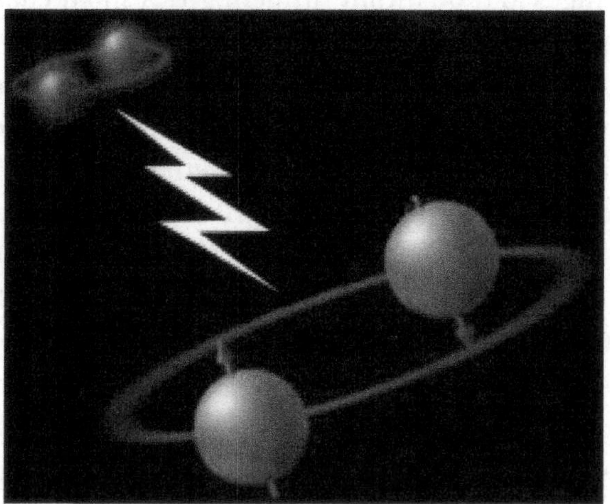

Figure 6. Ebit agency

The hyperdimensional quantum approach is important because it naturally supports maximally concurrent quantum states. This is important, because when concurrent states are translated into time, they generate frequencies similar to how computer programs generate time series data. Quantum states are little concurrent programs, each unfolding into time as a different frequency. Understanding the translation from concurrent states to time-based frequencies is part of the coupling between metric and nonmetric spaces.

We know from the Big Bang research that quantum states most likely existed before the universe started, so most likely spacetime itself emerges from the source quantum states, and therefore it is reasonable to assume that frequencies and wavelengths also emerge from quantum states, as do quantum field wavelengths, as defined by the Schrodinger wave equation. Frequencies and wavelengths arise from quantum states, just like probabilities, due to the fundamental nature of bit dimensions. Based on this premise that H-spaces contain the protofrequency and nonlocality mechanisms, H-space is most likely a superset of R-space properties. I talk in more detail about this in a later chapter.

Dr. Tiller: That is an interesting idea, that spacetime, frequency, wavelengths, and therefore all spacetime fields occur as a result of concurrent states. The double-slit interferometer experiment proved the wave nature of particles by showing that the quantum state (passing through slit 1) of a quantum particle can interfere with the same state (passing through slit 2) of that same particle. Even though this quantum explanation sounds counterintuitive, this is an example of quantum weirdness due to concurrent states. This seems even weirder since humans can directly interact with these states.

I also performed a prism experiment, with children as participants, that gives more insight into how concurrent quantum states have unexpected results. Some children are good at this experiment because they have not forgotten how to see auras. My research shows that when a conventional light source is split in a prism, in addition to the classical Newtonian bent-down spectrum, there appears to be an inverse, bent-up, mirror-like spectrum. We discovered this effect by creating an electric field through the prism using a large voltage source and recording the observations of children. They looked through a rotatable sight into the prism, rotating it to the angles at which they observed the mirror spectrum (Figure 7 and Figure 8). Here, we discuss the physics first, followed by the experimental details.

The term "speed of light" usually refers to the maximum speed of light through empty space, rather than through any material, such as air, water, or glass. Normally, when light hits the smooth surface of a transparent material, such as water or glass, part of that light is reflected off of the material and the rest is refracted into the material. This refraction is due to a change in the velocity of that light upon entering the medium. Every type of material has a different index of refraction, meaning each material slows and bends light to a different degree. In addition, different colors of light all entering the same medium slow down and bend by different amounts. Such slowing down in a glass prism reveals the colorful rainbow spectrum, a phenomenon first described by Newton.[88]

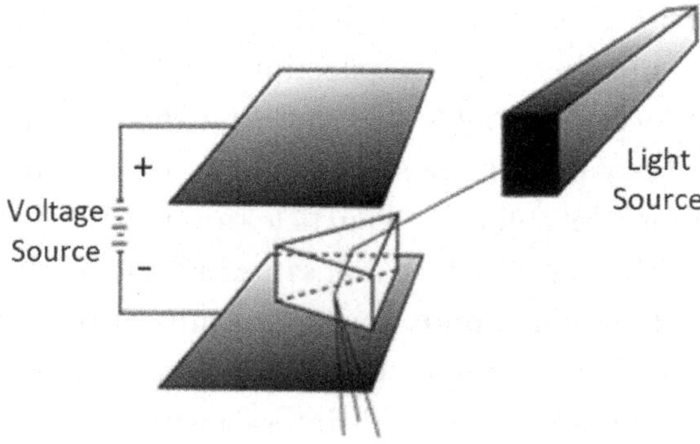

Figure 7. Prism experimental setup

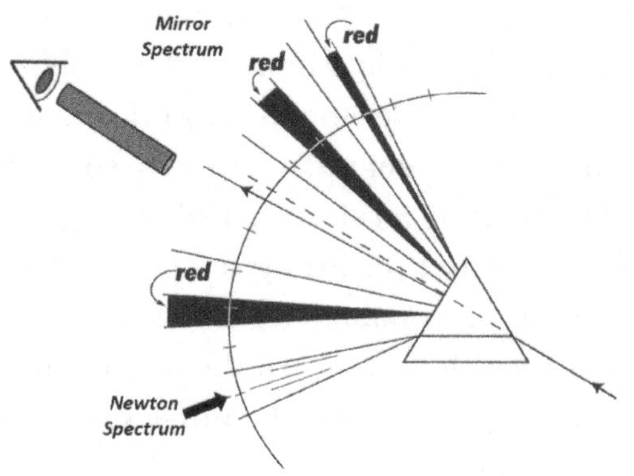

Figure 8. Mirror spectrum

All of the children could see the Newtonian spectrum with their physical eyesight. Additionally, some could also see (based on their innate ability to see auras) a bent-up spectrum at somewhat different angles with their auric eyesight. When our most gifted auric-sensitive child (Bobby) looked carefully through the sight, he observed not one but three distinct spectra, as illustrated in Figure 8. This is what we might expect if we are dealing with a bending of light around the edges of an object rather than a bending when entering a transparent object.

Because of this mirror principle in R-space, light hitting a prism speeds up instead of slowing down, and gives a reverse-order spectrum compared with the Newtonian spectrum order. I refer to this as "subtle realm light." Thus, if normal light contains at least the two components of being physical and subtle, then we should expect to see a refracted bent-down spectrum from the physical component and a diffracted bent-up spectrum from the subtle component, as illustrated in Figure 8. What are your thoughts on this, Doug?

Dr. Matzke: As usual, your research is original, insightful, and thought provoking. Since I focus on quantum states, I characterize the subtle light as quantum states and not as actual photons. Because of that distinction, there is no actual light traveling faster than the speed of light. Rather, the quantum states act as virtual photons, in that they have the same geometric topology as a photon, except without the energy, and they map to harmonically related locations on the bent-up path. Another way to think of this topology is as virtual-photons that are higher-dimensional structures equivalent to photons. In general, the individuals in your experiments who have auric vision most likely can directly interact with quantum states. This theme is repeated over and over in quantum-detection and quantum-affecting experiments. This model suggests that the mind may be the ultimate instrument for observing and affecting quantum systems.

The important aspect of this model is its universally applicable basis in math and geometry—bit dimensions are primitive for quantum states and, thus, form the basis of everything else.[89] Structure and orientation of mathematical bits do not need space or time. A vector, for example, defines it own magnitude and a direction, just as a stud in a house has a length and orientation, and can be joined with other vectors to create new structures in one, two, three, or more dimensions. Unlike trivectors, which are defined with three directions and thus can exist in 3D spacetime, single vectors and bivectors have only one and two dimensions, respectively, and do not define a 3D spacetime. These vectors define that space rather than existing embedded in the space.

We show later how the particle Standard Model can map to different numbers of dimensions. Bit-dimension vectors combine to form magnetic spinors (geometric precursors of spacetime magnetism), electric primitives (catalysts for electrically charged particles, such as electrons and protons), other quantum particles (such as quarks and bosons), and other phenomena (such as entanglement) and the mass primitives (the potential graviton).[90] Specifically, quarks are really the sum of a two-dimensional bivector and a one-dimensional bit-vector. Further, qubits, neutrinos, weak/strong force (Z/W bosons), and bivector spinors, such as possible magnetic monopoles, are all 2D constructs that do not interact as easily with other 3D particles. Finally, my geometric, mathematical model shows that entangled states are 4D and are the sum of two bivector spinors.[91] None of the fundamental objects described previously will likely ever be observed through particle accelerators or other traditional means. We have given a sneak preview of some technical terms here, but define them more fully later.

Any model or research that helps us to observe magnetic spinors indirectly is our best hope, as demonstrated through using electric fields in your prism experiments and magnetic fields in your pH water experiments. You appeal to the magnetic monopole concept—the idea that, just as an electron represents a point source for electrical charge, so the magnetic monopole represents a hypothetical point source for magnetic force. In my model, the point source for magnetic force is due to this 2D spinor, which is a plane that can be *oriented* in spaces conditioned by your IHD, but, consistent with traditional science, it does not yet exist as an independent 3D particle in spacetime. Conversely, my model represents the point source for electrical force as a 3D trivector, which is related to 3D electrons.

Dr. Tiller: My magnetic monopole and your magnetic spinor focus on the same problem. As a quantum computation engineer, you are looking at computational primitives based on topology, and as a material scientist, I am looking at primitive forces. In both of our cases, symmetry and consistency naturally arise from the mathematics, which is similar to how much of the modern Standard Model was also developed using a SU(3) symmetry.[92]

Bit Physics Gives Rise to Spacetime

Dr. Matzke: I am glad you and I agree on our collaborative objectives. In that spirit, let us discuss other properties of nonmetric geometries, the bit physics precursors of space, known as "protospace," and of time, known as "prototime." Now that we have set the groundwork, we can have a deeper discussion of the properties of nonmetric environments.

Since distance is not a valid concept in a nonmetric environment, the spatial idea of locality must be reconceptualized. For example, my research with hyperdimensional neural networks shows the formula for computing the similarity between two points uses the exact same mathematics as the traditional Euclidian distance metric (square root of the sums of squares of coordinate differences).[93] One of the properties of this hyperdimensional mathematics is that a point's coordinates in this realm is constructed by the point's content. For example, traditional data memories are like a coin placed on a table, where the value is either heads or tails. When content is the address, the left side of the table is heads and right side is tails. The addresses are also sparsely spread out so that finding points near each other represents a significant correlation between them. So, points near each other are correlated. This research is most commonly known as "sparse distributed coding" or "content-addressable memories" (CAMs).[94] The term for the generalized version of CAMs is "correlithms" (correlational algorithms).[95] The insight and significant details behind the mathematics for CAMs and correlithms is described at length in Chapter 4, where we show that correlithms naturally form the mathematical mechanism behind the Law of Attraction.

Entrepreneur and author Jeff Hawkins founded a machine intelligence (aka AI) company called Numenta that uses CAMs as their approach to AI.[96] Hawkins is such a believer in the mathematical properties of CAMs that he states in his YouTube videos (paraphrase), "If you want to build AI, you must use CAMs." His technology is called hierarchical temporal memories (HTM)[97] that uses a sparse distributed representation-based technology that looks for patterns in temporal sequences of data using CAMs and hierarchy.[98] As we discuss in more detail later, generalized correlithm approaches lead to macroscopic geometric properties, similar to those of quantum systems: orthogonal vectors, superposition properties due to phases, and probabilities due to phases. Let's now switch from talking about the bit physics properties of protospace to the bit properties of prototime.

Since time and, hence, duration are not valid concepts in a nonmetric environment, change is the only possible time primitive. If two states are unable to exist together,[99] and if both states have been observed, then one state must have changed into the other state. This is called a "co-exclusion," since the two states exclude each other. For example, if a dog can be either in my kitchen or in the yard but not in both places simultaneously, but I observe him in the kitchen and later observe him in the yard, then he must have changed his state from being in the kitchen to being in the yard. The "one and zero" states of a classical bit are another example of mutually exclusive states. Imagine all change being instantaneous from one to zero, or vice versa, without any global sense of time-based duration. Another way to comprehend this is: time is built on top of instantaneous primitive changes.

In the source science model, our normal notion of the arrow of time emerges from quantum versions of these primitive state changes. At the quantum level, only two kinds of state changes can occur: reversible and irreversible. "Reversible operators" do not erase information, and therefore an inverse operator exists that can undo changes and revert the new state to where it was in its original state. Such operators are able to perform this behavior without knowing what the original state was. For example, it is possible to flip a coin to the opposite side without knowing what side is currently facing up. Reversible quantum operations do this for all operations, since it is impossible to know the exact current state of the qubit phase state.

"Irreversible operators" erase information (are singular) and, therefore, no operator exists to recover the original unknown state. Normal quantum operators that simply change phases are reversible, whereas all quantum measurements return a probabilistic answer and destroy the information (upon measuring), and so are irreversible. The operator for creating quantum entanglement is defined as the "Bell operator," which is considered reversible in conventional Hilbert space mathematics. One of the significant results of my geometric algebra version of quantum computing for my PhD is that I proved that the GALG Bell operator is irreversible due to the erasure of information,[100] which is important to the fundamentals of the theory of entanglement.

In summary, I believe that time emerges from irreversible state changes, so represents a primitive "tick" (so all others are reversible), which most likely includes the creation of entangled states. All quantum operators affect change, but it is not clear what operators show up as temporal sequencing inside our spacetime. These ideas are related to the concept proposed by others that increase in entropy is related to the forward arrow of time.

I also believe that irreversible change gives rise to time—and that bit dimensions give rise to space. Essentially, protospace and prototime give rise to real space and time. There are still discussions within the physics community about the relationship between entropy, time, space, and gravity. For example, change may also give rise to gravity, since it is understood that whichever direction gravity is pulling is the direction of slower relativistic time, so entropy-related models that construct time's arrow may also construct gravity.[101] Just think, the deeper in any gravity well (like planet Earth), the slower the clocks run (due to relativity), which is why clocks on Earth run slower than clocks in satellites, so GPS satellites must correct for this.

Orthogonal states that can exist together and happen simultaneously are described as being a "co-occurrence."[102] For example, the dog can simultaneously be in the kitchen and be brown colored, without needing to switch from one state to the other. Mathematically speaking, the power of orthonormal states is that they can be concurrently combined without limit. I believe this concurrency property of orthonormal bit dimensions is the basis of all quantum computing and is the representation of all mental states, which gives rise to unlimited concurrency that supports supermind capabilities, as discussed in Chapter 4.

The key point here is that massively orthogonal bit dimensions are primitive enough to support the protophysics of similarity and change, thereby supporting the basis of any computation system: space and time. These bit dimensions have unlimited concurrency since they are not embedded inside spacetime, and thus define a pure informational representation. Therefore, I propose that this bit physics substrate has all the requirements to support thoughts and mind—especially supermind, telepathy, and auras—and that their fundamental representation is hyperdimensional and spacelike. The next level of details will be discussed in the next chapter.

Using this proposed bit physics infrastructure, we can provide more details regarding auras and telepathy. Bill, we have both worked with people who can see auras and are telepathic, so can you please describe your firsthand experience as an introduction to these important topics?

Seeing and Knowing Thoughts

Dr. Tiller: To gain insight into our prism and gas discharge experiments, my team collaborated with talented individuals who could see auras. The gas discharge experiment demonstrated that human intent could affect the cascade rate of a near-threshold gas discharge device, most likely by influencing the tunneling rates. Figure 9 shows the gas discharge experimental setup and visually illustrates the perceived influence mechanism in spite of the Faraday cages blocking all electromagnetic waves. Our observers reported seeing emanations from three of the seven different focal points for prana in the body interacting with the target device during successful trials.

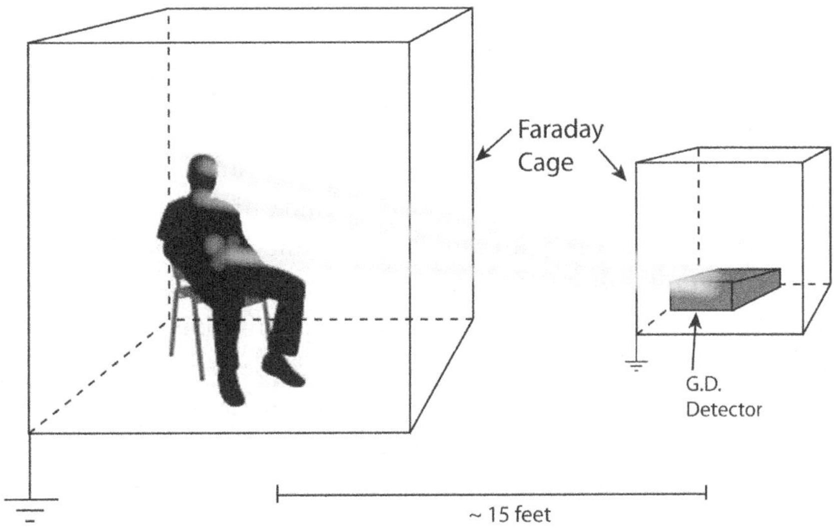

Figure 9. Gas discharge experimental setup

These points are known as "chakras" (discussed more in Chapter 7) and they were interacting with the target device during successful trials. There is a saying: "Where intention goes, prana flows."[103] People who read auras can readily see these bands of "light" (or aka cords)[104] between individuals. Even though there is no classical way to measure prana, this kind of connection is most likely occurring during all mental interactions, especially those involving PK targets. Clairvoyant people report that auras and their aka cord extensions look like filaments of light; similar to how halos are depicted around saints.

You and I agree that if the mind was composed of an extremely large number of bit dimensions, then it would create a mental image of this collection of dimensions as an aura of light filaments, since the topological structure of photons is three vectors. Other similar phenomena are orbs, which are free-floating aura balls that show up on photographs. Some orbs are reported to be minds performing "astral travel." There are documented cases where a telepathic connection to an orb was made and the orb was a known, living, telepathic autistic child.[105] This is consistent with our own source science model that describes our quantum mind as being telepathic and separate from our brain.

Suzy Miller, the multidimensional seer and author and a research colleague of mine, works telepathically with autistic children, and also teaches families to connect telepathically with their autistic family members.[106] Miller was originally taught this style of interaction by one of her autistic child clients. She calls this program "Awesomism" and states that, despite common perceptions, these children are mentally and energetically advanced. Unfortunately, their hyper-sensitivity makes it difficult for them to interact well with their own bodies or with other people. I believe you have some stories about this, Doug.

Dr. Matzke: I do. The photos in Figure 10 and Figure 11 were taken by my sister with her cell phone and show auras and orbs around her dogs. I also know many people who routinely use telepathy in both their personal and business lives. I have experienced telepathy myself with a few individuals and know many more who have reliable telepathic abilities. My particular interest in telepathy is because it seems to represent some universal meaning that is independent of traditional human languages. I believe that meaning is more primitive than language, because children learn languages by establishing meaning first and then attaching language labels second. I believe telepathy is due to correlithms and bit dimensions, which we discuss more in Chapter 5.

Figure 10. Aura photo around dog

Figure 11. Orbs photo around dog

Further, thoughts are balls or packets of meaning associated with the hyperdimensional nature of mind. Researcher, mystic, and author Robert Monroe defined the term "rotes" to signify those "thought balls,"[107] as bundles of meaning retrieved during remote viewing. Rotes are a representation of meaning independent of the brain. An example of learning-without-a-brain occurs when amoebas learn to anticipate being fed at regular intervals. This learning occurs even though an amoeba is a single cell (without a brain) but with the same complexity as a single neuron. Consciousness expert Dr. Stuart Hameroff offers the explanation that amoebas also contain microtubules, just like neurons.[108] Here are some other examples that rely on the meaning of thoughts being separate from the brain:

- Imprinting thoughts: in water, food, places, IHDs, blessing, curses, and common objects[109]
- Shared dreams: telepathy during dreams[110]
- Rotes and remote viewers: a "rote" is a bundle of meaning retrieved during remote viewing[111]
- Telepathy with orbs: some of these orbs are living autistic children[112]
- Astral travel and out-of-body experiences (OBEs): communication via pure thought with other astral beings[113]
- Near-death experiences (NDEs): communication via pure thought and lucid memories of experiences[114]
- Animal telepathy: Even animals can exchange thoughts with animal whisperers and telepaths[115]
- Channeling: channelers use telepathy to interact with spiritual guides[116]
- Past lives: people, especially children, can have deep knowledge of a deceased person's life[117]

Robert Monroe, founder of the Monroe Institute of altered consciousness, worked with people who could mentally travel outside their body (astral travel) and become aware of remote locations (remote viewing). Every time a remote viewer initiated a session, they did it with an intention or a request for information. His term "rote" was used to describe the resulting response—a mental packet of information containing the answer being sought. Remote viewers have told me that the meaning of the rote is symbolic and outside time, and they must decode it into sequential thoughts and language without projecting their own meaning into this process.[118] The decoding of rotes is similar to quantum measurement, in that in both cases bias can obscure the meaning. During the Cold War, the US government reliably used remote viewing to keep tabs on the Russians, and vice versa, and these programs are reputed to be active to this day.[119] There is, in fact, today a large remote-viewing community with its own annual conventions.[120]

Like you, Bill, I also know Suzy Miller. I found that her team's telepathy has evolved to the point where it is a new language on its own, in addition to the telepathic underpinnings. This "light language"[121] is noteworthy for future study because it is not a conventional human language. Video examples of Miller speaking this light language can be found on YouTube and represents an aha moment regarding psychic abilities, since it is trainable and repeatable.

I also have a friend who is telepathic and we recently had lunch.[122] While talking about telepathy, she made a comment that many of my thoughts have parenthesis wrapped around them. This was a particularly personal and revealing comment because I had been programming for more than thirteen years in the computer programming language Lisp, a language renowned for its extensive use of parentheses. This comment meant to me that the structure of my thoughts had been molded by my work environment, which she could directly observe.

One of my energy-sensitive friends can see auras. I originally met him when he was working as a barista at Starbucks.[123] One day I was ordering coffee and the cashier helping me seemed a bit scattered. I talked her through a quick thirty-second grounding exercise, which as it turned out, calmed her. As I moved down the line, the barista making my coffee asked me if I had just performed energy work with the cashier. Surprised, I answered, "Yes, how did you know?" He said he could see auras and could see the energy work I had just performed. We became instant friends as we shared our interest in and mutual experience with auras. At a lunch we did energy work on a patio and he described the halo persisting at our table, even as we walked away.

Telepathy and auras are related because they both involve the exchange of mental thought information. Auras are more visually oriented, so require some amount of deciphering. Telepathy can also be some combination of images, audio, feelings, or direct knowing of information. For example, one of my telepathic luncheon friends reported that one day she just started getting "downloads" of mathematical information and formulas. She politely asked that this information be redirected to someone else.

Bill, I am sure you have other interesting personal stories to share, especially ones involving the IHD.

Dr. Tiller: My research team included a gifted inventor named Randy who could also see auras and talk with spirit guides.[124] Randy was instructed by unseen helpers to build the IHD using a simple electrical memory semiconductor part. The IHD also contains a high-frequency electrical oscillator that establishes a resonance of the molecular elements of the unprogrammed chip. This continuous resonance is like a bell ringing nonstop. When intention intersects with this resonance, thoughts are encoded and rebroadcast like a standing wave, the same way that a laser beam recreates a holographic image. Randy can see the resonant beam, similar to how some people see auras.

Randy previously had a job finding misplaced equipment in a large industrial company. Once, he even used his remote viewing ability to discover the location of an expensive piece of equipment that had accidently been shipped to a warehouse in another state. Excited about the find, he reported the good news to his boss, who promptly fired him—his boss could not explain the find and so just assumed Randy must have purposely shipped this item to the wrong location to make himself look good.[125] This type of "shooting the messenger" is more common than many realize. My own experience is that a large number of people who have psychic abilities keep it to themselves, fearful that others will misunderstand them, ridicule them, or discriminate against them.

Dr. Matzke: Your story of the IHD is similar to my experience with imprinted cassette tapes. In the mid-1990s, I was part of a team that worked with Russian physicist Dr. Yuri Kronn, the inventor of the Vital Energy Technology, a type of prana generator.[126] The master device was not a tape but used mini florescent bulbs that varied in intensity based on sound patterns created by Kronn. These bulbs were specially prepared using noble gases, which when activated with a special machine that modulated the intensity of the plasma (hot gas atoms with electrons stripped off) based on specifically chosen audio band tones. All conventional florescent tubes work on the same principle that excited plasma generates light driven by standard 60 Hz power frequency, so if you are prana sensitive you might want to limit your exposure to florescent lights.

Healers and sensitives experienced the various light patterns as machine-generated prana, and many reported these patterns as being extremely intense. These prana patterns were later imprinted onto audio cassette tapes using a special process, along with an audio recording of specially designed music. What was fascinating is that prana sensitives would see the cassettes as life-force beacons, even without playing them. I have had many firsthand experiences where even nonsensitive people tended to be unconsciously attracted to the cassettes when our team carried them. Those tapes could be played through speakers, and sensitives and others would experience the prana, again some very intensely. I have many other firsthand stories about these tapes and have given several lectures and seminars on them.

My best description of the life force technology of the light device is that the vibrating plasma in the light bulb resonates with (or tugs on) the ether. This mechanism is similar to the IHD technology. In Einstein's theory of special relativity, any acceleration—such as a change in speed, direction, or, as in this case, oscillation—is indistinguishable from a gravitational force. Therefore, any technology based on any type of acceleration might have similar results. Examples include music (accelerating air molecules), spiritual drumming circles (accelerating drumheads), homeopathic succussion of water (accelerating water by striking the container),[127] radio frequency generators (acceleration of electromagnetic fields), and therapeutic sound tables and light tables (accelerating air or photons).

Quantum physics was just as unimaginable one hundred years ago as metaphysics technology is today. Without these advancements in quantum physics, there would be no transistors, computers, or lasers today to power our developed modern world. This supports our contention that the bit dimension realm offers the next information age beyond conventional computers and quantum physics,[128] if only society will be curious and disciplined enough to discover the next breakthroughs.

Chapter Summary

This chapter is a whirlwind of topics all related to the advanced properties of thoughts. Research shows that thoughts can directly affect the physical world, which invalidates the widely accepted Descartes assumption. Specifically, Bill's team used the intention host device, which can be imprinted with an intent that demonstrates psychokinesis in a laboratory setting.

Classical physics does not provide a mechanism for how the mind can affect the physical world, so we appeal to information theory and the quantum domain for a solution. This approach is supported by a large number of PK experiments, such as Radin's double-slit interferometer and Tiller's gas discharge device, in which the mind is shown to directly affect the quantum probabilities of the target. The direct connections between quantum computation, quantum probabilities, information theory, and entropy make this approach sound—any change in probabilities represents a change in the order of the system; a change in entropy has an associated effective energy available for affecting physical things.

We both agree that thoughts are nonbrain and information centric. The examples from this chapter illustrate that thoughts and mind cannot be limited to any purely classical physics or energy-based representations and, therefore, cannot be exclusively in the brain due to trans-spatial and trans-temporal behaviors. We collectively must realize that classical neural information models of brain are insufficient to account for psychoenergetic phenomena. We propose that the quantum mind is separate from the brain, which means the brain is a "quantum antenna." The source science model also proposes the bit dimension infrastructure of protospace and prototime is the quantum information basis for all phenomena: classical, relativistic, quantum, meaning, real intelligence, and psychoenergetics.

We further believe that those who think intelligence and auras might be explained using classical models are falling for the myth of AI, thinkism, and neglecting documented phenomena. People routinely exhibit abilities such as remote viewing, telepathic meaning, precognition, and retrocausation—all requiring information mechanisms beyond classical space and time restrictions.

Chapter 3: Thoughts on Source

Source science takes the approach that information represented as bit dimensions is the root of all laws in the universe. Even the conservation laws of physics are based on the conservation, symmetry, and consistency laws. The physical universe we experience runs on a bit-dimension quantum simulator. Like all other simulators, this computer exists outside of the resulting simulation. This exotic information system simulates in a self-consistent fashion the entire universe containing all of physics, chemistry, biology, neurology, thought, psychology, metaphysics, and all other phenomena we humans experience. This chapter introduces our bit-physics math that supports these ideas, allowing the readers to realize this is real science and not philosophy.

Many researchers and physicists believe that physics and computation are the same thing.[1] The 1981 PhysComp proceedings introduction says, "The conference brought together about sixty people who believe that physics and computation are interdependent at a fundamental level."[2] The scope of this protocomputer is extremely hard to comprehend, since it must support simulations of Planck length quantum states, black holes, and a spacetime universe having a 46-billion-light-years diameter of space and 13.8 billion years of time.[3]

This chapter defines the deep bit physics math that supports source science. We focus on the concepts of the math, and the algebraic formulas are presented for completeness but can be skipped over for those who are math averse. Focus on the concepts, which are real, since the math is real. The concepts are layered and build upon each other, so take your time, with the end goal of understanding how bit physics leads to the usefulness and magic of space-like mental states.

Bit Physics Is the Source of Everything

Dr. Matzke: Let us understand in more detail exactly the meaning of "source." A single bit dimension represents the smallest change to a black hole, and thus forms the link between information theory, entropy, quantum mechanics, and gravity. The surface area of a black hole is its entropy measured in bits and forms the boundary between the relativistic spacetime metrics "outside" the black hole and the nonmetric environment "inside" the black hole. We put quotes around the term "inside" since the surface area and circumference of the black hole can be computed, but the diameter "through" the black hole is always of length zero due to relativistic space contraction. The inside of a black hole is a single spacetime point, a singularity, which might have similar properties to the singularity that preceded the inflation of the Big Bang.[4]

The black hole topology is quite unintuitive because the volume of the hole is on its surface area. Math predicts the same result for high-dimensional spaces. For example, Claude Shannon, the father of information theory, speaking in Dallas in the mid-1980s outlined that he proved that the volume of a very high-dimensional sphere is increasingly located on its surface area as N increases. This is the same result we see in the black hole singularity.[5] In both cases, bits and high-dimensional spaces are interlinked with unusual and unintuitive geometry and topology.

A large collection of bits by itself has no meaning. But we show how bits can be naturally combined to form structures, such as qubits, ebits, photons, particles, rotes, and even thoughts. This journey starts with bits represented in a mathematical language common to both computing and physics.[6] Each bit mathematically represents a separate tiny protodimension, orthogonal to all others. Each protodimension is so primitive and small that it might never be directly measured by physicists, but we still know it must exist, due to its quantum math effects. What are your thoughts on this, Bill?

Dr. Tiller: In general, the properties of materials may be characterized in many ways (e.g., electric, magnetic, or optical). The total material could be described by a sum of complex vectors. Your research using geometric algebra showed that each primitive vector of one-unit length mathematically represents one bit.[7] This approach is both algebraic and geometric, where each unit-bit-vector is orthonormal (both orthogonal to all others *and* unit length). This approach allows mapping of the computer science concept of Boolean logic into the same vector mathematics language used by physicists. Orthogonal vectors are important to physics, since they are all ninety degrees and maximally independent to all others, which allows for parallel descriptions of concurrent processes.

Dr. Matzke: You are right about how important orthogonality is to math and physics. The next key idea is that these orthonormal-bit-vectors can be combined using addition and multiplication, where addition expresses concurrent states (the dog is both in the kitchen and brown-colored) and multiplication expresses operations on those states (the dog relocates to the yard or becomes yellow-colored). These operations, because they include both states and changes to state, represent Turing-complete computation. Most people are familiar with Boolean algebra and I now introduce the geometric algebra primitives, so stay focused on the concepts.

Unlike a vector, which has both magnitude and direction, a scalar has only magnitude. The everyday counting numbers are types of scalars, denoted like the familiar –2, –1, 0, +1, +2, and so on. For example, let us denote a unique vector of one-unit length as a bold symbol "**a**" with a positive or negative scalar unit length direction as "± **a**," and denote the space it exists in as $\mathbf{G}_1$, with a number of dimensions N as $\mathbf{G}_N$. If we add two vectors, ±**a** and ±**b**, both of G1, together as the multivector "±**a** ±**b**," they form the space $\mathbf{G}_2$. In general, each G_N contains 3^{2^N} total unique corner states due to generation of 2^N orthogonal elements with three possible coefficient values:

- Any dimensionless space $\mathbf{G}_0$ contains the three scalar states 0, +1, and −1. The shorthand for this set of states is denoted as {0, ±1}.
- Each 1D space $\mathbf{G}_1$ contains nine states—the same three scalar states and an additional six vector related states: 0, +1, −1, +**a**, −**a**, +1 +**a**, −1 +**a**, +1 −**a**, and −1 −**a**. The shorthand for this set of states is denoted as {0, ±1, ±**a,** ±1 ±**a**}, where the "+" operator is implied in "±1 ±**a**."
- Each 2D space $\mathbf{G}_2$ contains eighty-one states using the combinations of elements 0, ±1, **a, b,** and ±**a^b**. The symbol "^" is the traditional outer product and is used to denote graded elements described later.

The elements in any *N*-dimensional space $\mathbf{G}_N$ can be determined for the set of orthonormal vectors{a, **b**, ...} by expanding the expression (using geometric products) (1+**a**)(1+**b**)(1+...) ...:

- (1+**a**)(1+**b**) = + 1 + **a** + **b** + (**a^b**)
- (1+**a**)(1+**b**)(1+**c**) = + 1 + **a** + **b** + **c** + (**a^b**) + (**a^c**) + (**b^c**) + (**a^b^c**)
- (1+**a**)(1+**b**)(1+**c**)(1+**d**) = + 1 + **a** + **b** + **c** + **d** + (**a^b**) + (**a^c**) + ... + (**a^b^c**) + (**a^b^d**) + ... + (**a^b^c^d**)

What exactly are these newly created elements, such as ±**a^b**? Vectors **a** and **b** are grade-1 elements: since they are one dimensional, they are an oriented line. Grade-2 elements, such as ±**a^b**, are oriented 2D planes called "bivectors." Grade-3 elements, such as ±**a^b^c**, are oriented 3D volumes called "trivectors." In general, grade-*N* elements are *N*-dimensional *N*-vectors (high dimensional volumes or hyper volumes). This is how topological structure is created using only bits and geometric products. This is important because other kinds of vector mathematics do not have this structure building mechanisms (of bivectors, etc.), plus this they do not start with bit-vectors using real valued coefficients.

An important idea is that combining vectors as a concurrent sum, such as **a+b** or **a+b+c**, defines a $\mathbf{G}_N$ space and also automatically defines all the *N*-vectors associated with that space. Thus, changes of state due to operations on the vectors inherently define the states themselves as resulting vectors—another Turing-complete behavior.

The simplest example of a bivector is a complex number having both a real and an imaginary element.[8] Complex numbers seem mysterious to many but are required for finding such solutions as $x=(-3\pm3i)$ to equations such as $(x+3)^2=-9$, and are used extensively in physics. Geometrically, a complex number also represents a plane with a real axis and an imaginary axis (where the imaginary axis is $i=\sqrt{-1}$ or $i^2=-1$). Multiplying a state by i causes a rotation of state in the complex plane, per Figure 12. Alternatively, it is possible to define a planar equivalent solution to complex numbers by using grade–2 elements from geometric algebra. For example, in Figure 13, given orthonormal grade–1 vectors **a** and **b** in $\mathbf{G}_2$, we can define the typical vector expressions such as a+b and the geometric product **a*b** as the sum of inner and outer products, or formally **a*b** = **a.b** + **a^b**. When **a** and **b** are orthogonal then **a.b** = 0, so then **a*b** = **a^b**.

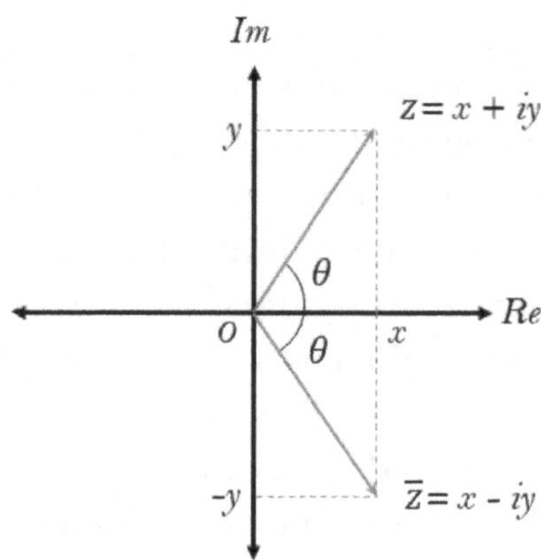

Figure 12. Complex–number Argand diagram

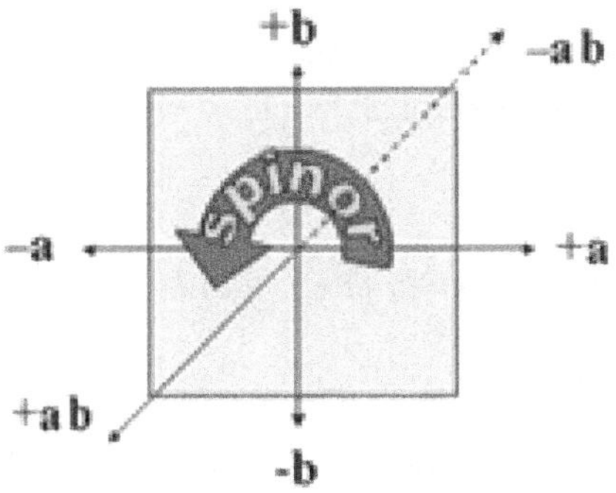

Figure 13. Spinor visualization

Since geometric algebra is noncommutative, then the products **a*b** = **–b*a** have different right–handed orientations that are anti-commutative. Using the right-hand rule, two orientations for this plane exist, in and out of the page. Now take the square of any bivector and that will produce:

(**a*b**)*(**a*b**) = **a^b^a^b** = **–a^a^b^b** = –1*1 = –1.

Therefore, the square of any bivector $(\mathbf{a*b})^2 = -1$ has the exact same definition as the square of the imaginary number $i^2 = -1$. The expression a*b = **a^b** is geometrically a plane and is referred to as an even, grade-2 bivector and represents a generalization of complex numbers, but in any pairing of dimensions, each with its own orientation. The orientation of the bivector, whether in or out of the plane, is also the mathematical equivalent to the traditional 3D cross product, but in any number of dimensions.

Likewise, the product **a*b*c** forms an oriented trivector **a^b^c**, etc., through arbitrary graded *N*-vectors. Since bivectors make it easy to perform rotations, all of the physics laws have been re-expressed by physicist Chris Doran as geometric algebra formulas, including all of relativity and quantum mechanics.[9] Each *N*-vector also has an orientation that can be treated like another vector and represents keeping track of hierarchy in the structure of graded elements.

The quaternions were defined by Hamilton in 1843 as an extension to complex numbers for 3D spaces with these anticommutative definitions.

$$i^2 = j^2 = k^2 = ijk = -1,\ ij = k,\ jk = i,\ and\ ki = j$$

The bivectors in $\mathbf{G}_3$ = {x, **y**, **z**} naturally have these exact properties and define a 3D volume {x, y, z} formed by the three oriented bivector planes, therefore quaternions are simply bivectors:

$$i = \mathbf{x}\wedge\mathbf{y},\ j = \mathbf{y}\wedge\mathbf{z},\ k = \mathbf{x}\wedge\mathbf{z}$$

Just like Boolean algebra expressions, conventional Boolean truth tables (that express all outcomes for all inputs) can be constructed for these geometric algebra (GALG) expressions using the addition and multiplication tables of the ±1 coefficients of the elements (see Figure 14). As the English description indicates, this math is exclusive-NOR logic dominated—change oriented—with different behaviors for when coefficients are the same versus different. The Boolean logic XNOR is true if both inputs are the same and false if different. The following tables are essentially addition (left) and multiplication (right) using mod 3 arithmetic of {0, 1, 2} transformed symmetrically, where 2 = –1 resulting in {0, +1, –1} = {0, +, –}.

+	+	–
+	–	0
–	0	+
If same then invert If different then cancel		

*	+	–
+	+	–
–	–	+
If same then + If different then –		

Figure 14. Geometric algebra prefix for addition and multiplication

Using a custom symbolic math program I wrote in Python,[10] it is easy to generate the truth tables for any GALG expression using these rules by iterating over all the ±1 coefficients permutations for each input vector and compute the sums of products of graded elements (see Table 1).

Table 1. Geometric Algebra State Table Examples for G_1, G_2, and G_3

```
>>> gastates((1+a))
<table for + 1 + a>
INPUTS: a | OUTPUT
--------------------------------
ROW 00: - | 0
ROW 01: + | -
--------------------------------
Counts for outputs of
ZERO=1, PLUS=0, MINUS=1
for TOTAL=2 rows
```

```
>>> gastates((1+a)(1+b))
<table for + 1 + a + b + (a^b)>
INPUTS: a b | OUTPUT
--------------------------------
ROW 00: - - | 0
ROW 01: - + | 0
ROW 02: + - | 0
ROW 03: + + | +
--------------------------------
Counts for outputs of
ZERO=3, PLUS=1, MINUS=0
for TOTAL=4 rows
```

```
>>> gastates((1+a)(1+b)(1+c))
<table for +1+a+b+c+(a^b)
+(a^c)+(b^c)+(a^b^c)>
INPUTS: a b c | OUTPUT
--------------------------------
ROW 00: - - - | 0
ROW 01: - - + | 0
ROW 02: - + - | 0
ROW 03: - + + | 0
--------------------------------
ROW 04: + - - | 0
ROW 05: + - + | 0
ROW 06: + + - | 0
ROW 07: + + + | -
--------------------------------
Counts for outputs of
ZERO=7, PLUS=0, MINUS=1
for TOTAL=8 rows
```

```
>>> gastates((1–a)(1–b)(1–c))
<table for +1–a–b–
c+(a^b)+(a^c)+(b^c)–(a^b^c)>
INPUTS: a b c | OUTPUT
--------------------------------
ROW 00: - - - | -
ROW 01: - - + | 0
ROW 02: - + - | 0
ROW 03: - + + | 0
--------------------------------
ROW 04: + - - | 0
ROW 05: + - + | 0
ROW 06: + + - | 0
ROW 07: + + + | 0
--------------------------------
Counts for outputs of
ZERO=7, PLUS=0, MINUS=1
for TOTAL=8 rows
```

```
>>> gastates((1+a)(1+b)(1+c) +
(1–a)(1–b)(1–c)) ← (addition of
two expressions from above)
<table for – 1 – (a^b) – (a^c) – (b^c)>
INPUTS: a b c | OUTPUT
--------------------------------
ROW 00: - - - | -
ROW 01: - - + | 0
ROW 02: - + - | 0
ROW 03: - + + | 0
--------------------------------
ROW 04: + - - | 0
ROW 05: + - + | 0
ROW 06: + + - | 0
ROW 07: + + + | -
--------------------------------
Counts for outputs of
ZERO=6, PLUS=0, MINUS=2
for TOTAL=8 rows
```

Since the GALG is XNOR oriented, it takes expressions using all the GALG elements to express the smallest addressable state, which is represented by one row in the truth table. The bottom quadrant of Table 1 illustrates that summing of any primitive states combines to create optimized equations. This result shows the row-states of the truth tables are linearly independent and that any truth table can be constructed. These row-states also are all simultaneously concurrent and when any output rows have a zero value, which means these zero states naturally do not occur. Essentially, the row-states in GALG are tristate values that include the value zero, which means they do not occur. What starts with binary bits naturally produces mathematically valid tristate values.[11] This is important when we embed topologies in higher-dimensional spaces.

The output column of these truth tables can be thought of as a vector of all the row-states, and such row-state vectors can be linearly added to give the same result as adding the symbolic equations. The mixed-grade GALG expressions have a reversible duality of algebraic vs row-states representation that automatically represents the concurrent states, including the zero states that do not occur. These zero states represent trinary values and cannot be expressed in conventional Boolean algebra with only binary values. Most importantly, these row-state vectors are truly concurrent states rather than the mutually exclusive states of Boolean algebra. Each GALG expression (denoted here in bold uppercase) is linearly independent of other expressions, and some multivector expressions **A** and –**A** co-exclude each other, since **A** – **A** = 0, same as where **a** – **a** = 0.

These sums of graded elements are exceedingly important because they represent the real structure of things in physics based on their dimensionality. In my dissertation, I expressed quantum computing qubits in geometric algebra as **A** = (**a0** + **a1**) and found that the entangled Bell states are really the sum of even-grade *bivectors,* not a sum of grade-one *vectors* (i.e., for qubits **A*B** = (**a0** + **a1**) (**b0** + **b1**) in $\mathbf{G}_{4,}$ then an ebit state is bivectors **a0^b0** + **a1^b1**).[12] Using this bivector structure, I proved the Bell operator is *irreversible* in $\mathbf{G}_{4,}$ which is a similar-looking expression but different meaning when compared to the equivalent but *reversible* vector interpretation created with vectors formed by tensor products (|00⟩+|11⟩ in Hilbert Space H4). I am currently further exploring the meaning of this result, because this irreversibility of Bell operator significantly impacts the meaning of entangled states.

Dr. Tiller: This geometric algebra approach using bits is quite appealing and your results are fascinating. What else can you do with geometric algebra besides represent qubits and ebits?

Geometric Algebra Reorganization of the Standard Model

Dr. Matzke: The Standard Model has been extremely useful since the mid-1970s when it was first developed. Most people might not know that the Standard Model is not finished, since physicists only recently confirmed the Higgs boson. From a historical perspective, the Standard Model is still changing, since several predicted particles have only recently been detected and officially accepted, such as the top quark in 1995, the tau neutrino in 2000, and the Higgs boson in 2012. With that said, we show next how this GALG model can make predictions about the Standard Model. All of the accepted particles of physics are described in the "Standard Model" as shown in Figure 15, which are subdivided into quarks (that make up protons and neutrons), leptons (the electron and neutrino particles), and bosons (including photons and other force carriers).[13]

By taking two orthogonal bit-vectors (**q0**, **q1** in $\mathbf{G}_{2:}$ a GALG of two dimensions), I showed in my doctoral research that a qubit **Q** = ±**q0** ±**q1** is formed with all the known expressions and other operators of qubits. This GALG approach is topology centric and does NOT assume the qubits were embedded in a 3D space. Likewise, by taking three orthonormal bit-vectors (**q0, q1, q2** in $\mathbf{G}_3$), we showed that a qutrit **T** = ±**q0** ±**q1** ±**q2** (which is a photon) can be represented, as can the other known Standard Model particles. These results are simply due to the mathematical symmetries and concurrency inherent in geometric algebra.

The Standard Model was finalized in the 1970s using gauge theory and helped guide most of high-energy physics ever since, including the forty-year search for the Higgs boson. Figure 15 is a typical illustration of the Standard Model showing the primitive definitions using mass, charge, and spin properties (not topology) for the seventeen primitive components, plus the twelve antiparticle versions of the leptons and quarks. Each particle has an antiparticle, for example, the negative charge electron has the positron, which has positive charge. The normal Standard Model is based on SU(3) symmetries.[14] The force carrying bosons are their own antiparticles.[15]

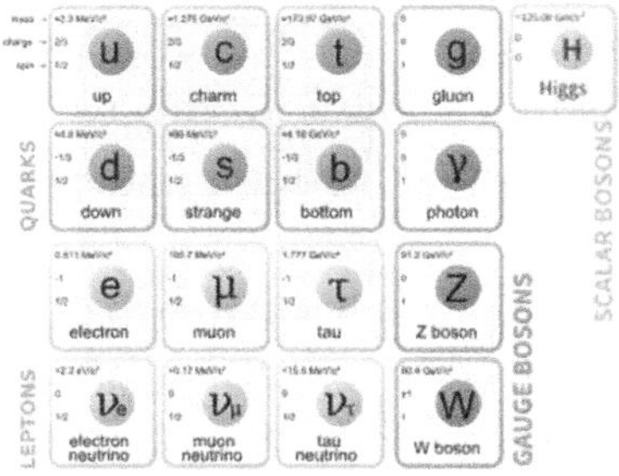

Figure 15. Approved Standard Model organization chart from Wikipedia

All of the following results came from the joint GALG research with Mike Manthey and me in 2010, specifically described nine surprising outcomes in my presentation[16] and video[17]:

1) We demonstrated that the W/Z gauge bosons emerged from the 2D $\mathbf{G}_2$ qubit space.
2) We determined that the elusive neutrino is the only particle that emerged from the 2D $\mathbf{G}_2$ qubit space.
3) We predicted a fourth neutrino pair and its dual antineutrino—the sum of three antineutrinos.
4) We identified that space itself is nilpotent ($B^2 = 0$, like other bosons) in $\mathbf{G}_3$, which might be the new proposed X17 boson.
5) We identified twice as many electrons, which represents the chirality variations (due to asymmetry mirror properties of left-handed vs right-handed particles).
6) We proved that the ebit Bell states have four dimensions in $\mathbf{G}_4$ and that the Bell/Magic operators are *irreversible* due to multiplicative cancellation.
7) We proposed in $\mathbf{G}_4$ the Higgs boson is the sum of three entangled states.
8) We identified in $\mathbf{G}_4$ eight quark-like dark quarks that are inseparable, just as are many other nilpotents, as potential dark energy candidates.

9) We identified in $\mathbf{G}_4$ that dark matter is the sum of four dark quarks in four dimensions and other particles. Metaphorically similar to how normal matter is made of three quarks.

This constructive approach to the Standard Model demonstrates that by using bit-vector topology alone (goal of the group Alternate Natural Philosophy Association—ANPA), it is possible to identify the Standard Model primitives. It all starts with the idea that bits are primitive and orthonormal vectors. I label them as "bit dimensions." Figure 16 shows our alternative structure for the Standard Model based on GALG topology.

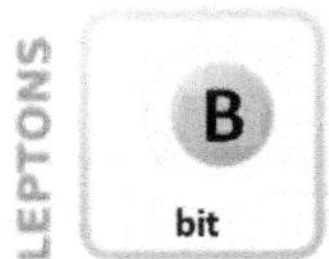

Bit in G_1

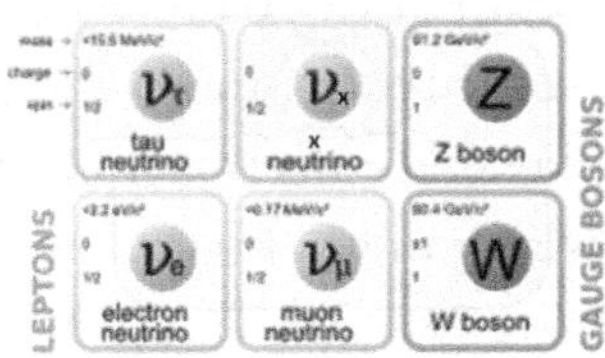

primitives in G_2 plus qubit

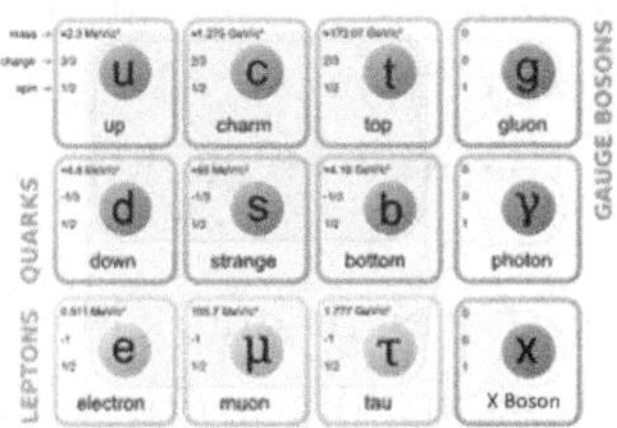

primitives in G_3 plus protons/neutrons

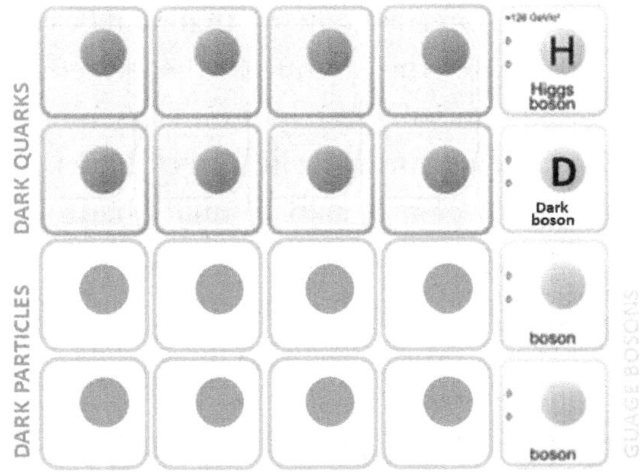

possible dark primitives in G_4 out of 43,046,721 total states

Figure 16. GALG topological reorganization of Standard Model primitives

With the GALG models, it is easy to discover that bosons **B** are nilpotent (where $\mathbf{B}^2=0$), particle expressions P are unitary (where $P^2=1$) and quarks are identified separately. When we reorganize the Standard Model primitives by the number of dimensions (in G_1, G_2, G_3, G_4), they might look like the graphics in Figure 16; for example, in the $\mathbf{G}_4$ space a total of seventeen particle signatures (unitary) and thirty bosonic signatures (nilpotent) are identified. See the detailed GALG signatures for nilpotents and unitary expressions later in this chapter.

Our classification is based on the number of unique corner states: in G_0 has 3, G_1 has $3^2 = 9$, G_2 has $9^2 = 81$, G_3 has $81^2 = 6{,}561$, and G_4 has $6{,}561^2 = 43{,}046{,}721$, so it is possible to completely classify all these states. However, it is impossible to iterate over all $(43{,}046{,}721)^2$ states of G_5, since that value of 1.85e+15 is roughly equivalent to the total age of the universe in hours.

Our results match particles that are being identified by other research groups. For example, a recent repeatable experiment suggests that an additional fifth force of low-energy protophobic X17 boson might match our nilpotent quaternion.[18] Other researchers are proposing a fourth sterile neutrino that matches our prediction of four neutrinos.[19] After the meson was discovered in 1936, scientists realized it is a member of the hadron class and consists of two quarks, while baryons are formed with three quarks. Scientists have also recently discovered 4-quark and 5-quark hadrons.[20] There are many additional proposed particles and bosons, all of which have indications of being results from some other modeling efforts. The Standard Model is still evolving, spurred on by its known deficiencies and new modeling efforts.[21]

Dr. Tiller: The GALG approach for organizing the Standard Model is ingenious, since it gives some insight about why 2D neutrinos are so hard to measure. Also, if the Higgs boson, dark energy, and dark matter are all four dimensional, then it might explain why they are also hard to detect. But, Doug, how does this connect with metaphysics?

Early Quantized Universe Based on Anu

Dr. Matzke: The history of the Standard Model is similar to the history of the periodic table of elements. New elements have been officially added as recently as 2015 (i.e., Oganesson element 118). About the same time that the periodic table of elements was being organized by Russian chemist Dmitri Mendeleev,[22] starting in 1895 some Theosophical Society members used their clairvoyance ability as a subatomic microscope and described the atomic structure of the known elements.[23] This work by Annie Besant and Charles Leadbeater occurred even before the discovery of electrons in 1879 and 1897, protons in 1911, neutrons in 1932, and quarks in 1964.[24] Their countable discrete constituents of the atomic nuclei were constructed as groups of "anu" (the Hindu word for atom) that seemed to have very similar threesome properties as quarks and anti-quarks. From a historical perspective, it is quite interesting to read the pdf version of this book *Occult Chemistry*, which can be found free by searching online.

Based on their descriptions, the images in Figure 17 are an artist's conception of the anu, which has ten bands wound into a loose ball, like yarn. These ten strands may be the equivalent to bits, string theory, or dimensions. Both right-handed and left-handed orientations of anu were observed and reported. It could very well be that the mind is the ultimate instrument to hold together the fundamental connection between us, physics, and the universe. This idea shows up repeatedly throughout this book.

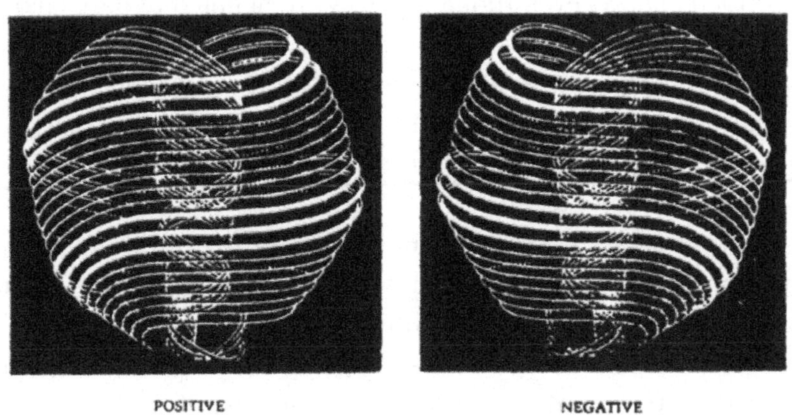

Figure 17. Artist drawing of anu from occult chemistry

Interestingly, Russian occultist and philosopher Helena Blavatsky founded the Theosophical Society in 1875, which she described as "the synthesis of science, religion and philosophy" and proclaimed it would revive the ancient wisdom which underlaid all the world's religions,[25] and in fact her doctrines influenced the spread of Hindu and Buddhist ideas in the West, as well as today is similar to the source science approach.

An interesting fact is the mathematical, physics, and metaphysical communities all predict quantized beginnings of our physical universe. We experience the world as continuous but in reality it has quantized or discrete roots, which is the root of quantum physics and apparently metaphysics. These quantized bits combine to form more complex structures resulting in the source of all we know. Also the idea of threeness appears in these domains. Bill, can you discuss how everything in physics appears to be continuous but is really discrete?

Dr. Tiller: As they say, all is not as it seems. We have already stated that a "quantum" is the minimum discrete amount of any physical entity involved in an interaction. This means all physical properties can take on only certain discrete or countable values. We already discussed that the smallest change to a black hole is a "bit." An electron is the smallest discrete amount of standalone electrical charge, even though quarks are deemed to have charge in one-third increments. A photon is the smallest discrete amount of light energy, while all the other Standard Model particles are also discrete and countable. Most people do not know that space is also discrete on the order of a Planck length because it is impossible to determine a position to a precision smaller than the Planck length using the known laws of quantum mechanics and the known behavior of gravity.[26] Similar arguments define "Planck time" as the smallest unit of time.[27] This spacetime discreteness is so small that it looks continuous, and this emergence of continuity from discreteness represents one of the big mysteries of physics.

Dr. Matzke: My own thinking on this has led me to conclude that since space is discrete, at the limit of size, then space can be thought of as grid of little blocks next to each other. From each block there are only six discrete next-door neighbors in a 3D space: left, right, forward, backward, up, and down. The amount of locality is proportional to two times the number of dimensions (2*N*). This is extremely important in physics and also in computing, since a classical and causal computation can only be made based on inputs reaching a common decision of a Boolean logic gate (like the AND/OR/NOT gates used to build computers). As the number of dimensions increases, the amount of locality increases, since there are more directional possibilities available.

The amount of locality is a property of the number of dimensions of the space. This locality metric is not related to distance but is a property of the adjacency in the space itself.[28] For instance, a 4D ebit has an increase in locality metric compared to 3D spaces.

To illustrate this further: knots can only exist in three dimensions, since a knot cannot be formed in only two dimension and can be pulled apart in four dimensions, due to the extra dimension. Similarly, neutrinos exist in two dimensions, quarks, electron, and neutrinos require three dimensions and ebits can only be formed in four dimensions.

As the number of dimensions increases, any Euclidian distance measurement expands, because more dimension segments contribute to the distance formula. For example, the diagonal of a unit square is $1.41 = \sqrt{1+1}$, a unit cube is $1.73 = \sqrt{1+1+1}$, and in general a unit N-cube diagonal $= \sqrt{N}$. So, even though all sides of the cube are size 1 and the volume is also $1 = 1^N$, the length of the diagonal grows as the square root of the number of dimensions grows. All distance calculations also grow with the number of dimensions—when very few items are near each other, sparse distributed coding occurs. This idea of the hyper-hypotenuse of the hypercube shows up again later in this book.

In this spreading out of distances as the number dimensions increases, each qubit has its own two private dimensions, and consequently each ebit has its own four private dimensions. This implies that to account for all ebits in the universe, there is a nearly infinite number of raw orthogonal vectors, plus all the graded elements built on those vectors to support quantum states. This interplay with a nearly infinite graded 1-vectors/N-vectors and sparse distances is how quantum dimensions are linked to content addressable memories (CAMs), and ultimately to the Law of Attraction. For example, for 300 qubits coupled in a quantum register, the 2^{300} number of orthogonal states is larger than the number of particles in the entire known physical universe. Anytime a large number of dimensions occurs, the CAM and correlithm mathematics also apply.

The hyperdimensional address represents the data in a CAM,[29] such that similar points are near each other in the correlithm space.[30] For instance, imagine that each thought is a point in a hyperdimensional CAM space. This point also represents a vector from the midpoint of the space (for unit *N*-cube the center is point [..., .5, .5, ...]). Assembling clusters of these dimensions allows the creation of large thought vectors for each unique meaning.

Since this high-dimensional thought vector representation (made of bits) does not have any metrics other than the number of dimensions and similarity measurements, it has no size, no mass, no distance, no time, and no scales, all of which allow for any number of dimensions and any number of thoughts. In contrast, a conventional matter/energy representation of information has a size, mass, energy, and bandwidth, etc., due to being embedded and distributed in three dimensions, which limits how complex the system can be to still remain as a whole. Information encoded as thought vectors also exists in the pure nonmetric space without any physicality limits. We discuss this in more detail in the next chapter.

Coin Demo and Space-Like States to the Rescue

Dr. Tiller: It is well known that a classical Turing machine, or any classical computer, cannot *efficiently* simulate a quantum computer. What is so different about quantum computing? We know the number of states (Shor-complete) and degree of entanglement (ebit-complete) are important, but is there anything else fundamentally different?

Dr. Matzke: All classical computation is causal, where inputs of logic gates cause the outputs to be computed, and generally uses electrons or photons to propagate the bit representations of any computation. Using the light cone in Figure 18, physicists classify the spacetime interval of classical computation as respectively either **time-like** (for electrons), where the spatial separation is less than the distance light travels, or **light-like** (for photons), where the spatial separation is equal to the distance light travels in a vacuum.[31] The path thru the light cone diagram is defined as the "world line" of the photon, particle, or computation.

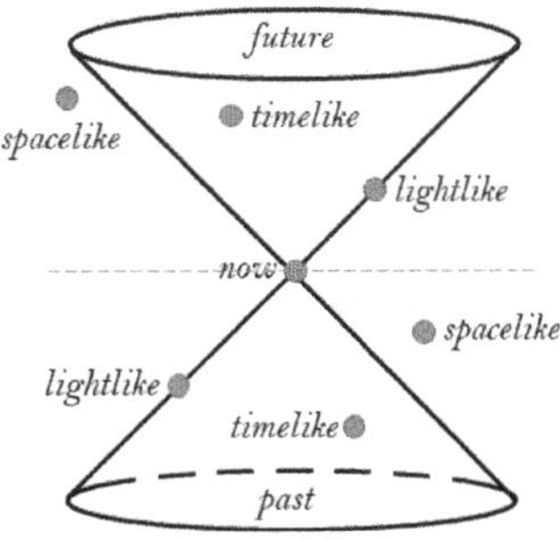

Figure 18. Light cone of physics

All classical computation falls inside the world line of the light cone reachable by light. Physicists also define the **space-like** interval, where the spatial separation is outside the light cone reachable by light. This includes points far away in space or time. Entanglement is an example of space-like states that cannot interact causally.

A very important feature of many aspects of source science requirements is they have space-like states. This space-like behavior also supports all quantum probability amplitudes: otherwise the collapse of entangled states would not appear to be instantaneous. Therefore, quantum states cannot be traditional classical waves; rather, they are a holistic, distributed, mathematically consistent wave-like probability property due to bits. Even gravity propagates at the speed of causality (also the speed of light), whereas all quantum states are fundamentally space-like in order to support entanglement.[32] These space-like states are extremely important because it proves the existence of a mechanism for outside spacetime behaviors, such as entanglement.

Quantum states are concurrent and this sum is synonymous with space-like behavior. This information property related to space-like states can be illustrated with the coin demo developed by my colleague and professor emeritus Mike Manthey—this same coin demo can also illustrate true simultaneity and non-Shannon information.[33]

Act I: *A person stands in front of you with both hands behind his back. He shows you one hand containing a coin, and then returns the hand and the coin behind his back. After a brief pause, the person again shows you the same hand with what appears to be an identical coin and again hides it, and asks, "How many coins do I have?"*

This is not a trick question, nor some clever play on words—since it is particular and straightforward. The known possibilities at this point are exactly one: the person has at least one coin, which implicitly represents *one bit* of information due to the two possible but mutually exclusive states: *state1* = "one coin" and *state2* = "more than one coin."

Act II: *The person now extends his hand and it contains two identical coins.*

We now know that there are two coins and have received one bit of information since the ambiguity is resolved. We have now arrived at an important dramatic insight:

Act III: *The person asks, "Where did that bit of information come from?"*

The bit of information originates in the simultaneous presence of the two coins—their co-occurrence—and encodes the now-observed *fact* that the two *processes,* whose states are represented by the two individual coins, do not exclude each other's existence. Thus, there is information on the environment that cannot be acquired sequentially, and true concurrency therefore cannot be simulated by a sequential Turing machine. Therefore, a given state of process ***a*** can exist simultaneously with a given state of process ***b***, and they do not exclude each other's existence.

In concurrent systems, this is the fundamental and important process distinction. Simultaneity from relativity is related to this, since not all observers perceive two events to be simultaneous, but we believe this kind of quantum concurrency is precise and therefore different because exactness in time represents a protospace building primitive, which is expressed as multivectors using addition in GALG. We know this to be true since all qubits, photons, and Standard Model particles do not dissolve due to changes in simultaneity under relativistic motion.

The coin demonstration shows that by its very existence, a two-co-occurrence like our qubit representation **A** = (**a0** + **a1**), contains one bit of information, compared to the two individual bit-vectors. Co-occurrence relationships are structural protospace and space-like in comparison to Shannon's time-like information. This space-like concurrency is distributed and produces globally coherent behavior due to the sum of all states, including zero states, which represents the photons, the quark structure of mesons and protons/neutrons, and ebit behaviors. Quantum concurrency is simultaneously everywhere and nowhere and is completely outside the scope of Turing sequential computation and Shannon's information. Quantum concurrency is fundamentally wave-like and space-like whereas classical computation is particle-like and sequential. Manthey proposes that awareness and consciousness are also space-like and, thus, wave-like.[34] I have coined the term "source-like" to emphasize that space-like concurrency is fundamental to source science concepts and properties. I believe the term "source-like" means the same as "thought-like." What can you add, Bill?

Dr. Tiller: True concurrency and simultaneity are hard to comprehend since most people and even scientists do not really understand what they mean, so we discuss this in more detail as we proceed. This idea that quantum concurrency is naturally space-like is also very interesting and useful, mainly because that kind of concurrency never shows up in classical metric spaces, except when dealing with entanglement. It is useful that the term "source-like" is synonymous with "space-like." Sir Roger Penrose established that human thought goes beyond the algorithmic, and we need to find a non-computable process that can account for it and it is not conventional, established quantum physics we are talking about.[35] I believe this source-like approach meets Penrose's noncomputational requirements.

The coin demo also demonstrates that concurrency of geometric algebra elements and states leads to changes in information content due to creation of new higher-dimensional constructs. This sounds strangely similar to the Bose–Einstein statistics that we know are part of the quantum infrastructure and related to indistinguishable states. In 1924, physicist Satyendra Nath Bose submitted to Einstein a pioneering paper on the statistics of indistinguishable states, which then became associated with his name and which forever influenced quantum mechanics.

We can give a clear analogy about indistinguishability by using a pair of normal six-sided dice (dice1 with value X and dice2 with value Y). Based on random throws, there are 6*6 = 36 total possible combinations. Of those, there are six possible pairs, ([1][1]), ([2][2])... ([X][Y]), where X=Y and which represents 6/36 = 16.66% of the possibilities. Of the remaining thirty states, there are fifteen pairs of combinations of ([1][2]) vs ([2][1]) and ([1][3]) vs ([3][1])... ([X][Y]), where X ≠ Y and cannot distinguish which dice is which. Specifically, if two dice yield a [1] and [2], those are indistinguishable from a [2] and [1]. If those fifteen pairs ([X][Y]) were indistinguishable, then only 6+15=21 total unique states would exist. Therefore, if dice obeyed the laws of Bose statistics, then the true pairs would represent 6/21=28.57% of the states. Dice do not work this way and Bose showed that quantum physics actually does work this way! Do the geometric algebra expressions and concurrent states have anything to say about indistinguishability?

Geometric Algebra States Represent Probabilities and Indistinguishability

Dr. Matzke: Since the GALG corner state expressions are countable, we could compute how likely each state is due to randomness, which defines the Shannon information content. Likewise, some GALG expressions are rotations of other states so have the same complexity and can be lumped into bins of indistinguishable states. The approach to reveal this uses Karnaugh maps thinking (an alternative grid-like form of logic truth tables) applied to GALG state tables.[36] For example, 1+**a** and −1−**a** have the same state complexity as +**a** and −**a**. Let us take the nine expressions for $\mathbf{G}_1$, compute the row-state vectors, count the number of each state, and then sort those counts, creating a state count list or tuple. Expressions with the same state count ratios have the same relative expressive power to distinguish states. The second half of the signature is related to the number of orthogonal *N*-vectors in the GALG expression, which when combined with the state signature forms a unique complexity signature to identify two bins for $\mathbf{G}_1$, as shown in Table 2. Notice how expression (± 1 ± **a**) represents a rotation of states using these transitions (± → 0, ∓ → ±, etc.) from the ±**a** states, so they have the same state complexity and therefore the same bin signature.

Table 2. One Dimensional Complexity Binning

Expression	Row-States	Signature	Bin #	Bin Count	Bin Statistics
0, ±1	[0 0], [± ±]	((0, 0, 2), 0)	1	3	3/9=1.585 bits
± **a**	[± ∓]	((0, 1, 1), 1)	2	2 of 6	6/9=0.585 bits
± 1 ± **a**	[0 ±], [± 0]	((0, 1, 1), 1)	2	4 of 6	

When this same approach is used for the eighty-one expressions for $\mathbf{G}_2$, then complexity signatures define four bins. This style of signature counts and statistics is equivalent to classical Shannon bits. As Table 3 shows, the difference between the bin counts for single elements versus two elements is exactly 1 bit = 2.170 – 1.170, which is identical to the coin demo. These bit measures are exact as shown in Table 3, because the counts are all integers out of the eighty-one total expressions.

Table 3. Two-Dimensional Complexity Binning

Signature	Bin Count	Example Expression	Row-States	Bin Statistics
((0, 0, 4), 0)	3	± 1	[± ± ± ±]	4.755 bits
((0, 1, 3), 3)	24	+ 1 + **a** + **b** + (**a^b**)	[0 0 0 +]	1.755 bits
((0, 2, 2), 1)	18	+ **a** or **a^b**	[− − + +]	2.170 bits
((1, 1, 2), 2)	36	+ **a** + **b**	[+ 0 0 −]	1.170 bits

Another way to look at these bins is that elements in each bin might be indistinguishable (where each set of indistinguishable items are counted just once), so the Bose information measure is just log2(number of bins), which gives a Bose measure of 2 bits for $\mathbf{G}_2$. There are 14 bins for $\mathbf{G}_3$, which gives a Bose measure of 3.807 bits, and 86 bins for $\mathbf{G}_4$, which gives a Bose measure of 6.426 bits. Each bin is just as likely when including indistinguishable states, since all items in that bin are counted just once, which is the important contribution that Bose made to physics.

When this same complexity measure is applied to $\mathbf{G}_3$, then each bin output states are the same; however, the example expressions look very different. There are four times as many expressions in bin ((0, 4, 4), 4) as compared to bin ((0, 4, 4), 1). Due to random processes, the higher the bit value, the more *unlikely* the states in that bin are expected to be. Out of a total of 6561 total expressions, Table 4 shows that one of the most likely states in $\mathbf{G}_3$ is the bottom row (+ a + b + c), which is the photon/qutrit signature; and the next most likely signature is + **a** + **b**, which is the qubit state. This is significant since photons and qubits are the most likely physics-related states to emerge from $\mathbf{G}_3$ topologies. The next most common states are variations of the mesons. The top-most likely state is ±**a** ±**b** ±**c** ±**x^y** (with bin statistics of 2.287 bits), which is the sum of a qubit and a quark or photon and spinor. These ideas may be important when applied to how particles might have been created from quantum dimensions during the Big Bang.

Table 4. Three-Dimensional Complexity Binning (Partial)

Signature	Bin Count	Example Expression	Row-States	Bin Statistics
((0, 4, 4), 1)	42	+ **a**	[- - - - + + + +]	7.287 bits
((0, 4, 4), 1)	42	+ (**a**^**b**)	[+ + - - - - + +]	7.287 bits
((0, 4, 4), 1)	42	+ (**a**^**b**^**c**)	[- + + - + - - +]	7.287 bits
((0, 4, 4), 4)	168	+ **a** – **b** + **c** + (**a**^**b**^**c**)	[+ - + + - - + -]	5.287 bits
((0, 4, 4), 4)	168	+ **a** + **b** – (**a**^**c**) + (**b**^**c**)	[+ + + - - + - -]	5.287 bits
((0, 4, 4), 4)	168	+ **a** + (**a**^**b**) + (**a**^**c**) – (**a**^**b**^**c**)	[- + + + + - - -]	5.287 bits
((2, 2, 4), 2)	252	+ **a** + **b**	[+ + 0 0 0 0 - -]	4.702 bits
((2, 3, 3), 3)	672	+ **a** + **b** + **c**	[0 - - + - + + 0]	3.287 bits

Are indistinguishable states based only on output state counts, or also on algebraic expression complexity? Alternatively, if we create a complexity measure that differentiates the expression based on counts of vectors, bivectors, and trivectors, we get forty-eight bins for $\mathbf{G}_3$ and a Bose measure of 5.585 bits. Table 5 gives the 1-bit coin demo result, including a bit value with unknown interpretation for the qutrit expression (+ **a** + **b** + **c**), which we believe is the photon.

Table 5. Three-Dimensional Coin Demo with Detailed Signature

Signature	Bin Count	Example Expression	Row-States	Bin Statistics
((0, 0, 8), (0, 0, 0))	3	±1	[± ± ± ± ± ± ± ±]	11.095 bits
((0, 4, 4), (1, 0, 0))	18	+ **a**	[- - - - + + + +]	8.510 bits
((2, 2, 4), (2, 0, 0))	36	+ **a** + **b**	[+ + 0 0 0 0 - -]	7.510 bits
((2, 3, 3), (3, 0, 0))	24	+ **a** + **b** + **c**	[0 - - + - + + 0]	**8.095** bits

This may need some more work to define the bins for indistinguishable states perhaps if only bosons (which are nilpotent where $\mathbf{B}^2=0$) are indistinguishable.

We are now going to list the detailed GALG expressions used earlier in the GALG topological reorganization of Standard Model primitives in Figure 16. There is one nilpotent form (eight variations) in $\mathbf{G}_2$, five nilpotent forms (eighty variations) in G_3, and thirty nilpotent forms (7,280 variations) in $\mathbf{G}_4$. The examples in Table 6 are the complete nilpotent list, and it is easy to identify the bosons in GALG. The GALG expression for quarks in G3 is (**±x ±yz**).

Table 6. Nilpotent Boson Signature Summaries for GALG

Size	Boson	Expression
$\mathbf{G}_2$	W/Z bosons	(**±a ±ab**)
$\mathbf{G}_3$	W/Z bosons	(**±x ±xy**)
	photon	(**±a ±b ±c**)
	X-boson	(**±ab± ac ±bc**)
	meson	(**±x± z ±xy ±yz**)
	gluon	(**±x ±y ±z ±xy ±xz ±yz**)
$\mathbf{G}_4$	W/Z bosons	(**±x ±xy**)
	dark boson	(**±w ±xyz**)
	Higgs boson	(**± ab ±ac ±bc ±ad ±bd ±cd**)
	Additional nilpotents	27 more

Now we present the complete list of identifiable GALG expressions for particles (which are unitary, $\mathbf{P}^2$=1), listed in Table 7. The total summaries of unitary states are: two unitary forms (twelve variations) in $\mathbf{G}_{2,}$ four unitary forms (ninety variations) in G_3, and seventeen unitary forms (12,690 variations) in G_4. More research on this is needed to understand these other particles in G_4.

Table 7. Unitary Particle Signature Summaries for GALG

Size	Particle	Expression
$\mathbf{G}_1$	bits	(**±x**)
$\mathbf{G}_2$	neutrinos	(**±a ±b ±ab**)
$\mathbf{G}_3$	electrons	(**±xy ±xz**)
	protons	(**±x ±y ±z ±xy ±xz**)
$\mathbf{G}_4$	graviton	**±wxyz**
	Additional unitary	15 more

Dr. Tiller: I particularly find it interesting that unitary neutrinos are two dimensional and this proposed nilpotent Higgs boson is four dimensional. What is interesting about the previous tables is that all primitives are expressed as concurrent sums of vectors, bivectors, trivectors, and 4-vectors. These topological structures and subsequent state vectors are completely unique ways of expressing the structure of the Standard Model and may give insights into how particles actually interact or their low ability to interact, as is the case of 2D neutrinos and 4D Higgs bosons.

Dr. Matzke: This is true; because our proposed Higgs boson is expressed as the sum of all possible bivectors (the complete even subalgebra of G_3) and we suspect that dark matter appears to be using the odd subalgebras (sums of vectors and trivectors). This might account for why they do not easily interact with standard matter and are so are hard to detect.

For completeness, I show the details of the Bell states that form the proposed Higgs boson. For GALG with qubits states $\mathbf{A}_0$ = (**a0**+**a1**) and $\mathbf{B}_0$ = (**b0**+**b1**) and where the spinors are defined as S_A = (**a0^a1**) and S_B = (**b0^b1**), then the Bell operator is defined as $B = S_A + S_B$ and the complex conjugate Magic operator is $M = S_A - S_B$. These operators are singular since B^{-1} and M^{-1} have been proven to not exist. Likewise, states shown in Table 8 are also singular due to multiplicative cancellation because $\mathbf{A}_0\ \mathbf{B}_0$ = **a0^b0** **– a0^b1 – a1^b0** + **a1^**b1 = $\underline{B}_3 + M_3$ and $0 = B{*}M_j = M{*}B_i = B_i{*}M_j$. This means any quantum register with two qubits is the sum of Bell and Magic states, so multiplying by either operator causes an erasure of states due to multiplicative cancellation.

Table 8. Bell and Magic operators with states for GALG

$B_{(i+1)mod4} = B_i\boxed{(S_A + S_B)}$	$M_{(i+1)mod4} = M_i\boxed{(S_A - S_B)}$
$B_0 = A_0\,B_0$ **Bell** = $-\,S_{00} + S_{11} = \Phi^+$	$M_0 = A_0\,B_0$ **Magic** = $+\,S_{01} - S_{10}$
$B_1 = B_0$ **Bell** = $+\,S_{01} + S_{10} = \Psi^+$	$M_1 = M_0$ **Magic** = $-\,S_{00} - S_{11}$
$B_2 = B_1$ **Bell** = $+\,S_{00} - S_{11} = \Phi^-$	$M_2 = M_1$ **Magic** = $-\,S_{01} + S_{10}$
$B_3 = B_2$ **Bell** = $-\,S_{01} - S_{10} = \Psi^-$	$M_3 = M_2$ **Magic** = $+\,S_{00} + S_{11}$
$B_0 = B_3$ **Bell** = $-\,S_{00} + S_{11} = \Phi^+$	$M_0 = M_3$ **Magic** = $+\,S_{01} - S_{10}$

With the singular and inseparable Bell operators and states defined, we can now show the tauquernions $\mathcal{T}_i$, $\mathcal{T}_j$, and $\mathcal{T}_k$ are a higher dimensional version of quaternions {*i*, *j*, *k*}, where:

> $\mathcal{T}_i$ = B = **(a0^a1)+(b0^b1)**, $\mathcal{T}_j$ = B_2 = **(a0^b0)–(a1^b1)** , $\mathcal{T}_k$ = B_1 = **(a0^b1)+(a1^b0)**
>
> $\mathcal{T}_i'$ = M = **(a0^a1)–(b0^b1)**, $\mathcal{T}_j'$ = M_3 = **(a0^b0)+(a1^b1)** , $\mathcal{T}_k'$ = M_0 = **(a0^b1)–(a1^b0)**
>
> $\mathcal{T}_i\mathcal{T}_j=\mathcal{T}_k,\ \mathcal{T}_j\mathcal{T}_k=\mathcal{T}_i,\ and\ \mathcal{T}_k\mathcal{T}_i=\mathcal{T}_j$ (plus the same for $\mathcal{T}_i'$, $\mathcal{T}_j'$ and $\mathcal{T}_k'$)
>
> $\mathcal{T}_i^2=\mathcal{T}_j^2=\mathcal{T}_k^2=\mathcal{T}_i\mathcal{T}_j\mathcal{T}_k=I^-$, where $(I^-)^2=I^+$ (sparse versions of ±1)
>
> I^- = +1–**a0^a1^b0^b1** = [0 – – 0 – 0 0 – – 0 0 – 0 – – 0] (sparse state version of –1)
>
> I^+ = –1–**a0^a1^b0^b1** = [0 + + 0 + 0 0 + + 0 0 + 0 + + 0] (sparse state version of +1)

By looking at the row-states, we discovered the ±1 sparse invariants are I^- = +1±**a0^a1^b0^b1** and $(I^-)^2 = I^+$ = –1±**a0^a1^b0^b1**, which are two out-of-phase sets $B^2 = I_b^-$, $M^2 = I_m^-$, $B^4 = I_b^+$ and $M^4 = I_m^+$, therefore $B^2 + M^2 = -1$ and $B^4 + M^4 = +1$. These are operator defined rings.

Now with the tauquernions defined, we can show that the Higgs boson $\mathcal{H}$ can be defined as the sum of three tauquernions $\mathcal{H} = \pm\mathcal{T}_i \pm\mathcal{T}_j \pm\mathcal{T}_k$, where $\mathcal{H}^2 = 0$, which produces sixteen nilpotent variations that represent the complete even subalgebra for $\mathbf{G}_4$ and are nilpotent bosons. There are also forty-eight variations, where $\mathcal{H}^2$ = ±**a0^a1^b0^b1**, which we believe is the mass primitive. Likewise, the $\mathbf{G}_5$ version of the tauquinions can be defined in a similar manner.

Another prediction is that Bell/Magic operators/states can be rotated with **(a1^b0^b1)**, producing odd algebra nilpotent forms of ±**w**±(**x^y^z**), which might be the 4D dark bosons. These higher dimensional states resemble 3D quarks (with form ±**w**±(**x^y**)) and the summation of four dark quarks are unitary, which might be the elusive dark matter. All these states are entangled.

Now that the Higgs prediction details are complete, Table 9 illustrates more detail about the previously stated prediction regarding the existence of four neutrinos. The top three rows of the upper-half of table are the three known neutrinos and the top three rows of the bottom-half are the three known antineutrinos. Neutrinos/antineutrinos all have the row-state signature of tuple ((0, 1, 3), 3), which is detailed in the middle 'vector' column. Notice there are eight states with this signature pattern, which strongly suggests the existence of an additional fourth neutrino pair. Also notice how the bottom row of each section illustrates; the new proposed neutrino is the sum of the three known antineutrinos, and likewise the new proposed antineutrino is the sum of the three known neutrinos. This kind of recombination or oscillation prediction can be validated in a laboratory.[37]

Table 9. GALG Signature and States Predicting Four Neutrino Pairs

Name	*Form*	*Vector* ($\mathcal{G}_2$)	*Signature*	*Bits*
ν	$a+b+ab$	$[- - -0]$	$(0,1,3),3$	1.75
ν_μ	$a-b-ab$	$[- - 0-]$	"	"
ν_τ	$-a+b-ab$	$[-0 - -]$	"	"
$\Sigma =$	$a+b-ab$	$[0 + + +]$	"	"
$\bar{\nu}$	$-a-b-ab$	$[+ + +0]$	"	"
$\bar{\nu}_\mu$	$-a+b+ab$	$[+ + 0+]$	"	"
$\bar{\nu}_\tau$	$a-b+ab$	$[+0 + +]$	"	"
$\Sigma =$	$-a-b+ab$	$[0 - - -]$	"	"

Emergence of Time Sequences and Spacetime from Quantum States

Dr. Tiller: It is great how your model identifies particles and bosons using purely topological considerations, especially your new predictions based on those same topologies. Now you are right that defining the indistinguishable states is a tricky problem. Even Einstein could not solve it until Bose came up with the idea of counting these states differently. Therefore, indistinguishable states were eventually named after him and called "bosons." Bose statistics (based on collapsing the counts for indistinguishable states) show that quantum probabilities are fundamental and especially related to indistinguishability. Also, true simultaneity is fundamental to quantum states, especially entanglement, resulting in no occurrence of time. Exactly how quantum processes and time emerge from concurrent bits is a fundamental mystery.

Dr. Matzke: Agreed. In computer science, the concepts of "wait" and "signal" are used to allow asynchronous processes to interact in controlled ways. For example, multiple computers sharing a printer must have a controlled way of waiting until the previous print job is complete. In GALG, there is a direct mathematical formulation for the synchronization primitives of wait and signal in which sequences are implemented as products, and concurrency states are implemented as sums. Mathematically, nilpotents are defined as N*N=0 and idempotents are defined as I*I=I.

> Waits (**W**) are implemented as nilpotents (**W=N**) because **W*W** = 0 (related to bosons).
> Signals (**S**) are implemented as idempotents (**S=I**) because **S*S** = **S** (related to measurement).

These computer science ideas are tied to physics because particles (**P**) persist since they are unitary (**P=U**) where **P*P** = 1. All particles **P** are related to measurement because it is easy to prove that for every unitary particle there is an idempotent measurement operator **I** = **S**, where signal **S** = –1±**P** (or **I** = –1±**U**). Because of these mathematical properties wait and signal exists, plus they form the basis for nondeterministic (or random) ordering of events (which can lead to the emergence of time) for concurrent processes, which in turn forms the coarse-grain skeleton of physical nondeterminism. The wait-and-signal capabilities define the operating system style primitives beneath source science based on the quantum simulation infrastructure of concurrency, bit-vectors, and *N*-vectors. This topic is even more scientifically and mathematically quite deep, so we do not delve into it any more here.[38]

Because our mind can directly influence quantum states (remember the quantum double-slit and gas-discharge PK experiments), as we have outlined, it must be part of these same quantum states and possess the ability to act as an operator on these states. Essentially, our thoughts are part of the source code of this universal quantum simulation. Bill, do you have anything to add to this complex topic?

Dr. Tiller: Causality and determinism are also deep topics that generally apply to physics. By extrapolation, some strict behaviorists also believe they apply to human behaviors as well, based on the contention that humans are just deterministic brain machines controlled by the laws of classical physics, which, if true, means that humans do not really have free will. Many proponents of determinism over free will also make false assumptions about the nature of the universe, our brains, and our minds that are inconsistent with modern quantum principles. Since nondeterminism has its roots at the quantum source level, which is the same layer where mind most likely exists, free will appears out of this wait-and-signal nondeterministic ordering of space-like concurrent states and probabilistic choices. If all choices are not deterministically made, then we can make choices that represent free will. We see more in the next chapter on Law of Attraction concepts about how thoughts affect choices that affect mental states that affect memory and decisions in a holistic manner. This wave-like nondeterministic method of living life is very different from preordained deterministic machine-like life.[39]

Dr. Matzke: At a very high level, most Turing computing machines are deterministic, with sequential time-like algorithms that stop when they find solutions or when they exhaustively find none at all.[40] Deterministic algorithms mean that if the same choices are made repeatedly, then the exact same answer will be repeatedly determined each time. If a random element is used in any algorithmic step, this is considered a "probabilistic algorithm." With the advent of parallel programming, all reasonably sized solutions can be computed in parallel, which might also be considered to be nondeterministic, since picking one of those solutions might be different each time, due to the order they finish or a different subsets of solutions. For example, an automated light bulb factory will make each bulb exactly the same, but at a coffee shop, different human baristas would vary the results, timing, and order for the line of people requesting drinks. For space-like quantum algorithms, nondeterminism is due to quantum probabilities, irreversible operators, uncertainty, and wait/signal ordering. As Chapter 4 discusses, you can also have quantum-like probabilities due to context of hyperdimensional states from probabilistic sparse distributed coding hyperstates.

There is an old adage about designing algorithms and writing computer programs. Originally, this saying contained only the items numbered below as 1, 2, and 6. I have expanded the list to include four more:

1) Thinking about sequential algorithms is hard
2) Thinking about parallel algorithms is hard
3) Thinking about quantum algorithms is hard
4) Thinking about space-like processes is hard
5) Thinking about hyperdimensional algorithms is hard
6) Thinking is hard, especially critical thinking
7) Not thinking at all is hard

Traditional time-like algorithms focus on items 1 and 2; items 3 and 4 are being investigated in quantum computing; item 5 represents correlithms; and item 6 is the traditional punch line. Item 7 is the deep state of meditation. The ones I added are based on the space-like source science perspective of hyperdimensional reality. There are many kinds of algorithms each with their own assumptions and techniques for how to apply them, which makes them hard to comprehend in order to use them appropriately.

Dr. Tiller: Your classification of the different kinds of computational algorithms is great, since most people do not appreciate the possible variety. Connecting physics and computation is really important, and recognizing that mind and thoughts are a space-like informational paradigm is even more important. The hyperdimensional nature of source science represents both the quantum simulator infrastructure as well as quantum operating system primitives that exist outside the spacetime box we call our universe. Adding the space-like paradigm to the existing light cone causality model clearly differentiates source-like thinking from traditional classical time-like or light-like computation models.

Exploring space-like concurrent states is interesting and novel, yet as a material scientist I want to know how do time and frequencies emerge? Frequencies imply a wave-like model, which is really a spatial concept since waves have values at each point in space and wavelength is also a spatial concept. Spacetime itself must also emerge at the Planck scale from this concurrent hyperdimensional substrate. Is that how you see it?

Dr. Matzke: Yes. But also, those quantum states are really space-like, because they are simultaneously both everywhere and nowhere. The row-state vectors described earlier represent the *concurrent* states equivalent to the possible states of a quantum finite state machine. Those states, when unfolded and mapped into spacetime, represent the structure of the wave pattern. In additional to concurrent row-state vector, there are also co-exclusions (states that exclude each other) that imply some reversible operators must also exist. These two mechanisms of concurrent row-state vectors and co-exclusion operators work together like an automaton to generate the spatial and temporal patterns we experience as fields and waves.[41]

A new example of this are time crystals—a new, bizarre state of matter with an atomic structure that repeats not just in space but in time, allowing the crystals to maintain constant oscillation without energy.[42] An analogy that demonstrates how different structures produce different wave patterns is: two inverting gates when cross-wired forms an oscillator and the components are used to determine the frequency. Another useful analogy is this: a slinky produces a pattern of walking down steps. In general, structures and state machines each produce different patterns in time, meaning quantum structures also produce different wave patterns.

Joseph Fourier proved in 1805 that any sequence of values in time or pattern in space can be represented as a weighted sum of frequencies.[43] The function that performs that conversion from time series to frequency domain is called a "Fourier transform" (FT). This transformation is reversible and represents a dual representation between spatial data and frequencies. The states of finite state machines (FSMs, sets of rules about how states change) and concurrent quantum states can also be transformed into the frequency domain using FT techniques. Functions that are localized in the time domain have Fourier transforms that are spread out across the frequency domain and vice versa. Further, this contrast between finite and infinite extents in dual representations is related to the uncertainty principle.

Parseval's identity, named after Marc-Antoine Parseval, is a generalization of Fourier's transform as applied to hyperdimensional spaces.[44] Parseval's original insight was that energy is equivalent even if measured in the frequency domain. This represents a hyperdimensional version of the Pythagorean metric because the frequency domain is represented as the length of the hyper-hypotenuse, which is sum-of-squares of magnitude of the side for that frequency component. Therefore, any hyper-hypotenuse also represents angles and frequencies, just like FT of time series or spatial patterns.

Deep Reality from the Planck Scale

Dr. Tiller: This mathematical insight also makes it clear how states can be mapped to frequencies, even in the hyperdimensional context. Our conversation here does not represent proof, but it does indicate a clear mathematical approach that is historically sound, based on Parseval's Pythagorean metric and Fourier transforms. I understand that the frequency domain is really a spatial concept, not a temporal one, and supports waves and fields defined by the wavelengths extended through space. This explains how states are mapped to wave-like patterns in space.

Another important question is, "How does classical spacetime emerge from quantum no time?" I would imagine this is directly related to the Planck units[45] down at the Planck scale, including the Planck length, etc.[46] These Planck scale terms are defined below, and the starting point for understanding this are the five universal constants and related physical theory:

1) Quantum theory: reduced Planck constant
2) Temperature and thermodynamics: Boltzmann constant
3) Electromagnetics: Coulomb constant
4) Special relativity: speed of light
5) General relativity: gravitational constant

These can then be rewritten to give the following five base Planck units, which are all described using only these five universal constants: Planck length, Planck time, Planck mass, Planck charge, and Planck temperature.

With these five base units, other Planck units can be derived for fifteen metrics, plus a few more of interest:

1) Planck units of area, volume, momentum, energy, force, power, density, energy density, intensity, angular frequency, pressure, current, voltage, impedance, and acceleration.
1) Planck frequency (reciprocal of Planck time), which can be interpreted as an upper bound on the frequency of a wave. This follows from the interpretation of the Planck length as a minimal length, and therefore a lower bound on the wavelength.
2) Planck epoch is the point in the Big Bang expansion when the universe was one Planck time old, one Planck length in diameter, and had a Planck temperature of 1, this represents the point at which quantum models are applicable.
3) Fine-structure constant (1/137.03599911) where combinatory hierarchy predicts 137=127+7+3.

Dr. Matzke: These five base Planck units of length, temperature, charge, mass, and time would have to be derived directly from first principles from hyperdimensional bit-vectors based on the principles of geometric algebra. Here is the approach:

1) Bit-vectors are directly related to quantized bit information and entropy measures.
2) Quaternions can be expressed using the three bivectors in $\mathbf{G}_3$, which can represent 3D spaces and rotations.
3) Tauquernions (three bivector pairs in $\mathbf{G}_4$) can express 3D quaternions projected from a higher 4D space. These bivector pairs are four Bell states (plus Bell operator) or four Magic states (plus Magic operator), so are entangled.
4) Tauquinions (six bivector and trivector pairs in $\mathbf{G}_5$) can express 3D quaternions projected from a higher 5D space. These are also entangled, like the quaternions.
5) The proposed Higgs boson is the sum of three tauquernions, so suggests mass is due to entanglement, which is based on bivectors.
6) In addition to the above topological principles, we believe:
   a. We believe magnetic and electrical properties are tied to bivectors and trivectors, respectively, plus the even grade 4-vector is related to the graviton.
   b. The fine structure constant 1/137 may be directly related to charge due to the combinatorial hierarchy of 3+7+127=137.

Manthey and I believe it is also possible to tie bits, electromagnetism, and gravity to the *N*-vector structures that emerge from geometric algebra. This brings a new question to light: How does time emerge from quantum no-time, which is essentially the same as asking how spacetime emerged initially from the Big Bang, and is also applicable to a discussion on how continuous spacetime emerges from discreteness.

The full answer is not known at this time, but a partial one says it is clear that quantum state dimensions exist outside of spacetime and create all fields, including spacetime itself since the Big Bang inflation. Primitive changes in quantum states must be self-consistent with energy spacetime models, so changes in states show up as changes in particles and rates of change in space. Thus, time is emergent from the low-level states changes. Even length contraction and time dilation of special relativity might be explainable due to limits imposed by Planck units.[47] Our tauquernion model proposes that the Higgs bosons are entangled due to bivector topologies—other scientists are also thinking about how relativity is derived from entanglement.[48]

Another aspect of *N*-vector hierarchy in geometric algebra is the larger the *N* in the *N*-vectors, the slower its orientation can change as individual vectors change. Each *N*-vector or the oriented sum of *N*-vectors is the holistic combination of all the individual vectors, and the change in final orientation to larger *N*-vectors represents the bubble-up of abstraction in a hierarchy.[49] The trickle-down represents the action from these changes. This orientation of an *N*-vector is orthogonal to all other vectors and orientations, just like any other vector, as input into each upper level of the hierarchy. This topological differentiation of vectors and *N*-vectors is obvious using geometric algebra.

All AI systems use some kind of hierarchy to build higher-level constructs. The GALG hierarchy is unique since it is maximally concurrent and space-like, leading to a holistic consistency that is not possible with object-oriented sequential computer systems. Each level in the abstraction hierarchy is first-class and has its own persistence rate based on valid row-state vector changes. These changes affect behaviors and time scales observed in the emergent spacetime—Mike Manthey's patented Topsy system uses GALG co-occurrences, co-exclusions, bubble-up, and trickle-down to naturally define this concurrency and hierarchy.[50]

An example of hierarchical persistence rates is when our conscious awareness of experiences makes the physical world appear to be stable. The reason for this is that our mind is spread through time. Our perceived "now" is really smeared through time, which can be affected in altered states. This is more space-like behavior than the typical sequential in-time behavior due to interacting with the brain. We do not perceive the world as a series of independent images, but rather as a sliding window of space-like states spread through time. Psychologists such as Robert Ornstein put forth that how we experience time is related to how we organize information.[51]

We also know that since source stuff is most likely a near-infinity of orthonormal space-like dimensions, some are associated with our physical universe and others define other universes in the multiverse. These hyperdimensional source bits form everything we know, including qubits, ebits, space, time, matter, energy, waves, fields, gravity, quantum states, thoughts, and mind. In the next chapter, we dive deeper into the strange reality of hyperdimensional environment of thought vectors.

Chapter Summary

As we mentioned in the introduction to this chapter, bit-vectors mathematics can lead to amazing scientific results, not just philosophic ruminations. Discrete orthonormal bit dimensions and GALG formalizations form the backplane of the unimaginably sophisticated and concurrent hyperdimensional source quantum supercomputer with built-in operating system primitives to self-consistently run the simulation of our universe. Everything we observe in it is based on the mathematics we defined and the reorganized particles and bosons in a dimensionally graded version of the Standard Model. This reorganization naturally identifies new particles and bosons, such as 4th neutrino pair, proposed X17 boson, Higgs boson, dark matter, and dark energy. It also shows that the GALG Bell and Magic operators are irreversible (due to multiplicative cancellation) and therefore Bell and Magic states are entangled. They are stable due to information erasure, which changes the way to think about space and mass since the Higgs boson and dark matter are also most likely entangled. We further developed how particle statistics can emerge directly from the state discrimination, topology, and symmetry.

These concurrent quantum states exist outside spacetime and are both wave-like and space-like, which we summarized as being source-like. We discussed how Planck-scale primitives, space, time, and frequencies might be derived directly from no-space and no-time primitives. The primitives of this source hyperdimensional supercomputer also include the behavior of nonphysical thoughts and mind, which means our mind, is part of the operating system of the quantum simulator. Our thoughts represent the source code of the universe and allow us to directly observe and influence the outcomes of the simulation of our physical world.

Chapter 4: Thoughts on Law of Attraction

The Law of Attraction (LOA)[1] is a spiritual and self-help concept with the simple definition of "like attracts like." The LOA concept was originally promoted through books such as *Think and Grow Rich*[2] by Napoleon Hill and *You Can Heal Your Life*[3] by Louise Hay. Starting in the 1980s, Esther Hicks and her husband Jerry Hicks held live channeling workshops on LOA and ultimately published many *New York Times* bestselling books.[4] Esther's work is particularly interesting since her messages are channeled from a spiritual being called Abraham.[5]

Influenced by Esther's work, the film *The Secret*[6] was released in 2006 by Rhonda Byrne and subsequently the companion book later that year.[7] As the title implies, people in power in earlier times did not then, and those in power still do not now, want the masses to know or understand about this ancient LOA knowledge. *The Secret* was a massive international sensation that brought LOA out from the shadows, and inspired megastar Oprah Winfrey to further help promote LOA concepts and authors.[8]

Abraham reports that it represents a collective of beings that is sharing the Law of Attraction message through channeling with Esther. Abraham also describes itself as infinite intelligence and its message is amazingly consistent over the years:

> Thoughts are things that affect the world; and thoughts attract like thoughts and, therefore, we create our own

> reality. By following these teachings, we can tap into the source that is the energy that creates worlds. Meditation and positive emotions are a big part of achieving success at getting tuned in, tapped in, and turned on. Abraham states that the LOA is absolute and universal, just like gravity or other laws of physics.

In fact, because of these described LOA behaviors, we believe LOA is essentially information centric, occurs naturally, and is fundamental in the universe and to therefore in source science.

The Math Beneath the Law of Attraction

Dr. Tiller: What does "like attracts like" mean? To most people, it means like-minded groups of people are attracted to one another for a common purpose, such as companionship, family, religion, politics, sports, or entertainment. However, to a scientist it means some physical force, such as magnetism or electric charge, is at work. To a computer scientist, it can only mean content-oriented lookup (CAMs, content addressable memories) that are based on the properties of hyperdimensional math.

So, here is the dilemma: do opposites attract or do likes attract? Physicists know that opposites attract when talking about positive and negative electrical/magnetic poles. For example, a positive electric charge is attracted to negative electric charge. Gravity is the only physics field where like attracts like, since all matter is attractive due to its mass. Opposites attract for both electrical/magnetic poles due to classical energy laws, however in spite of the similarities with attraction for electric charges and magnets, there is no free-floating magnetic particle (the hypothetical magnetic monopole) equivalent to an electron.

Dr. Matzke: From the perspective of information laws, "like attracts like" in people because the mechanism of meaning of shared ideas is required. There is no energy-based classical physics mechanism that exists to support meaning of thought for Law of Attraction, but the mathematics of hyperdimensional spaces naturally supports this idea using CAMs and correlithms. Therefore, opposites attract due to energy principles, except gravity, whereas likes attract due to some meaning mechanism. Let me introduce how correlithms can solve this problem.

I start with the neurological insights, but the result is based purely on mathematical and probability principles. The neurons firing in the brain appear to be random, and this randomness is the key to correlithms. Imagine choosing a random point (values from 0-1) in a 3D unit box with coordinates **x**, **y**, and **z** (Figure 19). Now imagine choosing a point in a 100D box (**a0**, **a1**,…, **a99**) and this would look like the image in Figure 20. If you pick one thousand random points in each box, what can you say about those points? Previously, we discussed that as the number of *N* dimensions increases, the points appear to move farther apart.

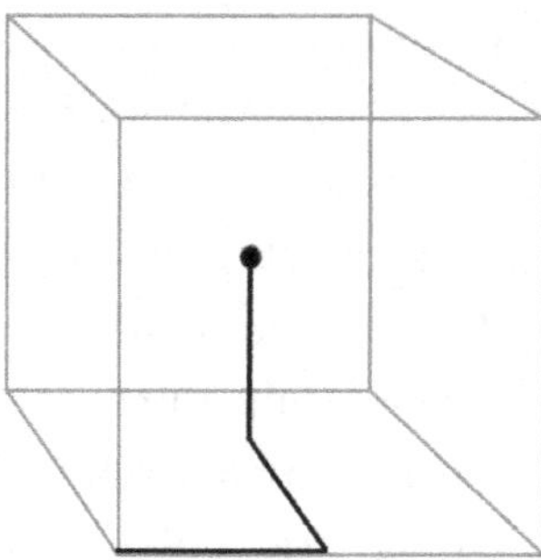

Figure 19. Point in 3D space

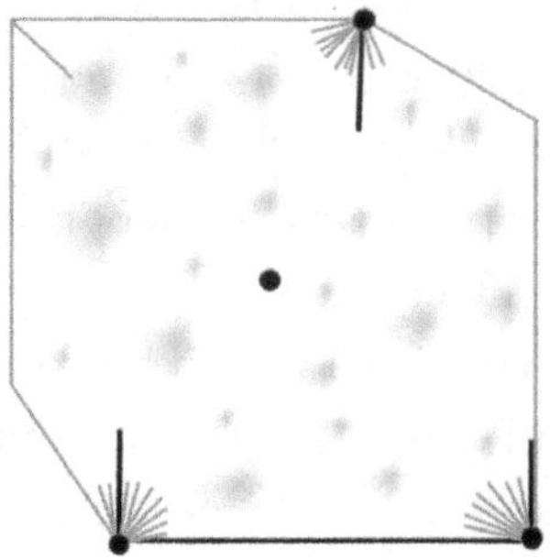

Figure 20. Point in ND space

You can create the charts shown in Figure 21 if you compute the distance between any two random points (see **p** & **q** in Figure 22) and gather these standard distance statistics. The key is that the average distance keeps growing with *N* dimensions, but the shape of the distribution stays the same because the randomness contained in each dimension tends to average out and cancel each other during the distance computation. It is relatively easy to show programmatically that for any unit *N*-cube there exists a standard distance that is exactly $\sqrt{N/6}$ and the standard deviation of those distance is exactly $\sqrt{7/120}$=0.2415. These exact values were derived with the Mathematica symbolic math tool. Also, random corners **d** are $\sqrt{N/2}$ away from corners **c** or **o**. For example, with $N = 24$, the standard distance is $2 = \sqrt{24/6}$; this means that all the random points are more than eight standard deviations away from each other (because $2 \div 0.2415 = 8.281$). For $N = 96$, the standard distance is $4 = \sqrt{96/6}$; this means that all points are more than sixteen standard deviations away from each other (because $4 \div 0.2415 = 16.563$). Anything more than six standard deviations are considered highly significant. These correlithm points form a probabilistic geometry and represent a noise-immune way of expressing unique tokens, using random points.

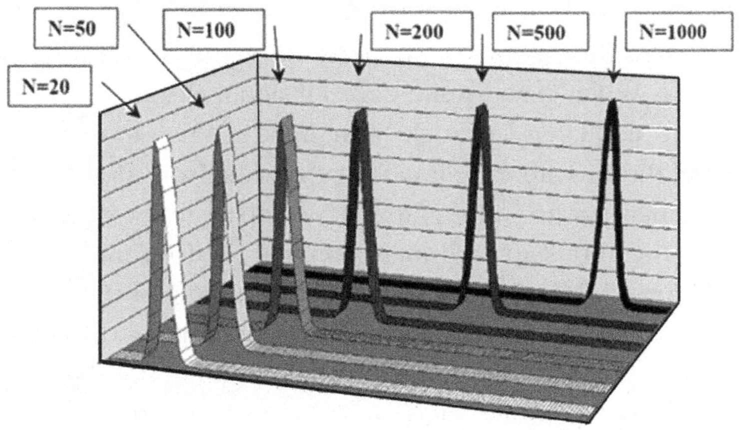

Figure 21. Standard distance vs dimension

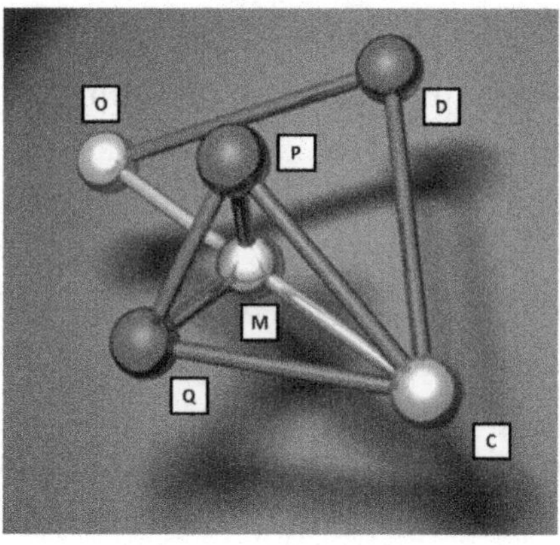

Figure 22. Probabilistic geometry tinker toy model

This idea is powerful because random points represent an ideal way to store unique thoughts so that they do not run into each other. Thus, in any *N*-space, all random points are approximately a standard distance apart from all other random points. This is hard to visualize, so in Figure 22 we built the probabilistic geometry ball and stick model where **p** and **q** represent any two random points and **m** is the midpoint of the space. Point **c** is a corner of the *N*-cube, **o** is the opposite corner, and **d** is some other randomly selected corner. We already know the distance **co** $=\sqrt{N}$, since it is the diagonal of the *N*-cube and half that amount is **cm** = **om** = $\sqrt{N}/2$ or $\sqrt{N/4}$.

Here is the geometric understanding of this probabilistic geometry. When three points are all equal distance apart, it is called an "equilateral triangle" (for $N = 2$). When four points are all equal distance apart, it is called a "tetrahedron" (for $N = 3$). For $N + 1$ points that are all equal distance apart for $N \geq 100$, we can essentially call this an "*N*-dimensional tetrahedron" or my term of "equihedron." For all *N*-equihedrons, the middle of the *N*-cube **m** is [… .5, .5…] and the distances from any point to the midpoint can be computed for **mp** or **mq**, which we call the "standard radius" with the exact average value $\sqrt{N/12}$ and standard deviation of exactly $\sqrt{1/60}$, which is independent of *N*. Figure 23 and Table 10 show these relationships.

When all other distances are normalized by this standard radius, then **mq** = 1, **pq** = $\sqrt{2}$ and the **pmq** triangle forms a right triangle, since $\sqrt{2}^2 = \sqrt{1}^2 + \sqrt{1}^2$. Likewise, you compute the normalized values of **cm** = **dm** = $\sqrt{3}$ (midpoint to corner), **cp** = **cq** = $\sqrt{4}$ (random point to corner) and **cd** = **od** = $\sqrt{6}$ (random corner to random corner). All random points are orthogonal to each other (from the midpoint perspective) and so all angles from point **m** are 90°. Also, since $\sqrt{6}^2 = \sqrt{3}^2 + \sqrt{3}^2$, then all random corners are orthogonal to each other (from the midpoint perspective), which replicates Pentti Kanerva's CAM work.

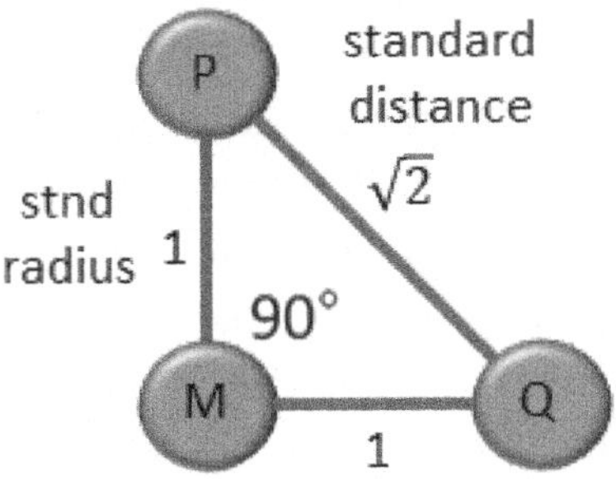

Figure 23. Standard distance normalized by standard radius

Table 10. Raw and Normalized Standard Distance

Lines	Average Raw Distance	Normalized Distance
mq=mp	$\sqrt{N/12}$ (standard radius)	1
pq	$\sqrt{N/6}$ (standard distance)	$\sqrt{2}$
mc=mo	$\sqrt{N/4}$ (½ diagonal)	$\sqrt{3}$
cp=cq	$\sqrt{N/3}$ (point to corner)	$\sqrt{4}$
dc=do	$\sqrt{N/2}$ (Kanerva)	$\sqrt{6}$
co	$\sqrt{N}$ (diagonal)	$\sqrt{12}$

CAMs use inner products for nearness computations (using phase), whereas correlithms rely on normalized distance metrics. The generalized results using correlithms was invented and patented by Nick Lawrence and was augmented by me with identifying the standard radius and cell generalization.[9] This standard radius perspective is mathematically important because it shows that correlithms form near-orthogonal vector sets that contain phase angles, just like qubits. This means the correlithms have the orthogonality expressed by matrix math and the phase angles of quantum computing. These properties emerge robustly when the number of dimensions N is much greater than 20 ($N >> 20$).

These random points in a hyperdimensional space are the thought vectors we discussed earlier. When each bit dimension is some small attribute or characteristic, then similar ideas naturally are near each other, since the content features form the address. We describe how this works for thoughts later in the chapter when we discuss submodalities. In mathematics, the orthogonal vectors **A** and **B** can be compared using the inner product where **A.A** = 1 means 0° and **A.B** = 0 means 90°. So, when spiritual people say that they are aligned, they are intuitively saying that their thought vectors have an inner product of 1. Since this N-space is not in our brain, we can all share subcomponents of thought vectors, which is how rotes and telepathy work.

Correlithm math is unintuitive, just as quantum computing concepts are hard to understand. The hyperdimensional nature requires a mathematical approach to comprehend either domain, since we have very little common sense about hyperdimensional spaces due to the 3D experience from our daily lives. The most common example of this class of technology is a dating web site. There exist numerous attributes about a person and the goal is to match that person with similar people. Bill, what do you think about this approach for understanding the geometry of nonmetric hyperdimensional spaces?

Dr. Tiller: This takes some imagination to visualize this N-dimensional equihedron geometry, so we have to rely on the math to gain intuition about how it works. The best part of this hyperdimensional solution is that it transcends traditional neurology and quantum physics. Though most quantum researchers still assume that all quantum events happen inside spacetime, we both know that is incomplete, because entanglement, thoughts, and psi phenomena cannot be explained by any purely classical representations only existing in 3+1 spacetime geometry.

Law of Attraction Is Built on Space-Like Bit-Vectors

Dr. Matzke: Quantum entanglement requires these vast hyperdimensional *N*-spaces, since each ebit has their own four private bit dimensions (are not shared and are not curled up). Most physicists just wave their hands at this mathematics and do not understand the reality of those dimensions. These private dimension sets are real orthogonal dimensions and not just mathematical constructs, and actually represent bits, which we know from Landauer's principle, are physical. These bit dimensions are the infrastructure of a giant quantum supercomputer that simulates our classical world. These bit dimensions are also the basis of LOA, based on correlithm math. Hollywood examines these ideas of simulated reality with the holodeck concept from the Star Trek series, and there is no spoon, from *The Matrix* movies.[10]

Orthogonal bit-vectors are literally classical bits, since each bit-vector has two orientations; for example: +1 = Heads and –1 = Tails (Figure 24). As described earlier, when two bit-vectors are combined they form a qubit, where each state is its own orthogonal vector—the qubit states are 90° rather than mutually exclusive classical states of 180°. This state decoupling means it is possible to represent a 45° phase angle so that the actual measured state is probabilistically half and half. This superposition feature of spin ½ qubits introduces bivectors, phase, and probabilities as being fundamental in physics and also the root of entanglement. Figure 25 illustrates the Hilbert space version of the same.

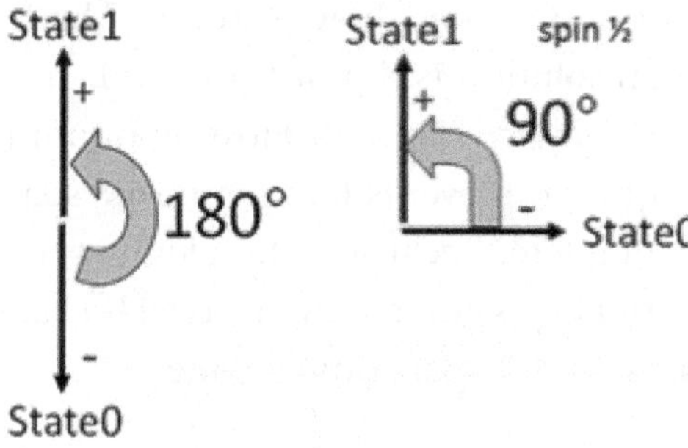

Figure 24. Bit and qubit in geometric algebra

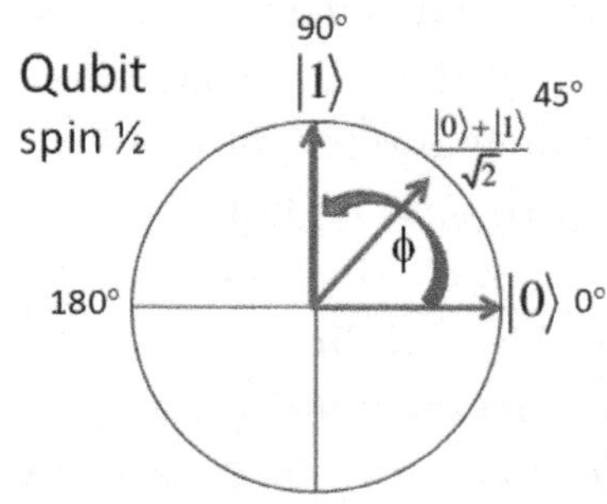

Figure 25. Qubit in Hilbert space notation

Similarly, all random correlithm ensembles represent big vectors that are also virtually orthogonal, which means it is rare to have truly mutually exclusive thought vectors. For example, the correlithm thought vector for the complex concept "light" is 90° orthogonal to the correlithm thought vector for "dark"—this means they are not opposite states. In quantum computing, the "inversion" operator is different than the "not" operator. According to Abraham, LOA is built on the inclusion principle, since "any thought" (X) and "not of any thought" (not X) both represent the opposite ends of the same thought vector (either X or Y in Figure 26). According to Abraham, there is only attraction due to thought vector inclusion, and pushing thoughts away is not possible in LOA, or the quantum world either. If you want to stop thinking about pink elephants, you have to pick some other thought, rather than repeating "Do not think about pink elephants." In short, only hold the thoughts you want to persist. Abraham/Esther uses the food buffet analogy, where you only choose food you *want* to eat.

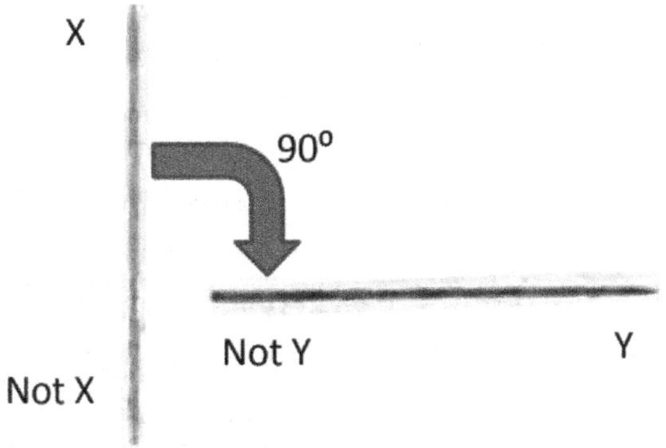

Figure 26. Orthogonal thought vectors from LOA

The true comprehension of orthogonality and how they build superposition and entangled quantum states has a profound impact on all of physics. A recent book, *Spooky Action at a Distance* by George Musser, describes in great detail the complete dissolution of the notions of space, time, matter, energy, etc., due to quantum wave mechanics and entanglement.[11] This represents the same story we are telling, plus we add correlithms. Information is physical and bit-vectors reign supreme as the root of source science. These bit-vectors underlie all of physics as ensembles of bits and represent the vibrations of the Law of Attraction and the strings of string theory.

Thought vectors are also first-class elements as defined in this geometric algebra constructed correlithm model. We borrowed the term "first-class" from computer science (and mathematics), which means any thought is just as primitive as any other thought and can be handled uniformly without restrictions due to the space-like concurrency of bit-vectors. Historically, humans learn by building hierarchy from primitive ideas to more complex ideas, in a process that builds computational efficient semantic hierarchy without end. This is relativity applied to hyperdimensional spaces of ideas and thoughts—space-like concurrent states create first-class hierarchy—but it does not work for classically represented information, since the hierarchical complexity boundaries can never be removed or renormalized.

This has been a real problem for computer scientists. For example, the company Cycorp has created the Cyc software, a "common sense knowledge" system that contains a large ontology of concepts (>500k), relationships (>17k), and assertions (>5M) as a set of object relationships. Cyc uses pointers between elements to define a hyperdimensional space where each object considers itself the relative center of the graph universe. This hyperdimensional graph is so interrelated that it cannot be mapped to a lower-dimensional graph. In reality, each object is discreet and separate from all others, thus not resulting in real meaning. Object boundaries exist because they are represented as separate objects in a discrete metric environment in space and time.

A good example of a common sense representation defined in Cyc is a restaurant scenario in which the hours of business, restaurant building, the door, conversation, waiter, tables, chairs, dishes, silverware, menu, ordering, drinks, food, eating, taste, cost, the bill, money, the tip, and exiting are all interwoven into a sequence. These are all independent elements but tied together under the scenario of dining out. It is interesting to note that computers do not comprehend these kinds of general scenarios and autistic children generally also do not understand scenarios easily.

Cyc's system contains almost 6 million independent primitive elements and we strive to place all of them at addresses in a hyperdimensional space according to "likes are near likes" in very high degrees of locality. The location of those points in a hyperdimensional space represents learning or training from an AI perspective. Having a nonmetric space-like representation dissolves the boundaries between objects and gives the basis of true meaning and knowing: the thought vectors. Trying to do this training in a traditional quantum computer would not work, since quantum computers have no longer-term memory, so how do humans do this?

The "I" Observer Frame and Knowing Are Relativistic

Dr. Tiller: I agree that knowing needs to be completely relativistic, such that any thought vector is as primary and first-class as any other thought vector. Knowing also needs to be holistic, such that thoughts naturally include all the nearby related ideas, like you described in a correlithm space. Each thought can best be described as a hyperdimensional version of an observer frame (from physics) that gives the uniformity of behavior no matter the location, orientation, or velocity.

Physicists have taken great care to express the metric-space-dependent laws of electromagnetics and relativity so that they apply to any observer frame. Einstein's relativity is all about formally expressing all the laws of physics so that all references frames are equivalent (isotropic properties independent of direction, velocity, and acceleration). We experience thoughts as relative and isotropic—most likely meaning is also relative and isotropic in the hyperdimensional nonmetric space of thought vectors. Thoughts and mind represent the ultimate observer frame mechanism, since meditation, dreams, remote viewing, clairvoyance, astral projection, near death experiences (NDEs), and PK could all be explained as the mind controlling the observer address of "I." Essentially, the mind's eye is the ultimate observer.

Dr. Matzke: In his book series starting with *Teachings of Don Juan*, Carlos Castaneda introduced the concept of an assemblage point.[12] The shaman Don Juan could directly shift assemblage points so that Carlos could experience for himself other universes and realities. The literature on assemblage points represents the same source science ideas of mental observer frame constructed from a proto-dimensional substrate supporting the full multiverse. What is interesting here is that in physics an inertial frame cannot be acted up, since is not a thing, yet assemblage points appear to be manipulated. Verbnoun balanced thoughts act as both states and actions.

Another important idea is how structures form in the correlithm space. As discussed in Chapter 3, a new breed of physicists are using a relatively new class of mathematics called geometric algebra to show how physics combines vectors to construct complexities such as motion, fields, and relativity. I researched the combination of ideas for a government research grant and learned a great deal about how this novel geometric algebra interacts with correlithms.[13]

For example, when I talk about hyperdimensional spaces, I think of more than just bit-vectors; I also include additional GALG multivectors and *N*-vector structures. Correlithms can be defined with bits, qubits, ebits, and graded elements because correlithms can be defined by ensembles of cells using any cell representation. Ensembles of qubits are called a "quantum register." Each *N*-space defines its own built-in standard radius and standard distance, which represents a built-in unit measuring stick for that type of cell and ensemble size of *N*. Each correlithm space also renormalizes using that unit stick the same way that quantum probabilities are renormalized to a probability of 1.

This combination is critical since correlithm space-like ensemble properties cooperate with cell-complexity building constructs, including entangled elements. Graded and entangled elements give another kind of space-like wholeness because multiple aggregated elements can interact as one. Particles and thought packets can be formed from the sums of these graded primitives, similar to how internet packets can be defined from nested headers.

Dr. Tiller: This is exactly the kind of representation needed for thoughts to support my intention host device (IHD) results. A nonphysical thought packet contains the specific thought structure needed for rebroadcast. It also defines a structured, yet unobservable element that could interact with quantum PK/REG devices. Some structure is required to differentiate the intentions from my two experiments to change the pH up or the pH down, resulting in two separate meanings that affect the physical world differently.

This brings up the topic of how different thoughts and meaning are represented as different nonphysical structures. Maybe a better way to ask this is how do people have sensory or direct knowing during psi phenomena? Doug, do the quantum correlithm structures support those different modalities of information?

Law of Attraction and Neurolingistic Programming Submodalities

Dr. Matzke: "Modality" is the ideal word here since it is used by the Neural Linguistic Programming (NLP) community.[14] Most people think by using one or more dominant modalities of visual, auditory, kinesthetic, and auditory digital concepts/beliefs. The founders of NLP, Richard Bandler and John Grinder, discovered that when people are thinking, their eye movement patterns reveals their thought modalities in that moment—when under stress, people tend to revert to their dominant modality. Our eyes move while dreaming during rapid eye movement (REM) due to the same NLP mechanism, since eye movement is not suppressed during dreaming.

Bandler discovered that when someone's eyes look up, that person is accessing visual information; when their eyes look to either side, that person is accessing auditory information; and when their eyes look down, that person is accessing auditory digital feelings and concepts/beliefs.[15] Each of these four modalities has even more refined submodalities, such as brightness, orientation, frame, color, hue, loudness, tone, etc. These submodalities form a space of more than one hundred distinct features that define how we organize and access mental information. I know that using these submodalities are effective since I trained for five years in NLP and earned the distinction of Certified Master Practitioner.[16]

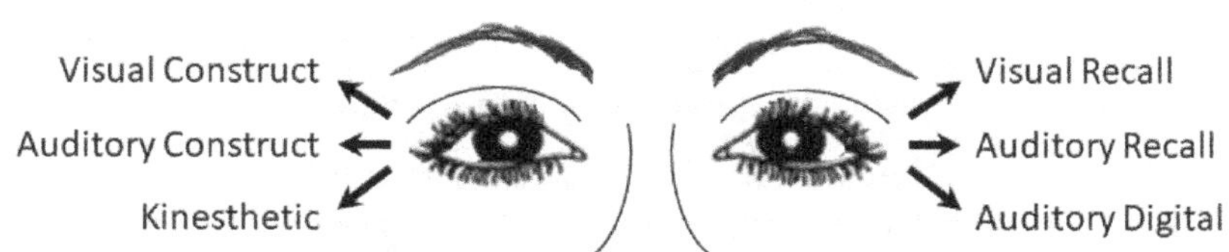

Figure 27. NLP Eye positions as viewed when facing another person

In addition, when facing out, for most people the left side represents recalling the past and the right side for constructing the future; this makes sense because most people experience time as flowing from the left in the past toward the right in the future (some people have these reversed). NLP has also adopted the Hawaiian timeline therapy, which entails mental time travel to reorganize past emotional states—this suggests a nonlocal or outside time mechanism.[17] Timeline therapy acts like superposition of your future self with your younger self and correlates with experiments on retrocausation. I have also participated in NLP sessions where nonlocal effects were experienced and reported by other remote people linked to that specific healing session.

NLP has many techniques for using submodalities to reprogram how a person thinks and feels about their past in order to be more effective in their future. For instance, Bandler created an extremely effective phobia cure using submodalities and temporal manipulation.[18] Submodalities are particularly interesting from a computation perspective, since any systems with >100 features have extremely strong correlithm properties.[19] Additional features of NLP modalities are: the visual modality is related to spatial properties, auditory is related to time/sequencing, and feelings are related to the present moment—all three tap into spacetime protoproperties of the unconscious mind.

NLP courses train people to use all their modalities but especially the visual, since it is the dominant one and represents seventy percent of all information received during most interactions. With practice, people can have rich internal visual experiences, to the extent that external signals arriving from their eyes are blocked out. If you are a good visualizer, be cautious while driving a car so that you are not distracted by other thoughts (music, radio, phone, or conversations) that might block the images from your physical eyes. Hands-free operation does not shut down these internal visual images. Even congenitally blind people have visual experiences, since the mind's eye has a built-in visual modality. NLP submodalities naturally have correlithm properties, which is why they work so well during NLP processes.

Let us talk about how sequences of thoughts are related to modalities. Sequences and scenarios are supported in correlithms, so the related item is closer than are other random items. Correlithms can also be characterized as remembering sequences, such as alphabets, music, processes, scenarios, and storytelling. This sequencing is called "string correlithms" in Nick Lawrence's research,[20] where related items are not orthogonal vectors, but are closer or rather a smaller angle. Figure 28 represents a vortex-style nearness plot for string correlithms.

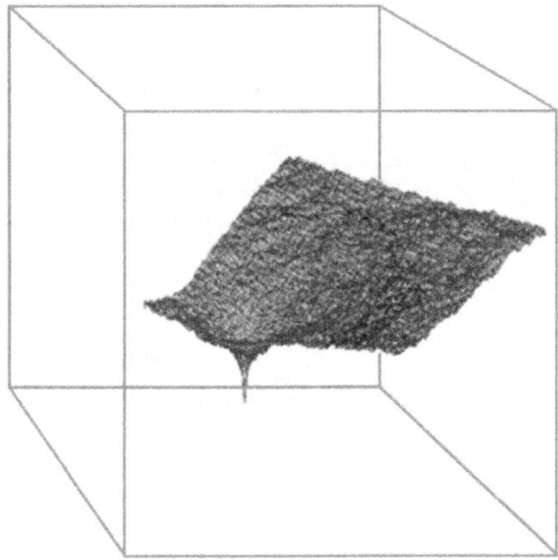

Figure 28. String correlithms vortex using toothpicks algorithm

An example of an autistic savant remembering sequences is Daniel Tammet, who is diagnosed with Asperger's syndrome and has synesthesia for emotions, numbers, and words. Daniel is the European champion for memorizing number of digits of PI (22,514 digits) and authored his memoir *Born on a Blue Day* in 2006.[21] He reports that each positive integer up to 10,000 has its own unique shape, color, texture, and feel, and his rich encoding of information is using NLP-style submodalities at a genius level. As depicted in the movie *Rain Man* with Tom Cruise and Dustin Hoffman, when autistic people have islands of genius abilities, it is called "savant syndrome."[22]

Other amazing examples are people who instantly become savants, sometimes due to neurological injury. This instant onset shows up in many forms, but often it is through music, art, or math. There are many names for this, including "instant savants"[23] or "sudden savants."[24]

We would expect modalities to be built into the mind and thoughts, since lucid dreams, astral travel, OBEs, NDE, eidetic memory (ability to see images after eyes are closed), and photographic memory (ability to remember most things they have ever seen) all have strong internal nonneural-based modalities. Modalities and submodalities are the primary feature categorization dimensions of thought vectors. In the next chapters, we add more detailed characterization from a correlithm perspective. Savants somehow tap into the apparent built-in quantum speedups using modalities, and this cannot happen with any kind of finite classical computation model. This is important and is a major clue that mind is separate from the brain!

Dr. Tiller: This awareness that built-in mental modalities and submodalities that are separate from the brain represent a BIG idea, because it suggests that the brain structure may have developed to support these modalities. This is a real chicken-or-egg philosophical discussion. We see this effect with neuroplasticity where the brain restructures itself due to brain injury. For example, blind people can experience low-grade visual images using a grid array (12x12 electrodes) that stimulates the tongue.[25] Synesthesia is defined where sense information crosses into another sense representation. For example, some people experience colors with sounds.

Now if the mind, with its proposed correlithm-based submodalities, is more fundamental than the brain, then how do the mind and brain interact? Doug, do correlithms and the Law of Attraction have anything to say about this mechanism?

Combining Qubits and Correlithms Defines Brain–Mind Bridge

Dr. Matzke: During my research with correlithms, we were exploring the relationship between high-dimensional correlithms and high-dimensional quantum models. The results showed that correlithms can be built with ensembles of any type of cell, such as bits, unit *N*-cubes, numbers, complex numbers, thermometer codes, qubits, or ebits. Correlithms also support tokens as large orthogonal vectors built from arrays/ensembles of smaller random cells. As we already discussed, this representation naturally gives noise immunity to thoughts (or tokens), because that infrastructure builds unique vector tokens from pure randomness of cells, naturally placed very far apart from each other, so are nearly orthogonal. We shall see how this is good for interacting with the brain using the same representation.

Repeatable processes would produce repeatable tokens with some noise, but greater than 20 (>>20) standard deviations away from any other tokens. These big correlithm vectors are nearly orthogonal, so they also support superposition and probabilities, because two similar thought tokens have an equivalent phase angle. For example, if we define orthogonal thought vectors "light" and "dark," then there exists a vector at a 45-degree angle between them that is a 50/50 mixture, which we would call "gray." The probability of landing within a hyperdimensional bullseye near another point represents information. Points that are near each other are extremely unlikely occurrences, due to random processes, so information is represented by nearby points with similar meaning, and therefore gray is similar to both white and black.

The big outcome of our research was this: We created random arrays of qubits and discovered some new properties using that configuration. We initialized the two qubits ensembles for X and Y to lists of random phases from 0° to 90°.[26] These resulting ensembles had just as many qubits of every phase (uniform distribution), and each iteration of the experiment produced exactly the same repeatable qubit phases for each ensemble **X** and **Y**. Since **X** and **Y** are both distinct qubit ensembles, it was easy to show for qubit correlithm ensembles the standard distance is $\sqrt{2N}$ and standard radius is $\sqrt{N}$. The measurement receivers of quantum correlation ensembles **X** and **Y** also had uniform random phase (repeatable for each trial) and no prior phase-related knowledge of or relationship to **X** or **Y**.

A general problem with quantum computing is that a random result occurs when a single qubit is measured from some unknown angle, which typically can be as bad as a 50/50 chance. With the uniform phase qubit ensemble, though, all phases are equally represented. Qubits measured at 45° get purely random results, and anything closer to phases of 0° or 90° has more-predictable results. The net result of measuring these repeatable qubit ensembles is that it is *possible* to distinguish **X** and **Y** without any phase information of the ensembles. Repeated trials produce answer bit correlithms that are 50 percent the same, which means they are apart only 70 percent of standard distance (Figure 29) due to contributions from less random phases. Therefore, in spite of the randomness produced by qubit measurement, the results of repeated X values are correlated and distinct from repeated Y values (Figure 30). This is important, because as we describe next, this process represents a way to exchange tokens between the brain and mind.

This is an extremely important patented result[27] because, in spite of the unknown starting and measurement phases, the repeatable uniform phase invariant ensembles can easily be distinguished from each other. The graphic in Figure 29 shows the distributions of answers after one thousand iterations for two ensemble sizes, where standard distance is the right edge of the graph. We believe that any process that produces uniform-phase invariant quantum ensembles in the brain could convey unique tokens between the brain and mind. The graphic in Figure 30 illustrates how the two ensembles produce probabilistic clusters that are distinct for **X** and **Y**, since the self-correlation is maintained even after measurement.

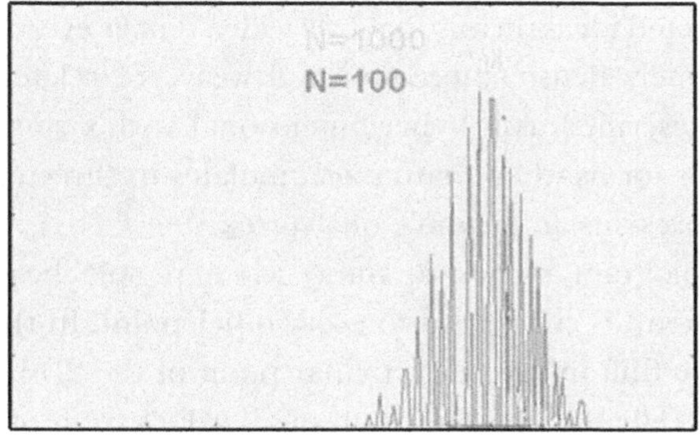

Figure 29. Distance plot for uniform phase qubits

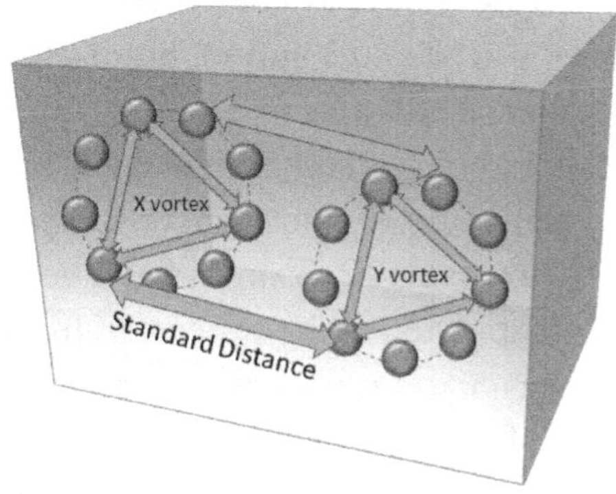

Figure 30. Cluster distance visualization

These random-phase qubit ensembles act like noisy semi-classical ensembles even though the cells are made of random qubits. The source phases and measurement phases must be repeatable for each trial for this to work, but both can initially be randomly selected. This important idea means that each brain could automatically bootstrap all the individualized vectors associated with thoughts between that individual mind and that individual brain.[28]

Based on the Law of Attraction, each cluster of results represents a vortex or bull's-eye. The LOA vortex is an epicenter for thoughts that tend to be near other similar ideas. Creating rich interconnected ideas means that every idea is near every other idea. This extremely dense interconnected weave of related thoughts could be described as a hyperdimensional vortex similar to how gravity wells forms when matter accumulates in three dimensions. Figure 28 presents an example of a vortex.

The hologram comes to mind when people hear the idea that each point is connected to every other point. In the case of a holographic film image, a particular point in the 2D holographic space is literally the weighted sum of all values from other points, so individual items are no longer distinguishable. In the case of a correlithm vortex, each point in a hyperdimensional space is a unique thought vector observer frame constructed from distinct dimensions. When a hologram is cut in half, the entire image is still represented but with less resolution. Similarly, as a correlithm loses some dimensions, it still acts like a noisier version of itself, as long as the dimensionality N is still higher than $N \gg 100$.

The mind's eye appears to know where the point of attention is in the thought vector hyperspace and what labels are attached to each point. Self-introspection is the process of finding other labels and points near the current observer perspective (or observer frame). An observer frame can change to other nearby observer frames in hyperdimensional spaces just by moving the point of attention, like moving the "mind's eye" in a mental spaceship. For these reasons, the hyperdimensional observer frame idea is a much more powerful information approach than are holograms, yet both use similar language to describe interrelatedness. Holograms fuse the information but in a way that cannot be introspected. Also, holograms are not Turing-complete, not Shor-complete, not quantum computing-complete, and do not support distinct entanglement. Neural networks also act like holograms, since each node is a weighted sum of all the training data and, thus, have the same lack of introspection problem as holograms.

This correlithm vortex idea allows "like" aggregation similar to how mass accumulation bends space, so the more repetition of a thought vector, the more that idea persists (Abraham calls this a belief or rut). Since the brain contains billions of neurons, the thought vectors contain billions of attributes, many with neural modality correlations. The more complexity the vortex contains, the more bit-equivalent effective energy it represents, and, likewise, the more space-warping effective mass that represents. The idea of bending hyperdimensional protospace due to information complexity is a good way to envision the vortex. Abraham states that ideas and beliefs have momentum, making it sometimes hard to change ideas once they are stuck in a vortex of thought. Or, as John Wheeler said, "Spacetime tells matter how to move; and matter tells spacetime how to curve." Given that thought dimensions are equivalent to spacetime, and rotes are equivalent to mass, this is a verbnoun-balanced arrangement.

More on Law of Attraction and Abraham

Dr. Tiller: I have hoped that real equations would be found to support the LOA. The mathematical topology of correlithms you describe appears to be a built-in formulation of such laws. You stated that Abraham has referred to the Law of Attraction as a "law of the universe," and the mathematics behind correlithm standard distance/radius appears to be a naturally occurring mathematical expression of LOA.

Dr. Matzke: My observation is that nonmetric hyperdimensional correlithms do not contain a complexity limit, since this collection of bit-vectors is source-like. This may allow unlimited collections of bits to support the complexities of savant, genius, supermind, and infinite intelligence. The source-like and nonmetric space properties of the correlithm could also support telepathy and orbs. Even though they are both made of bits, an orb is on the opposite appearance scale as a black hole—very large mass causes a black hole to become invisible, and increased complexity causes a nonmatter orb to become visible as it forms a hyperdimensional massless ball of light intersecting with our 3+1 spacetime world.

If we assume our mind is formed from hyperdimensional bit dimensions, then it must have unusual properties. Just as a knot does not stay looped in four dimensions, it is at least theoretically possible to astral project into a sun or a black hole and still escape again, since gravity does not trap the hyperdimensional nonphysical mental body, since those mental dimensions are not part of our physical universe.

The source science approach of representing a thought as an address in a hyperdimensional bit space solves the problem of the mind being outside and separate from yet interacting inside with the brain. Since these same bits appear to be the source of both mind and protophysics, the mind can be used as the ultimate instrument for intuition, invention, and discovery of source science knowledge. For example, the idea for the double-helix structure of DNA came to James Watson as a dream about a spiral staircase. Not surprisingly, there are numerous reports about inventions having been inspired by dreams.[29]

Since thoughts do not exist in the brain, or space or time, they interact with "like thoughts," no matter where or when those thoughts occur. From our 3D perspective, this interaction appears to be nonlocal in both space and time.

Two other reasons why a primitive nonbrain, source-like Law of Attraction representation must exist to support mind, thoughts, and psi-related phenomena are:

(1) Abraham's concept of attracting cooperative components requires a nonbrain meaning model because the effects are not limited to an individual's head/body. Abraham says our unconscious and spirit guides are continuously inspiring each of us to connect with related ideas and other sources that facilitate our goals and intentions. They add that our insights and coincidences are really LOA in action. Once you calm your mind, it is easy to identify when arriving thoughts have been attracted, since attraction of meaning is due to nonphysical rotes outside spacetime. Esther initially tried to ignore these ideas coming from Abraham, but eventually acknowledged them. The IHDs tap into this same mechanism.

(2) Abraham is a nonphysical entity that labels itself as infinite intelligence. But being able to receive channeled information from this infinite intelligence requires telepathy from thought beings that apparently have no brain. People such as Esther, who regularly channels, exhibit an amazing talent for high-bandwidth information transfer at the speed of thought, and guides such as Abraham indicate that the infinite intelligence thought forms are not fluid with our typical grammar and words, thus making Esther's abilities even more remarkable. My favorite atypical grammar phrase from Abraham is when, ready for a break, they say: "It is a good time for a segment of refreshment."

As we discussed earlier, living in a classical metric-space world makes most of our Western human languages noun-centric. However, Native American Indian languages are verb dominant. Due to this verb-dominant characteristic, Native American Indian languages also allow chaining of verbs, which is why their sentences sound irregular to English speakers. Abraham's channeled sentence construction tends to be verbnoun-hybrid-centric, which offers another example of the kind of duality that arises in nonmetric environments.

This leads us to understanding that any sequence of reversible quantum operations can be compressed into a single composite operation by multiplying all the operators together to form a single super-operator. The combination is not possible with conventional computer programs, because sequential computer data and irreversible primitives are distinct and cannot be compressed into a single concurrent operation. Any thought also acts like an action, so a calm state of being affects all around you (and even non-locally) as an action. Most conventional computer data is not executable, except those specially designed and written by humans with meaning to be compiled into programs without errors. Because of the laws of thermodynamics (where disorder happens due to entropy increases), arbitrary data does not self-organize into executable code, whereas most thoughts appear to be self-organizing and form vortices of thought due to LOA mathematics.

Nonmetric space solutions such as correlithms built on quantum computing using geometric algebra representation are a balanced quantum computing-complete system, since all GALG expressions and all correlithms act as both/either a state and/or an operator. This is very different from matrix math representations of quantum computing, where states and operators are disjointed mathematical representations. The segregation of states/operators also leads to problems for Hilbert spaces in representing some states. Using GALG notation, my proposed Higgs boson state is the sum of a Bell operator and Bell/Magic states, which cannot be expressed in Hilbert space notation.

Correlithm systems are also Turing-complete and support a quantum computing-complete architecture using mental observer frames. Both of these system elements are verbnoun balanced, and thus are capable of self-evolving using self-modifying program concepts from Turing, von Neumann, and NLP. This verbnoun balance is naturally part of source-like quantum representations, which extends into correlithm/LOA states and to spatial and temporal changes.

The mathematics of quantum computing in geometric algebra is change centric using XNOR-based logic (exclusive NOR). As we previously stated, even though XNOR logic is universal, it is harder to comprehend because humans traditionally use NAND (inverted AND) or NOR (inverted OR) logic. XNOR logic is oriented around sameness and differences, and, therefore, is more holistic and requires more logic terms to express the same state discrimination compared to AND or OR logic gates. The advantage of XNOR logic is that it is balanced and takes the same complexity to represent both AND or OR logic.

What are your thoughts on how balanced representations support parallelism?

Dr. Tiller: Abraham uses the pronoun "we" to describe the dozens of beings that share their wisdom through Esther. Since a nonmetric hyperdimensional environment does not have distance, these beings are distinct but not separated, similar to how cellphone bands are all broadcasting simultaneously but do not affect each other. Also, just as thoughts combine to form larger first-class thoughts, Abraham is a collection of individual consciousnesses that are distinct collections of their bit dimensions that cooperate together, like the coin demo. An orchestra represents an auditory example of this blending of the different instruments. Abraham embodies the perfect simultaneous duality of wholeness and separateness, all without the presence of a brain. This Abraham collective is only possible with massively concurrent representations of thoughts. We should talk about how this is related to meaning.

Law of Attraction and Meaning

Dr. Matzke: I connect the quantum mind of infinite intelligence concept reported by Abraham by using the term "quantum oracle." Mystics describe and can access the "Akashic Records," which contain all information from all time that is accessible in some eternal virtual library.[30] The Bible states that God is all-knowing and all-powerful. All these concepts map directly to the source science duality of information and energy. All of these topics share the same model: Complexity of meaning can be aggregated infinitely in some representation outside classical spacetime. If data is stored as any matter/energy representation, then the information can only support time-like and light-like access and causal computations; the data is distributed and, therefore, is not holistic, plus the complexity/density/integration is limited by the black hole limit (where if the mass density is so great it would create a black hole).

Please be aware that the words data, information, bits, semantics, meaning, and knowing are related but not interchangeable ideas. Data is typically a noun-dominant concept and stored in a classical matter/energy representation separated by distance in an addressable metric space, such as data stored on disk sectors. Information has a formal mathematical nature, since is used as a measure of complexity or uncertainty of outcome. Many people equate data and information, but random data contains no information. Bits are the primitive units of measurement for data, information, and entropy.

As humans, we take meaning for granted, but meaning originates in our mind and is projected out at the speed of thought and assigned to objects in our environment.[31] So if a tree falls in the forest it does make a sound, but if no one is present to hear it then the *meaning* of "fallen tree" is not present. Further, our mind is the source of all meaning, and computers do not have any built-in meaning of their data.

Traditional computer programs only simulate meaning with patterns and what-if rules programmed by a human, which is fast, useful, and sophisticated trickery, but possess no real meaning. Programs might act intelligent enough to pass the Turing test (whether or not a computer is capable of interacting like a human), but that does not indicate that the program understands the meaning of any of the data, questions, or answers. Humans apparently do possess meaning, based on all the reasons we are discussing. Our minds are the source-like source code of the universe that contain meaning based on space-like correlithm-organized bit dimensions, which is why we can design, plan, self-organize, and create complicated systems. Meaning guides us to achieve the end goal, even if the goal criteria are unknown and still evolving. Creating a new arbitrary planning system with evolving goals requires meaning, since it cannot be done efficiently using random processes.

Some gestalt informational mechanism/representation must exist that supports built-in meaning to underlie rotes and telepathy. "Knowing" is being conscious of meaning—knowing that you know—so meaning and knowing are as fundamental as consciousness and awareness. Knowing is most likely source-like because both consciousness and awareness are source-like. Computers are fast and useful, but they are stuck inside spacetime so do not have the richness of source-like, nonmetric thoughts/minds that exhibit meaning, knowing, understanding, dreaming, telepathy, or psi. Some of these ideas have been discussed in other texts, and I see them mapping literally to our source-science way of thinking.

The Seven Universal Laws

Dr. Tiller: According to Tania Kotsos, there are seven universal laws by which everything in the universe is governed. This material was derived from two sources: The 1923 book *The Science of Being* and the 1908 Hermetics book *The Kybalion.* Together, the material shows how the source science ideas are very similar to many other schools of thought from other spiritually oriented sources. The following are excerpts from Kotsos's book explaining the seven universal laws.[32]

> The Universe exists in perfect harmony by virtue of these Laws. Ancient mystical, esoteric, and secret teachings dating back over 5,000 years from Ancient Egypt to Ancient Greece and to the Vedic tradition of Ancient India, all have as their common thread these seven Spiritual Laws of the Universe. Once you understand, apply, and align yourself with these Universal Laws, you will experience transformation in every area of your life beyond that which you have ever dared to imagine.
>
> **The Immutable and the Mutable:** Of the seven Universal Laws, the first three are immutable, eternal Laws, meaning they are Absolute and can never be changed or transcended. They have always existed and will always exist. The other four laws are transitory, mutable Laws, meaning that they can be transcended or at least "better used" to create your ideal reality. This is not to say that you should ignore these four Laws or attempt to defy them, for even if you do they will still govern your existence. Your aim is to master each of the seven Universal Laws and only then learn to transcend the mutable ones.

- **The Law of Mentalism (Immutable):** The first of the seven Universal Laws tells us that "The All is Mind – The Universe is Mental." Everything we see and experience in our physical world has its origin in the invisible, mental realm. It tells us that there is a single Universal Consciousness—the Universal Mind—from which all things manifest. All energy and matter at all levels is created by and is subordinate to the Omnipresent Universal Mind. Your mind is part of the Universal Mind—the same in kind, with the only difference being one of degree. *Your reality is a manifestation of your mind.* This is true Mind Power.
- **The Law of Correspondence (Immutable):** The second of the seven Universal Laws tells us "As above, so below; as below, so above." This means that there is "harmony, agreement, and correspondence" between the physical, mental, and spiritual realms. There is no separation, since everything in the Universe, including you, originates from the One Source. The same pattern is expressed on all planes of existence from the smallest electron to the largest star, and vice versa. All is One. The Ancient Greek Temple of Apollo at Delphi was referring to this great Law of Correspondence in the inscription "Know thyself and thou shalt know all the mysteries of the gods and the Universe."
- **The Law of Vibration (Immutable):** The third of the seven Universal Laws tells us that "Nothing rests; everything moves; everything vibrates." The third and last of the immutable Universal Laws, tells us that "The whole universe is but a vibration." Science has confirmed that everything in the Universe, including you, is pure energy vibrating at different frequencies.

  The axiom that "like energy attracts like energy," upon which the Law of Attraction is based, has its foundation in this Law. Everything that we experience with our five physical senses is conveyed through vibrations. The same applies to the mental realm. Your thoughts are vibrations. All your emotions are vibrations, where unconditional love is the highest and most subtle of the emotional vibrations and hate is the densest and most base. *You can learn to control your mental vibrations at will.* This is true thought power.

- **The Law of Polarity (Mutable):** The fourth of the seven Universal Laws tells us that "Everything is dual, everything has poles; everything has its pair of opposites; opposites are identical in nature, but different in degree." It is also the first of the mutable or transcendable Universal Laws. It means that *there are two sides to everything.* Things that appear as opposites are, in fact, only two extremes of the same thing. For instance, heat and cold may appear to be opposites at first glance, but in truth they are simply varying degrees of the same thing. The same applies to love and hate, peace and war, positive and negative, good and evil, yes and no, light and darkness, energy and matter. You can transform your thoughts from hate to love, from fear to courage by consciously raising your vibrations. This is what in the ancient Hermetic Teachings is called the Art of Polarization.
- **The Law of Rhythm (Mutable):** The fifth of the seven Universal Laws tells us that "Everything flows, out and in; everything has its tides; all things rise and fall; the pendulum-swing manifests in everything; the measure of the swing to the right is the measure of the swing to the left; rhythm compensates." It is the second of the mutable or transcendable Universal Laws and means that the pendulum swings in everything. This principle can be seen in operation in the waves of the ocean, in the rise and fall of the greatest empires, in business cycles, in the swaying of your thoughts from positive to negative, and in your personal successes and failures. In accordance with this Law, when anything reaches a point of culmination, then the backward swing begins almost unnoticeably until such time that any forward movement is totally reversed, then the forward movement begins again and the process is repeated.

- **The Law of Cause and Effect (Mutable):** The sixth of the seven Universal Laws tells us that "Every cause has its effect; every effect has its cause." In accordance with this Law, every effect you see in your outside or physical world has a very specific cause, which has its origin in your inner world. This is the essence of thought power. *Every one of your thoughts, words, or actions sets a specific effect in motion which will come to materialize over time.* To become the master of your destiny, you must master your mind, for everything in your reality is a mental creation. Know that there is nothing like chance or luck. They are simply terms used by humanity in ignorance of this Law.
- **The Law of Gender (Mutable):** The last of the seven Universal Laws tells us that "Gender is in everything; everything has its masculine and feminine principles." This mutable Universal Law is evident throughout creation in the so-called opposite sexes found not only in humans but also in plants, minerals, electrons, and magnetic poles, to name but a few. Everything and everyone contains both masculine and feminine elements. Among the outward expressions of feminine qualities are love, patience, intuition, and gentleness, and of masculine qualities are energy, self-reliance, logic, and intellect. Know that within every woman resides all the latent qualities of a man and within every man those of a woman. When you know this, you will know what it means to be complete.

The Law of Attraction as Part of the Equation: You will notice that the Law of Attraction is not specifically mentioned as one of the seven Universal Laws. This is not to diminish its importance but rather to highlight that it is the foundation which runs through all seven Universal Laws. It holds everything together. It is through the knowledge of the Law of Attraction that one can rise above the mutable Laws of Polarity and Rhythm and gain a better understanding of each of the seven Universal Laws.

Dr. Matzke: There is significant overlap with these seven Universal Laws and the source science perspective, however source science takes each of these ideas and expands on them slightly with mathematical rigor.

Chapter Summary

"Opposites attract" is an energy principle and "likes attract" is a meaning-based mechanism. The correlithm mathematics naturally supports the meaning laws associated with attraction. We described a patented quantum-based correlithm with unexpected properties that can act as a self-defining bridge between the brain and the mind. The human mind is organized around $N \gg 100$ NLP-based submodalities that act as a natural representation for exchanging sense information and organizing mental encodings using NLP modalities. A common LOA saying is, "Thoughts are things" in the brain, but due to space-like concurrent quantum constructs, we restate that as "Thoughts are quantum source things" that are not in the brain and yet can affect the physical world.[33]

Once a bridge between the brain and quantum mind is established, the human mind can then tap into the vortex of our higher self, access infinite intelligence, and enable cooperative helpers of LOA. Correlithm mathematics allows hyperdimensional thoughts with similar meaning to aggregate and create vortices. Self-organization essentially is a source of information, which forms a vortex of energy or negentropy (negative-entropy). The negentropy comes from the coin demo and a correlithm-related similarity associated with LOA vortices, and is only possible when the quantum and string correlithms are tapping into the vortex defined by the space-like concurrency of bit-vectors in nonmetric spacetime. These mechanisms represent the verbnoun balance source-code of our mind that can affect anything we attract by tapping into the source that creates worlds.

Chapter 5: Thoughts on Emotions, Feelings, and Memory

A key ingredient of the Law of Attraction is the choice to control your emotional state. Abraham introduces the emotional ladder as a tool to evolve your emotional state from a less-resilient one to a more-effective, positive one. Table 11 presents Abraham's emotional ladder as published in the book *Ask and It Is Given* by Esther and Jerry Hicks. The goal is to develop your emotional guidance system by moving up the ladder to more-positive emotional states.[1] The goal is to feel good by being aligned with the inner vortex of your true self.

Emotional states help structure thoughts, in addition to modalities and submodalities. This chapter discusses the LOA connections between emotional states, memory, and correlithms.

Emotions Are a Major Factor for Structuring Thoughts and Memories

Dr. Matzke: My personal experience with emotions is that they significantly affect what memories I can access. *Abraham has stated that the emotional state of any problem only contains the problem details and that the solutions can only be found in a different emotional state.* I have further observed: People who experience strong emotions seem to get stuck there: People in love stay there for long periods of time, just as people with rage or anger do. People who have been seriously abused spawn multiple whole separate personalities to isolate their emotional memories from each other. Thus, emotions act as an additional major contributor to a state address, beyond modalities and submodalities, for our mental correlithms.

Table 11. Law of Attraction Emotional Ladder

The Emotional Guidance Scale
1. Joy, Appreciation, Empowerment, Freedom, Love
2. Passion
3. Enthusiasm, Eagerness, Happiness
4. Positive Expectation, Belief
5. Optimism
6. Hopefulness
7. Contentment
8. Boredom
9. Pessimism
10. Frustration, Irritation, Impatience
11. Overwhelmed
12. Disappointment
13. Doubt
14. Worry
15. Blame
16. Discouragement
17. Anger
18. Revenge
19. Hatred, Rage
20. Jealousy
21. Insecurity, Guilt, Unworthiness
22. Fear, Grief, Depression, Despair, Powerlessness
From the book *Ask and It Is Given*, 114

There are also neural correlates of emotions, because chemicals that support emotional states bias the neurons to oscillate at different vibratory rates. This change in brain pattern addresses a different set of vortices in our individual mental correlithm-related memories. Every distinct emotional state really acts like a separate emotional personality, with separate memories and thought patterns, which then affects our memories and decisions. The emotional body has a strong effect on the memories, thoughts, and decisions due to the same correlithm mechanism as modalities/submodalities. Figure 31 is just as valid for either clockwise or counter-clockwise dependencies. Based on this understanding, people can choose their emotional states. As Figure 32 illustrates, the traditional view of emotions is based on the body and chemicals triggered by external events, whereas feelings are the mind's awareness of the body and emotions.[2]

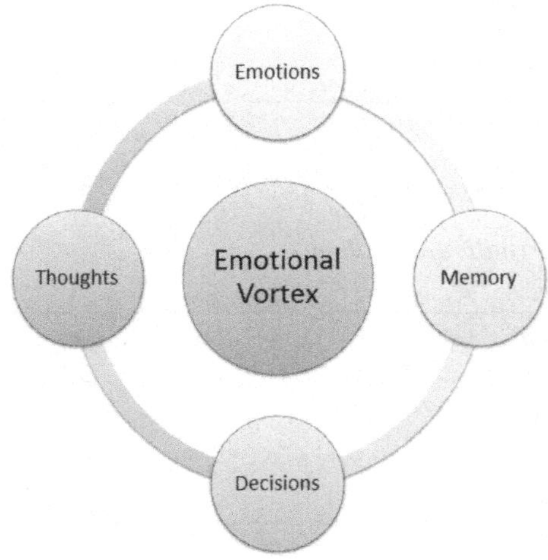

Figure 31. Emotional vortex circle

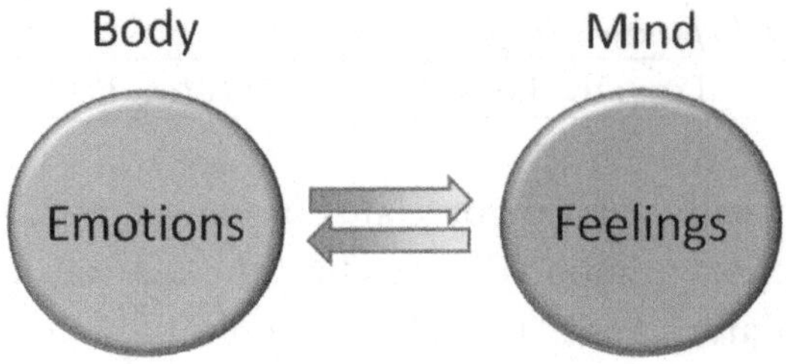

Figure 32. Traditional emotions vs feelings

From a survival perspective, there is a benefit when danger triggers instant adrenaline to fight or flight. Alternatively, the emotional ladder instructs that you can completely redirect your mind by choosing what feeling you want, and then your body will respond with the preferred chemical and emotional response. This is self-evident with thoughts that lead to deep states from meditation, laughter, or sexual arousal. Physical sexual arousal can occur with similar speed from external stimuli or internal thoughts. Surely, there is a connection between emotions and feelings, Bill.

Dr. Tiller: I see this really as another chicken-and-egg paradox, since it is not clear which comes first, emotions or feelings. For example, during times of stress the unconscious mind can reach forward to react to future emotional chemical states in a presentient or retrocausation presponse. Or, during near death experiences (NDEs), the mind can experience calm, utter elation, joy, and love, in spite of the body being injured and the brain appearing to be unconscious. People also report extreme emotions of sadness and joy while performing meditative breathwork, with virtually no external stimuli except breathing, and lucid dreamers can have extremely intense emotions that drive the brain to appear to be conscious

Just as with modalities, strong emotions appear to have a built-in nonneural basis independent of the physical brain/body/chemical layers. This is required since emotions must have a nonneural mechanism to support emotional states and LOA-based memories separate from the brain. How do you see this as it relates to LOA?

Emotions and NLP Anchoring

Dr. Matzke: I see each emotional state having a separate unique LOA vortex that is also supported by chemical/neural correlates. Each emotional state then dominates its own complex thought vector and they are all orthogonal to each other, which means we mostly experience one deep emotion at a time. From a source science perspective, we know that emotional states are LOA-meaning vectors, so it is possible to mix emotions using emotional superposition.

For example, many people have experienced being simultaneously both happy and sad. This emotional mixing is only possible with a superposition-based concurrent state vectors representation for emotions.

"Anchoring" is another great example of how mixed emotions occur.[3] Anchoring is a primary NLP technique where an external stimulus can be associated with an internal state (i.e., Pavlov's dog salivating when a bell is rung). It allows for a reprogramming of your mental state. The basic NLP technique for anchoring allows shifting your emotional state vectors. Below are simple steps for anchoring to be performed sitting down with your eyes closed:

1. Imagine an unresourceful emotional state A for 30 seconds while touching your left knee.
2. Lift your hand and break that state by thinking of some mental task, like counting backward from 100.
3. Deeply imagine a big positive state B for 30 seconds and touch your right knee.
4. Lift your hand again and break that state by thinking of some mental task.
5. Now fully engage state A and touch your left knee for 10 seconds.
6. Now add the touch to your right knee and switch to state B for 10 secs (superposition).
7. Experience the mixing/shifting of your two emotional states.
8. Finally, lift your left hand from your knee and hold the positive state B for 30 seconds more.

When this anchoring procedure is performed, the stuck negative state A is influenced by the positive state B, just like a tow truck pulling a car out of a ditch. When this technique is finished, the original state A will feel completely different or actually be gone since its phase state has moved like a quantum computation but using an emotional state vector. If needed, repeat this process multiple times to unstick the intensity of the state A feeling. Anchoring works best when experiencing the states completely by engaging fully in the now with all the visual and auditory modalities, plus emotions. Once these states are reprogrammed, those pesky memories and emotions will begin to dissipate and no longer have an impact on you. Anchoring is more action oriented using reprogramming compared to LOA, where the LOA activity involves you stopping paying attention to unwanted states by choosing and amplifying others instead, which is sometimes hard to do.

Anchoring is such a powerful technique it is used heavily in sales jingles, slogans, and images. Anchoring has also recently been utilized to trigger a psychoneuro-immunological response for cancer drugs.[4] For example, the treatment anchored the drug to a uniquely strong taste or smell. Subsequent treatments are then reapplied with this external anchor and with a lower drug dosage—the anchor stimulates the body response as if a full dosage had been given. When used for remote healing, nonlocal effects are also possible with other people by applying anchoring. Since anchoring affects the nonphysical thought vectors, any anchoring also affects your prana light bodies.

A 2015 animated movie called *Inside Out* featured emotional personalities (joy, sadness, disgust, fear, and anger) inside the head of an eleven-year-old girl Riley. In the beginning of the film, each long-term memory had predominantly one emotion. But by the end, the emotions were more blended for each long-term memory. This blending/superposition of emotional personalities is exactly what occurs with Abraham's multi-being and gives a superset unified perspective that is not possible by simply switching sequentially between emotional personalities. This superposition of beings helps construct infinite intelligence.

This ability to blend emotional states is a hyperdimensional quantum superposition capability using emotional correlithm thought vectors. This supermind state vector represents an observer from a superposition-balanced vantage point above the individual emotional states, rather than being stuck in the limitations of any single emotional state. The ability to integrate emotional states and to be an observer above any single emotion is the goal/outcome of many advanced spiritual practices. Simply avoiding negative emotional states does not enable the integration to occur. Meditation, grounding, and dreaming essentially allow integration of emotional states by taking these higher vantage points. Higher states of consciousness do not mean faster frequencies, but instead mean choosing mental observer perspectives from different "I" observer points to include multiple traditionally isolated and orthogonal emotional states. Thus, integrating more states make us more balanced and smarter.

This same technique of integrating emotional states was once applied to patients with severe cases of multiple personality disorder. Hypnotherapists used hypnosis to switch between identities as a group session in which they were unaware of each other and then merged them together, to become a new multi-being formed by combining the previous personalities.

Another useful NLP therapeutic technique is called "spatial anchoring," an idea discovered by ancient Greek messengers to help them remember long decrees from their governors by associating the parts of the message with landmarks along their journeys through the empire. Spatial anchoring associates memories and states with spatial locations, rather than with auditory or visual anchors. Spatial anchoring is so useful that students are advised to study for final exams in the same room where the exam will be held and to associate different subjects with various corners of the room. This technique can also be useful when doing "parts work" to facilitate switching between emotional subpersonalities. For example, using your shy personality anchored to the corner of the room facing out and your assured personality anchored to the middle of the room facing a wall. It is much easier to switch between emotional personalities by assigning each one a specific location. The final step in spatial anchoring is to merge the personalities by imagining standing in both places at once and then moving toward the final positive state. If imagining is too hard, chose the original two locations two to three feet apart and merge by straddling with one foot on each location.

Carlos Castaneda and his teacher were always manipulating his assemblage points. He described his teleportation process as being a variant of spatial anchoring where he imagined himself sitting on two park benches and then shifting his awareness from the first bench to the other, resulting in teleportation. According to his book series,[5] a Yaqui sorcerer must pass the final test of the impeccable warrior by jumping off a cliff and keeping his emotional composure to teleport to safety before hitting the ground. Many believe that these books are fictional, but people have personally reported to me their ability to teleport.[6] Likewise, historical documents describe that saints must have been able to bilocate because they were seen the same day at multiple far-apart locations. One of the other key ideas from these Castaneda books is seeing that our aura is a natural part of the energy of the world.

Emotions, Coherence, and HeartMath

Dr. Tiller: "Emotional energy" is more than just chemicals or organs in the body. I consulted with the HeartMath organization founders during its inception. This group teaches the idea of heart intelligence, which is where it is possible to apply scientifically developed techniques to shift the focus from brain (logic) to heart (emotions). This is their mission statement:[7]

> The mission of the HeartMath Institute is to help people bring their physical, mental, and emotional systems into balanced alignment with their heart's intuitive guidance. This unfolds the path for becoming heart-empowered individuals who choose the way of love, which they demonstrate through compassionate care for the well-being of themselves, others, and Planet Earth.[8]

Many cultures believe the heart is considered the focal point for emotions, especially those positive ones related to love, joy, appreciation, laughter, and compassion. There is a large overlap in the functions of the heart, which causes confusion when talking about this. The heart:

1. Is the engine for pumping blood for the body
2. Is the dominant (by 60X) electrical signal source that synchronizes the body with others
3. Has heart rate variability metrics that can influence the rest of the body
4. Contains more than 40,000 neurons
5. Contains its own thoughts and voice
6. Is located near the heart chakra

According to HeartMath, hearts can become the focal point instead of brains for heart-based thinking and can drive the rest of the body based on controlling heart rate and heart-rate variability. This results in more coherence from the heart and heart chakra. This heart coherence is then sent to the brain and to the entire body neurologically, biochemically, biophysically, and energetically, and also encourages coherence with others.

HeartMath teaches their techniques as self-help classes to individuals and corporate seminars. Many people find their techniques useful by switching from fear-based logic to heart-based love, and therefore can make better decisions. How do you interpret the HeartMath results based on the source science model?

Dr. Matzke: I have taken classes at HeartMath and studied their research. I am quite impressed with their people, research, and programs. My main observation is that they are marketing their techniques and products as a bridge to the same source science ideas we discuss here. An excellent video below from their website demonstrates this bridge:[9]

www.heartmath.org/resources/videos/hearts-intuitive-intelligence/

The term "coherence" is used in both quantum computation and HeartMath literature, except I believe the meaning is slightly different in both cases. In quantum computation, decoherence means some noise disturbed the sensitive entanglement quantum state, thereby destroying the state of interest. Coherence is also used in lasers, such that all the photons are statistically very similar, which causes the light to be amplified and hence does not get cancelled out. I believe that HeartMath is using the term "coherent light" as it is used in lasers, such that the emotional state is big enough to keep the heart, brain, mind, and energy field all correlated to each other, thereby making the resulting human energy system brilliant like a laser. This coherence affects the people in your local environment, but also a global coherence affecting the whole planet.

This specifically includes the chakra and prana systems so that the space-like states dominate, leading to greater intelligence and heart-based innate wisdom. This occurs when the heart/mind switches from in-time linear thoughts to out-of-time concurrent thoughts with the heart chakra completely open, plus aligning with the emotional vortex of love. This coherence is therefore space-like, which is more connected and coherent with the hearts/minds of others involved. This kind of description matches the positive emotions and outcomes discussed in the HeartMath literature. Their hearts-intuitive-intelligence video also does a great job in visually representing this same message.

Amplification of positive emotions and opening the heart chakra can be achieved using many techniques, including simple grounding and meditation. I use the following four-step visualization with members of chorus I sing with, to help lift the singers to being bright and coherent with each other and the audience:

1. Ground and activate your feet using whatever metaphor works for you (roots, etc.).
2. Deep, slow, and aware breathing with full exhales/inhales.

3. Appreciation in the heart, with focus and guiding breath to the chest.
4. Spin the prana from the heart out the left side connecting with others and back in on the right side.

This combination of grounding, breath, attention, appreciation, and spinning amplifies the source prana systems and when performed in a group makes the prana states coherent and interconnected. The singing also helps to get the performers and audience's brains into a coherent state, which is why sound is often used in rituals, such as chanting, toning, singing bowls, and drumming. Think of this state as a positive emotional form of mob mentality, which can be common in any concert setting. Also, nature is full of prana, especially trees. The Japanese developed the concept of forest bathing,[10] which means connecting outdoors with living plants, trees, and nature. Appreciation helps amplifies these states even more.

This coherent heart technique starts with individuals but is amplified nonlinearly when groups of people work together. Just like the number of quantum states grow exponentially to 2^Q states based on the number of Q qubits, the size N of the group state also grows 2^N as long as everyone is in the same heart-based state. For example, ten people have $2^{10}=1024$ times the impact as one person, and twenty people have 2^{20} or more than a million times the effect. Abraham would refer to this amplification as "alignment" and state that it would enable you to tap into the energy that creates worlds.

This idea has been demonstrated by the Transcendental Meditation (TM) group where they lowered the crime rate of cities in the United States for periods of time. This Maharishi Effect predicted that meditation by a TM group that was larger than $\sqrt{1\%}$ of the population of a region could lower the crime rate. For the US study in 2007–2010, that number for the United States was 1,725 people meditating, which they maintained over a four-year period.[11] The TM group uses the terminology "the positive effects of coherence and field effect of the consciousness." This result is similar to the effect from Dr. Tiller's IHD research, where focused intention can affect groups of people. Leverage can come from group size and intention on amplification, as well as from IHD-style technology.

Bandler uses this same terminology to amplify positive states by making the submodalities brighter, bigger, and more colorful. My understanding is that it is easy to amplify positive emotions since they are space-like states that are maximally concurrent, connected, and flowing, whereas negative emotions are stuck, heavy, and more time-like. Bill, what are your thoughts on amplifying prana?

Hyper-Emotional States as Entanglement

Dr. Tiller: Amplifying prana is an important topic and can lead to amplified feelings. This concurrent space-like state of positive emotions is hard to describe. Just like the question of what is hyper-intelligence or hyper-awareness, there are related emotional questions, such as what is hyper-joyfulness or hyper-intimacy? "Intimacy" is that desired special connection you have with another person, with nature, or ultimately with source. Intimacy is a two-way connection that is blissful, calm, and deep. Intimacy is important and fulfilling because the native state of mind is in intimate connection with the divine states of source. Outside the metric spacetime, there are no distances, so our native divine states are all intimately connected, which means intimacy and feeling of the divine may be related.

Dr. Matzke: I agree. I believe that intimacy is the feeling of a deeply shared connective state between two entities. Psychics would see that connection as aka cords, and I would describe it as a superposition with entanglement of two sets of quantum-based thought vectors. Once those thought vectors are interconnecting, they can become entangled, leaving two entities acting as one. Intimacy is really the feeling and awareness of that entangled state, which feels extremely good, similar to the descriptions of near-death states. I believe telepathy is also entangled, so it feels intimate as well. Knowing is also very intimate due to that same deep connection.

Connecting and entanglement are related to thought/emotional superposition. In pure quantum theory, superposition and entanglement are distinct properties even though ebits act like a conglomerate of a qubit superposition, because entanglement is built upon superposition and represents superposition embedded into a higher dimensional space. This ebit symmetry, where two things act as one, is due to graded elements and hierarchical symmetry. Since thought vectors exhibit superposition and can use graded elements, they have the elements to produce thought vector entanglement where two sets of states act like one. Bill, you are a long-term meditator, so what are your thoughts on this emotional superposition and entanglement ideas?

Dr. Tiller: Emotional superposition rings true to me. The goal of most spiritual practices is the integration of many emotional states into one unified super-state. The sum of the emotional state ensembles is larger than the sum of the parts, and produces an integrated and balanced emotional state. When the emphasis is on the positive emotions, then the negative emotions are deemphasized in this blending. Connecting to larger and larger sets of positive emotions and amplifying them by IHD, meditation, NLP, and group coherence techniques can definitely affect the world in a nonlocal fashion by forming conditioned spaces. This is only possible with a source-like representation for thoughts and emotions. These ideas are supported by source science model and matches up with teachers from Law of Attraction, TM, HeartMath, and NLP.

Chapter Summary

Emotions have meaning and this meaning is supported as emotional vectors at the space-like states of mind. Emotions play a major factor when accessing memories, since a major component of thought includes emotions and neural correlates of emotions in addition to other submodalities. These emotional vortices not only affect memories but indirectly affect how you make decisions. Choosing the most positive emotional state possible at any time is the LOA process of moving up the emotional ladder.

Anchoring and emotions are strongly related and allow for the ability to reprogram a person's emotional landscape by using positive emotions to get unstuck from negative emotions potholes, similar to using a tow truck to get unstuck from a ditch, a negative landscape. Many spiritual practices are essentially also manipulating the emotional correlithms by choosing a more resourceful observer "I" that is above, and a superposition of, other more positive emotional states. Other cooperating components are attracted to this new emotional address. This occurs with a source-like representation of thoughts and emotions independent of the brain/body.

HeartMath, NLP, and other techniques amplify the positive states as a hyperdimensional vortex where similar thoughts/emotions reside. The larger this positive emotional vortex, the larger the momentum is to stay in that vortex, to affect all your subsequent thoughts, emotions, memories, and decisions. Coherent and aligned thoughts mean that mental, emotional, and spiritual thoughts are singularly focused, thereby reinforcing rather than canceling each other out.

The unification of emotions using emotional superposition techniques also creates a unified panoramic view of all emotions. This makes us less reactive to negative emotions and more naturally observant to experience the state of heart-based love.

Chapter 6: Thoughts on Gender, DNA, and LOA

Another major factor in adding structure to your thought vectors is the role of your DNA and gender. Even though the modern world has many transgender people who do not identify with their birth gender, the physical and hormonal aspects of the body gender greatly affect the thought vortices, with significant hormonal, chemical, and neural correlates. We are of the belief that at the spiritual level we are all androgynous, but the physiology of gender does affect how we experience our lives.

Gender Effects on Thought Vectors

Dr. Matzke: Just how submodalities and emotions greatly affect our thought vectors, so too do body gender-based chemistry and hormones. Man and woman both have hormone-based and stereotypical thought patterns or archetypes, which represent a unique thought vector for each gender. These "male" and "female" are orthogonal thought vectors that are not mutually exclusive, so it is possible to create states of balanced gender thinking by forming gender superposition. "Androgynous" can mean either (1) having a mixture of gender characteristics or (2) indistinguishable gender characteristics. For the purposes of this LOA gender superposition, we focus on the first definition.

Balanced gender thinking allows people to be a blend of these characteristics, as appropriate.[1] Generally, people believe these traits are mutually exclusive, but since all thought vectors are orthogonal, they can in fact be mixed together using superposition of emotional states, which allows for a choice of responses based on conditions. My view of a balance of emotional superposition includes this list, which could be defining characteristics of gender stereotypes:

1. Facts *and* feelings
2. Strong *and* compassionate
3. Fierce *and* loving
4. Focused *and* holistic
5. Logical *and* emotional
6. Aggressive *and* tender
7. Physical *and* contemplative
8. Informative *and* sharing
9. Ritual *and* sacred
10. Achievement *and* relationship
11. Doing *and* being
12. Visual *and* auditory
13. Winning *and* bonding

Just like there are archetypes for thoughts and emotions, the gender archetypes are universal nonphysical source vectors that exist independent of the physical bodies. If you believe that mind does not exist in time, then we may have reincarnated many times in different physical genders. This would lead to feelings that many transgender people report: they identify with a gender personality other than their current birth gender. Here is a related thought-provoking passage by Val Valerian in talking about Robert Monroe:[2]

> You may believe you "are" a "male/man," or a "female/woman," when you as an androgynous *spiritual being* operating *through* a body *buy into* the cultural lie and the DNA programming that says or makes it seem *you "are"* your body and the *gender* of the body. Are YOU really a "male" or a "female"? No! However, most incarnations here *think*

they *are*! When you read the term "male/man" or "female/woman," the author is talking about *those who at this time believe they are their body and gender, not the spiritual being who they really are.*

We can believe humans are androgynous spiritual beings, yet our physiology can change daily, leading to broader changes in neural/chemical correlates driving our neural frequencies and source vibrations, and thus impacting our overall mental correlithm states.

Dr. Tiller: Once again, this leads to another chicken-or-egg problem. Which comes first: the gender mind preference or physical gender body? The androgynous mind that is a mixture of all the male/female traits is how Abraham is defined. Even God and angels are most likely androgynous, though our cultures and language patterns tend to assign gender labels to our deities.

Dr. Matzke: Carl Jung developed the idea of anima and animus to discuss the conscious versus unconscious aspects of gender in his theory of the human psyche.[3] He believed that universal, mythic characters—archetypes—reside within the collective unconscious of people the world over. Archetypes represent fundamental human motifs of our experience as we have evolved, that we believe archetypes exist in the quantum hyperspace. Consequentially, archetypes evoke deep emotions related to the totality of unconscious psychological qualities:

1. "Anima" is identified as the unconscious *feminine* qualities that a man possesses
2. "Animus" is identified as the unconscious *masculine* qualities that a woman possesses

These terms are the archetype of the collective unconscious rather than the individual unconscious and not an aggregate of father, mother, brothers, sisters, aunts, uncles, or teachers, though these aspects of the personal unconscious can influence the person for good or ill.[4] Archetypes have all the same properties as meaning and emotions that define our source science approach to LOA. Thus, we believe that they contribute to our overall source thought vectors using correlithm mathematics.

To put the archetypes in context, Jung believed that the human psyche was composed of three subsystems:

- The *ego* represents the conscious mind
- The *personal unconscious* contains memories including those that have been suppressed
- The *collective unconscious* contained all of the knowledge and experiences we share as a species

Jung identified four major archetypes and believed that there was no limit to the number that exists. Below are the four original archetypes he described:

- The persona: how we present ourselves to the world as different social masks that we wear
- The shadow: part of unconscious of repressed ideas, desires, instincts, and shortcomings
- The anima/animus: represents the true self rather than the image we present to others
- The self: represents the unified unconsciousness and consciousness of the whole individual

Dr. Tiller: Many people believe archetypes are based on genetic passed memories, but a source science approach gives a nonphysical representation for them. Based on work by Rupert Sheldrake, we know that even DNA can have a source science representation. Morphic resonance, archetypes, and thought vectors are implemented using the same mechanism.

Dr. Matzke: Right. Another important set of additional dimensions to our light body is our DNA. Sheldrake introduced the model of morphic resonance in his book *A New Science of Life* in 1981.[5] He writes that genes and DNA are controlled by a resonance field that is nonlocal and that these biofields influence the DNA to act as organizing memory that encodes habits of successful DNA—essentially, DNA is an antenna to these successful morphic resonance fields. Rupert also believes that social memories for birds and fish usually are related to accessing DNA passed memories through morphic resonance.

The hypothesized properties of morphic fields at all levels of complexity can be summarized from Sheldrake's website, with *my* emphasis in italics.[6]

- They are *self-organizing* wholes.
- They have both a spatial and a temporal aspect, and organize spatiotemporal *patterns of vibratory* or rhythmic activity.
- They *attract the systems* under their influence toward characteristic forms and patterns of activity, whose coming-into-being they organize and whose integrity they maintain. The ends or goals toward which morphic fields attract the systems under their influence are called *attractors*. The pathways by which systems usually reach these attractors are called *chreodes*.
- They interrelate and coordinate the morphic units or holons that lie within them, which in turn are *wholes organized* by morphic fields. Morphic fields contain other morphic fields within them in a *nested hierarchy* or holarchy.
- They are structures of *probability*, and their organizing activity is *probabilistic*.
- They contain a *built-in memory* given by *self-resonance* with a morphic unit's *own past* and by morphic resonance with all previous similar systems. This *memory is cumulative*. The more often particular patterns of activity are repeated, the *more habitual* they tend to become.

This language of morphic fields exactly describes the same kinds of concepts as source science hyperdimensional information system of mind and being. Since morphic resonance transcends time, I will not call it fields, since fields only exist in time. The

DNA represents approximately 25,000 genes that contribute to the address of the correlithm memory of thought vectors, in addition to the neural, chemical, hormonal, and emotional components. Sheldrake's body of research clearly overlaps with many source science topics, in particular on two principles: (1) source is dominant over the physical, and (2) the physical can influence source.

Dr. Tiller: This proposed relationship between collective DNA morphic fields and source science can be reinforced with the DNA research performed by the HeartMath scientists, where they have researched the effect of attention and coherent emotion on DNA. Since we know that thoughts and intentions can affect quantum systems, water, and the previous lists of PK effects, it is reasonable to conclude that the mind would be able to affect DNA using the same mechanism as described by morphic resonance.

The HeartMath DNA experiments researched the effects of coherence heart emotion on DNA and yielded the following results based on intention:[7]

- Unfolding rates of DNA: the higher the coherence, the more the DNA unwound
- Folding rates of DNA: the higher the coherence, the more the DNA wound
- Phantom DNA: DNA can make patterns for photons, even after the DNA has been removed

This ability for coherent thought to affect the rate of unfolding/folding for DNA is important, since this is how DNA replicates. This is reminiscent of my pH experiments where two opposite effects could be controlled with intention—up/down for pH or wind/unwind for DNA. We also know that the intention can insert noise/order into quantum systems, which could affect the number of errors when DNA is copied. If coherent emotion-based thought can affect both the pH of water and DNA, then that is the basis for life. The HeartMath phantom DNA experiment performed by Vladimir Poponin also shows another interesting interaction with DNA and light.[8]

Dr. Matzke: A word of caution is appropriate here. Much of the research HeartMath discussions are on the electromagnetics of the heart in conjunction with coherent emotion as related to the coherent effects on groups of people and DNA. We know from previous discussions that purely classical EM mechanism for mind/intention/emotions does not support nonlocal effects in space or time. Please remember that the measured electromagnetics are not the cause of these effects, but rather they are also results correlated with these coherent emotion-based intentions of thought.

Just like in the Copper Wall experiments we discussed earlier, people with a classical perspective read this kind of research and assume that it represents proof of EM-based heart-mind. But we know from all the other source science-based research (remote viewing, IHD, morphic fields, double-slit, retrocausation, archetypes, etc.) that nonlocal quantum states and nonlocal time mechanisms must be at work to support nonlocal DNA winding and morphogenesis. Our individual unconscious model of reality does indeed affect how we each interpret research results, and the goal of this book is to remind us all that we are source science-based beings. I believe that the HeartMath EM phenomena are correlated and not the cause of these effects.

Chapter Summary

The idea that emotions and archetypes that are typically associated with gender can also be understood within the source science model of LOA superposition of thought vectors. Creating a superposition of gender emotions leads to more balanced and androgynous gender-based thought patterns. The gender-based archetypes are also blended with the neural – and hormonal-based source vectors due to physical gender, and these vibrations all blend together to form the being we identify as "self." And even though our physicality may tend to label us as one gender, we believe that our higher spiritual self is androgynous. DNA is also a morphogenesis-based survival archetype that primarily works at the unconscious level but can also be influenced by coherent heart-based emotions and intentions. These capabilities can be eloquently understood using source science models.

Chapter 7: Thoughts on Prana, Chakras, Auric Bodies, and LOA

The last several chapters show the structuring effects of modalities, physiology, and emotions on thoughts and memories as related to correlithm mathematics of the Law of Attraction. The chakras, prana, and auric bodies also add hyperdimensional structure to thoughts, emotions, and memories.[1]

Chakras and Thought Vectors

Dr. Matzke: The seven main chakras have historically been depicted as symbols that increase in complexity from lowest color red to highest color purple. Table 12 contains the commonly accepted symbols, colors, and meanings for each chakra.

Table 12. Chakra Symbols and Descriptions

Chakras	Simple Description and Meaning
Crown Chakra	7) **Violet:** Top of the head – Spiritual – I understand
Third Eye	6) **Indigo:** Center of Brow – Perception – I see
Throat Chakra	5) **Blue:** Throat – Expression – I Speak

Heart Chakra	4) **Green:** Heart in Center of Chest – Love – I Love
Solar Plexus	3) **Yellow:** Solar Plexus – Power – I do
Sacral Chakra	2) **Orange:** Lower Abdomen – Sex – I feel
Root Chakra	1) **Red:** Base of the spine – Survival – I am

The chakras are described as vortices from each point in the body, as illustrated in Figure 33.

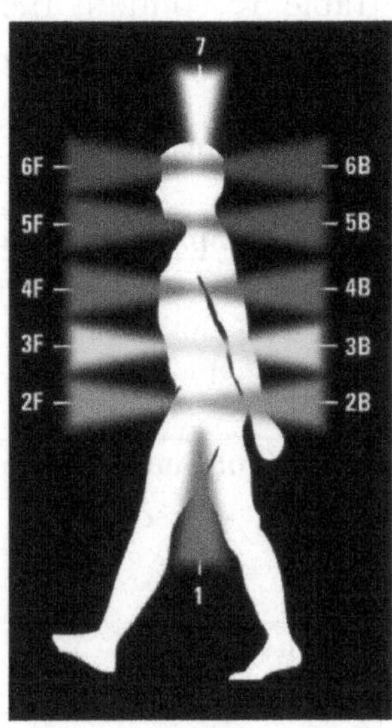

Figure 33. Chakra vortex placements

Complexity was equated with frequency, but based on the number of petals for each chakra symbol we propose in Figure 34 that "higher" chakras are related to increasing *complexity*.

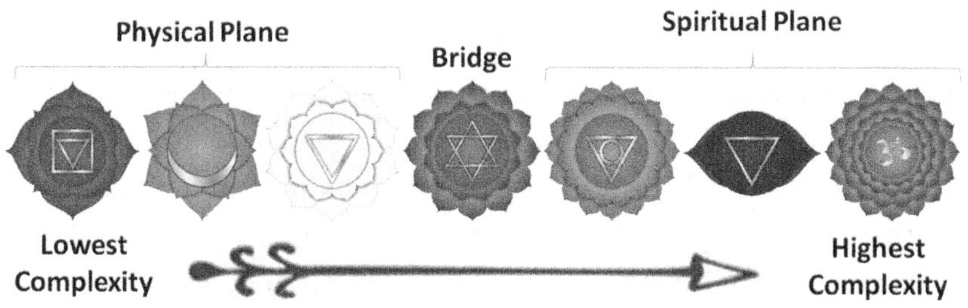

Figure 34. Chakra complexities

Abraham states that people feel bad when they are not aligned with their own inner vortex of truth. If the vortex is defined by all your submodalities, emotional states, thoughts, and corresponding auric bodies as the major thought vector, then choosing some other suboptimal thought vector would lead to much less mental connection with your primary source of prana. Anytime we choose a negative emotional state, we are starving ourselves of the connection with our full prana vibratory dimensions. Any process that pumps up the connection with prana, like breathing or laughing, causes the body to feel better due to an increase in the amount of prana intersecting with the physical body. Most of us feel bad due to prana starvation, which Abraham calls "misalignment."

Many yoga instructors teach that the breath *is* prana, yet there are many ways to actually build your prana. My preferred visualization exercise is a progressive relaxation style that spins all seven chakras using focused breath and attention, preferably in a group setting. Another effective visualization is using your breath to fill a body-sized balloon with prana. Anyone can accumulate prana forming a giant vortex by focusing the breath and attention on the physical body and/or chakras. We talked about some other examples in Chapter 5 regarding amplification of prana.

Experiment and discover your own techniques that make you feel great, and always remember to add grounding to your prana-building approach. Negative emotional states can turn off the chakras, especially the heart chakra, and causes the prana to barely trickle into the body, thereby making you feel bad. Choose positive emotional states, such as appreciation, to keep aligned, heart open, and prana flowing. We also discuss in Chapter 10 how to use Richard Bandler's hyperesthesia techniques to build and amplify positive emotions by stepping out of spacetime.

Prana is like a flowing river, not static like a filled lake, so is verb-noun balanced. Grounding and opening the heart chakra are the keys for boosting your prana flows. Thus, the HeartMath organization teaches techniques to use the neurons in your heart to relax and balance the neurology of your brain and body. HeartMath's heart intelligence is another set of neural correlates that can help you control your thought vortex.

Dr. Tiller: What you said is so true. Prana has no place to flow without grounding. So, after opening your heart chakra with appreciation and a smile, then put your bare feet on the grass and send mental roots to the center of the Earth, and breathe. Remember that Earth's radius is almost four thousand miles deep, so grounding works anywhere, even when in a high rise or jet. The Earthing website promotes grounding products that can keep us electrically connected directly to the Earth even while indoors and sleeping, with significant benefits for mental clarity, sleep, and overall health.[2] Essentially, you are entangling the prana of yourself and the entire Earth, so what a boost that will give.

Dr. Matzke: "Chakra" is a Sanskrit word that means wheel or vortex (as shown in Table 12 and Figure 33) and is drawn like a vortex. The anu is pictured as spinning ball of yarn. LOA also uses the concept of a vortex. "Quantum spin" is a built-in concept from quantum computing, and the anu also has a spin shape. Correlithms also depend on vortex or "bulls eye" formation. This repeated spinning idea is directly related to quantum thought vectors, and the mathematical structure comes directly from the bivector spinors.

Now to tie those chakras to the additional nonphysical prana states is what we call the "auric bodies." What is interesting about the auric bodies is that their source exists outside spacetime and might represent the model or blueprint by which our physical bodies are constructed.

Auric Bodies and Thought Vectors

Dr. Matzke: So far, we have identified many physical, DNA, biochemical, neural, attention, thoughts, archetypes, chakra, and prana factors that determine the size, complexity, and coordinates of your overall LOA vortex. The gestalt sum (more than the sum of its parts) of all these characteristics determines the primary thought vector of your vortex, of your "self."

Here is a list of all the primitive dimensions that contribute to each of our overall vortices of thoughts. Please remember that we are also holistically connected via a collective archetype version of these properties from everyone in your family, town, state, country, and planet.

1. DNA and quantum correlates of neurons
2. Modalities and submodalities neural correlates (including touch, smell, taste, etc.)
3. Emotions and emotional states (thoughts/chemicals bias the neural resonance)
4. Meditative and relaxed states
5. Archetypes, thoughts, attention, and beliefs
6. Breath and breathing
7. Chakras, auric bodies, and prana flow
8. Grounding and Earth-energy resonance

The number of bit-vector dimensions that these characteristics represent for each person is virtually infinite. We are beings of light dimensions where each bit-vector cluster acts like light filaments and appears as a halo or orb. This makes total sense from a LOA and correlithm perspective because all of these characteristics have a gestalt effect on our mental state. Bill, how do you view these characteristics layered in the auric bodies?[3]

Dr. Tiller: Many mystics who see auras report that our prana aura is layered from denser physical layers to much lighter outer layers. These layers are called the auric or etheric bodies and each one has a dominant kind of informational characteristics associated with that layer. The emotional body represents the nonneural information layer we have been discussing related to emotional memories and emotional thoughts. Just as visual modalities have a nonneural basis, so emotions have a nonneural basis in the emotional body. The importance of the graphic in Figure 35 is that it emphasizes the number of dimensional characteristics associated with the list above, especially the emotional body.

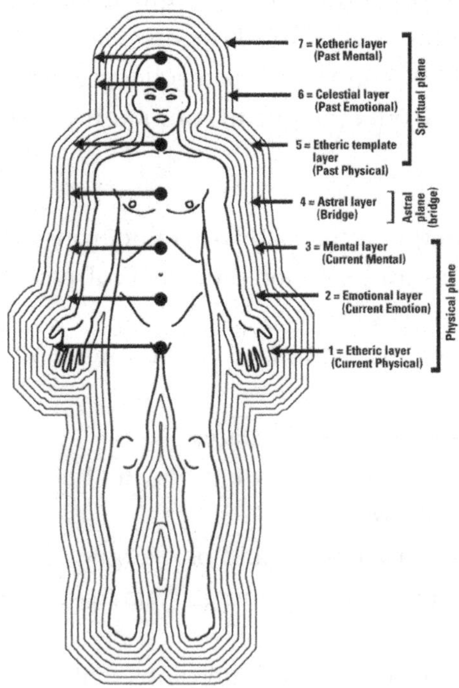

Figure 35. Astral and chakra mapping

Dr. Matzke: Assuming the physical body is level 0 and there are seven auric bodies related to the seven chakras, here are my descriptions of categorization where layers 1–3 are bound to spacetime and layers 5–7 are outside spacetime. Layer 4 is astral body, which is a bridge between physical spacetime planes and spiritual nonspacetime planes:

1) **Physical: Etheric (Physical) Body:** Related to all neural/chemical correlates associated with NLP modalities and submodalities (i.e. visual, auditory, space, time, etc.)
2) **Physical: Emotional Body:** Related to all neural/chemical correlates associated with NLP kinesthetic modality (i.e. emotions, feelings, present moment, etc.)
3) **Physical: Mental Body:** Related to all neural/chemical correlates associated with NLP auditory digital modality (i.e. self-talk, beliefs, abstract thought, mathematics, etc.)
4) **Astral Body:** Related to the heart chakra which is a bridge from physical correlates to the nonphysical
5) **Spiritual: Etheric (Physical) Body:** An out-of-time version of level 1
6) **Spiritual: Celestial (Emotional) Body:** An out-of-time version of level 2
7) **Spiritual: Causal (Mental) Body:** An out-of-time version of level 3

Mapping the structure and meaning of auras and astral bodies is an art form, which allows for many variations of these descriptions and illustrations. Figure 36 is an illustration of how Deborah Singleton visualizes the auric body. You can check out similar inspiring images by the famous artist Alex Grey on his website.[4]

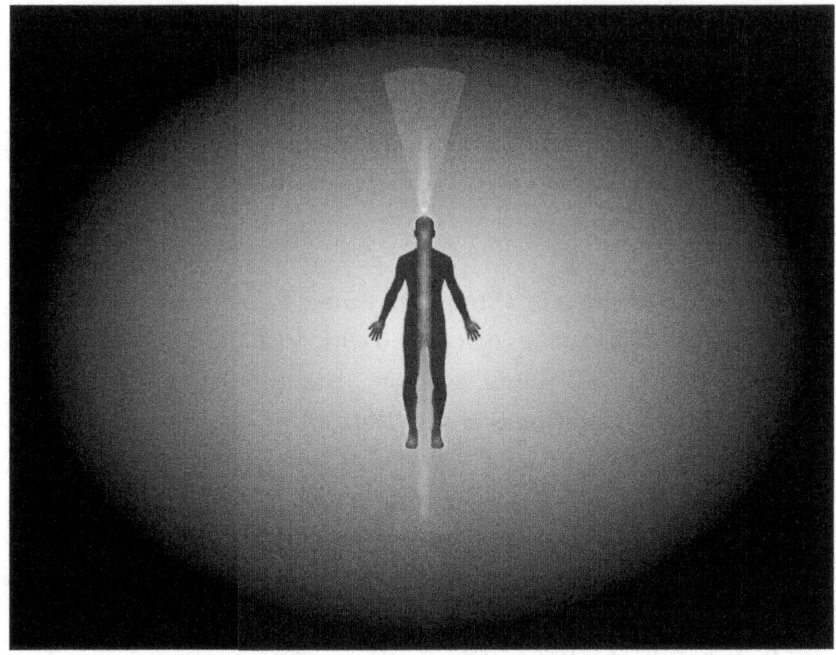

Figure 36. Chakra and auras visualization

Dr. Tiller: Besides visualizing these source layers, people can also use other modalities, such as touch, to interact with them. "Scanning" is a technique used by healers to use this sense of touch and awareness to find the edges and unevenness of auric bodies. You can even feel your own auric body by slapping your hands, rubbing them, and then feeling the energy balloon between your hands. "Energy combing" is another visceral technique where you can imagine your fingers as being very long and combing them through another person's auric body. This is easy and fun, so play with awareness of your source body.

Dr. Matzke: There are countless ways of becoming more aware of your source body and aura. This direct awareness is the key to source-like and space-like mind, where we are smarter than our mind focused on time-like brain.

The number of source dimensions associated with auric bodies is many, many orders of magnitudes greater than those directly associated with the cells, neurons, and chemicals in our bodies. In fact, the source-based source-like mind is infinitely bigger, maximally concurrent, and more heart intelligent than any classic computing-based brain. We can tap into our infinite heart intelligence by stepping out of time, which involves slowing down thought and enabling more space-like parallelism to become holistic. Talking less helps us detach from time.

Intuitive insight is another clue that you are tapping into your source intelligence, since according to Abraham cooperative components are based on the Law of Attraction of all vibrations of your source dimensions. The more dimensions from body, cells, neurons, chakras, and auric bodies, the bigger the vortex you have to attract like-minded helpers. The more complexity you aggregate, the smarter and more holistic you become due to source-like quantum parallelism and superposition of thoughts. You have to recognize and allow this external help.

Dr. Tiller: Related to this is something called "Kundalini." It is described as a prana energy that starts in the root chakra and rises and twists like serpents and causes a dramatic semi-persistent change in awareness. Figure 37 is the symbol for Kundalini. Notice its similarity to the traditional caduceus medical symbol in Figure 38.

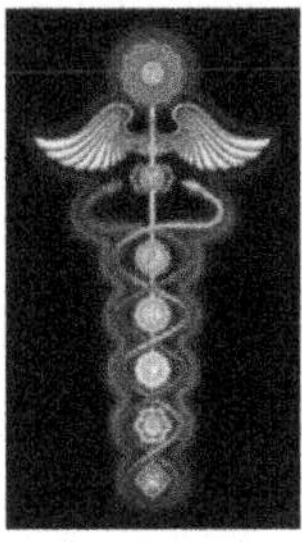

Figure 37. Kundalini symbol

Figure 38. Caduceus (symbol of medicine)

Based on the source science model, Kundalini is most likely a self-organizing set of source dimensions that reaches a threshold such that the traditional organization of them shifts into a more stable version of a vortex, experienced as a column of light up the spine. Kundalini is not explainable using a classical model of the brain or nervous system.[5]

Chapter Summary

The nonphysical source dimensions associated with prana, chakras, auric bodies, and Kundalini can all participate in the LOA and correlithm related to the true structure of our being. When complexity increases to some threshold like meditation, breath work, or Kundalini, then the mind is too complex to fit in the brain. This is a funny way of saying that we switch from the traditional time-like classical mind that focuses on brain, to the space-like quantum mind that taps into infinite intelligence.

Part II: What Does Source Science Mean?

Our discussions in Part I describe how source science reinforces the deep reality concept that the universe is constructed from hyperdimensional protophysical bits that support quantum physics, classical physics, Law of Attraction, and mind. This source science model changes many of the unconscious assumptions and beliefs we have about ourselves and how we exist in the universe.

Part II applies source science to the way we think about our world. It examines and reorients our unconscious beliefs, thereby giving us the true meaning of who we are as citizens of the universe. Just a note: some of this may seem repetitive, but that is by design because change can sometimes require a lot of dialogue. These conversations are not a set of arguments but rather a discussion tying the axiom "If X is true" to the consequences "then Y is also true." Typically, these consequences are hard to accept if axiom X is unconsciously believed to be false.

In the same manner that quantum physics behaviors and models require reinterpreting much of physics, so too do source science models of unusual behaviors require a reinterpretation of research results from human neurology, physiology, psychology, and spirituality. Both quantum mechanics and source science also rely on a hyperdimensional representation that exists outside spacetime, and are intrinsically related to information, meaning, and geometric topology.

Chapter 8: We Are Nonphysical Beings of Light

Source science describes that human minds are built with bit-vectors that can be viewed through clairvoyance as auras, halos, or orbs. Many people believe that humans are just classical meat machines, but we know that model is incomplete—from the source science perspective, we are beings of light.

We Are More Than Our Physical Bodies

Dr. Tiller: In reality, we are more than our physical bodies and brains. The prevailing thought is the brain is purely classical, yet metaphysical experiences demonstrate nonclassical behaviors, such as consciousness, awareness, psi, and supernormal intelligence. If the brain and mind are truly separate, then much of our every-day experiences, models, and research must be reinterpreted. Our mind is really an extremely large hyperdimensional set of space-like bit-vectors that appear as an aura.

This is not a new idea. Explorers such as Robert Monroe have been saying this for fifty years, while shamans and gurus have been saying the same for thousands of years.[1] Likewise, many statistical studies have documented peoples' experiences of awareness outside of their physical bodies.[2] Indeed, it is much more commonplace than expected. A conservative estimate is that 35 percent of people have experienced out-of-body awareness. This percentage suggests that more than 100 million people in the United States alone have experienced that they have awareness, mobility, and a separate existence outside their own body. Being even more conservative and using an estimate of only 15 percent, then about a billion people on Earth have experienced this phenomenon.[3]

There are many names for this other than "brain system." These labels include "mind," "soul," "spirit," "aura," "consciousness," "astral bodies," "chakras," and "source," and all of these refer to nonphysical and nonclassical elements of our being. This reinterpretation is not easy to absorb, since so many of our assumptions, unconscious beliefs, and instincts are challenged. That is one reason why the many labels can help us to focus on certain aspects of the reinterpretation. Here is a list of common brain/mind models and their primary focus (most can be found on Wikipedia). We provide this side-by-side comparison to illustrate the diversity of the models and their differences.

- Traditional brain as mind: reinforces the classical world view by ignoring major research areas
- Thoughts are things: focuses on thoughts without talking about their true physics representation
- Holographic mind: talks about holistic/gestalt/oneness properties but without math, physics, and computation theory
- Metaphysics, OBE, NDE, remote viewing: focuses on *proving* unusual behaviors exist but not models
- Quantum computation: focuses on abstract math algorithms without relating to human domains
- Bio-body suit: Good start by focusing on the separation of mind/soul from the brain
- Quantum mind: Begins to focus on the hyperdimensional and computational side of the mind
- Spiritual beings: focuses on spiritual/soul of the nonbrain duality but limited to philosophy/religion
- Panpsychism: Consciousness, mind, or soul is a universal and primordial feature of the universe

- Universal mind: A single universal consciousness is the source of everything in the universe
- Law of Attraction: combines many of the above ideas, with a spiritual/psychological perspective
- Source science: model combining these ideas with mathematics, physics, information, and computation

My preferred language for this idea is that our mind/spirit wears a bio-body suit to interact with 3+1 spacetime reality. This is metaphorically the same as wearing a diving suit for underwater exploration. Sometime before birth, our mind links with the body/brain, thereby allowing us to exist and interact in 3+1 spacetime causal reality. However, this is foreign to the outside spacetime nature of our hyperdimensional being.

The true nature of mind presents itself when we dream, meditate, have out-of-body experiences, have near-death experiences, or even die. In fact, researchers have found that when people are prohibited from dreaming, after several days they begin to exhibit immune, metabolic, and depression problems. Dreaming is a process of detaching from the brain and stepping out of spacetime. Lucid dreaming is when people awaken in their dream state,[4] and significant research and online resources exist about this fascinating ability.

The Brain Is a Quantum Correlithm Transceiver

Dr. Matzke: Your bio-body suit model is great. There are many proposals on how the mind interacts with the brain. My preferred description labels the brain as a "quantum transceiver," because it is so much like our cell phones, sending and receiving information as text messages, email, voice, and video conversations. Our body is like an extremely immersive virtual-reality environment where our observer "I" is somewhere else interacting with 3D bio-body suit via visual, auditory, taste, smell, tactical, temperature, and other sensory modalities. I prefer the term "quantum mind" when talking about brain/mind, since it reminds me that the mind is primarily informational, and especially not classical, not energy, and not matter. All of these requirements add up to an informational mechanism outside space and time, which is most likely, the source-like quantum states.

This idea of an independent yet linked brain and mind is critically important because this duality requires a mechanism for our brains and minds to interact. We have discussed our proposed brain/mind interaction using quantum correlithms, and this hyperdimensional solution links the architecture of the physical brain with the hyperdimensional structure of the quantum protodimensional reality. In addition, our source science solution shows mathematically how to inject order into a random system. Even alternative approaches must still meet the transceiver requirement that supports injection of order. It is a fact that any and all hyperdimensional spaces have the mathematical features of correlithms.

More succinctly, the brain is not a computer. It is a folded 3D antenna system that maps hyperdimensionally encoded information of mind into a 3D space. Any time a higher number of dimensions are mapped imperfectly to a lower number of dimensions, there is a loss of fidelity, which is called a "projection" and acts like a 2D shadow made by a light source from a 3D object. The brain axon/dendrite structures may also create an apparent dimensionality higher than three, which would help with the projection mismatch. The brain most likely is a 3D folded antenna that uses probabilistic mechanisms to control the firing rate of neurons.

Alternatively, synapses can be quantum mechanically influenced since the synaptic gap is very narrow at the level of quantum tunneling, where quantum states appear to traverse or tunnel thru a higher energy threshold. Additionally, the pyramidal brain cells of the motor cortex might also have some special structure to support the reliable firing of these motor neurons. We propose that more PK-style research should investigate these possibilities. The brain/body does have some autonomic systems, such as heart rate and breathing, that are self-regulating and represent neural/biochemical feedback control loops. These autonomic systems are separate from the mind itself, yet well-established biofeedback techniques can be trained to influence them.[5]

Dr. Tiller: This PK-driven mechanism is directly tied to much of my research. According to the second law of thermodynamics, disorder always increases in closed systems. For the brain state to change to more order, information must be injected. That information has an effective energy. For example, intent can change the probabilities and create the unlikely state of firing the motor neuron to move your finger exactly when you intend it to. This model does not violate the second law of thermodynamics, because the hyperdimensional nature of mind means that our brain is not a closed system. This model does not violate Landauer's principle either, because the changes in probabilities act like a change in information content, which acts like an effective energy injection. The brain is quantum mechanically not a closed system.

Brain Is a Quantum REG PK Device

Dr. Matzke: I agree and essentially the brain is a very high-gain random event generator (REG) PK device, where the mind inserts order into the brain. This model can be tested by building an electronic version of the brain, an ehostbrain that acts like a high-gain PK device.

For example, researchers are currently using memristors[6] to design a large-scale neural network where this architecture assumes that the brain is a classical neural structure.[7] Memristors are programmable resistor-based quantum tunneling gates being developed as next generation non-volatile storage. This same memristor technology could be used to build an electronic ehostbrain that assumes the brain is a quantum PK device, similar to a large-scale gas discharge system with hundreds of billions of nodes. My prediction is that as large-scale memristors arrays go online, they will be impacted by consciousness, just as other quantum electronics have been influenced, because every transistor can be biased to act like a quantum tunnel diode,[8] which would act like a miniature gas discharge device and be influenced by intention. These kind of mental influences on a variety of devices have been known for a long time.[9]

Dr. Tiller: Your design should be one of my lab's future experiments. Intention starts as a special state in the mental state space, which then forms a thought, which then triggers the neural correlate of that thought in the brain, and which finally fires the motor neuron. We know that intention cannot start in the brain, because the IHDs can directly affect the physical world (without a brain) after being programmed with a desired intention.

In another related research, our team had access to a touring exhibit of relics of Buddha. We predicted that these Buddha relics would be sacred and would act like the IHD. We suspected that the IHD and sacred relics might create the same kind of ordered states. We were right. Also, the Buddha relics can directly affect the pH of water ten times more than the IHD, again without any brain involvement.[10] We call this affect a conditioned space, which influences the probabilities similar to how normally randomly oriented magnetic poles can be aligned to produce detectable magnetic or electric fields. The Buddha relic research was motivated by Dr. Nisha Manek, who has been a member of my team for many years and has released a new book about her research and experiences with my laboratory research and team.[11]

These conditioned spaces of thoughts have been documented before in both psychological and metaphysical research. For example, mob mentality could be viewed as a form of coherent thought that affects others around them, causing normal people to behave unexpectedly. The Copper Wall experiments documented how meditation can cause a detectable alignment in the electromagnetic fields.[12] Most notably, the TM researchers also documented how hundreds of TM meditators can lower the measured crime rate of a targeted city over a weekend or longer. Finally, the IHD broadcasts research demonstrates an influence on many targeted systems.

Dr. Matzke: Most people think that the brain is the source of thought, and this is mainly due to there being nothing else classical that can be measured except the neurons. But with our alternative source science model where the brain is a two-way transceiver, the neural correlates have a matching thought states, and vice versa.[13] Even research where doctors directly stimulate neurons does not prove the brain *is* the mind, due to these two-way correlations. Our recommendation is that any research that assumes the brain is the mind can and should be reinterpreted with the alternative source science model. So, beware of scientists who have the assumption the brain equates to mind, since that obsolete model does not encompass all the known space-like phenomena, especially the well-documented metaphysical, nonlocal, or precognitive information related human behaviors.

Can you talk about causation?

Dr. Tiller: Causation and correlation are not the same, either. Just because two things are correlated does not mean they cause each other. In fact, quantum entanglement statistics are correlated and connected but it is not possible to use them for a causal communication channel. Quantum states are directly represented as quantum probability amplitudes without using matter, energy, fields, space, or time representations. Because brain states and mind states are co-correlated, this represents a co-causal system. You described to me how this has a similar interaction pattern as communicating sequential process (CSP) events, which are acausal since not a single participant of the event is the cause of the event.[14]

As you have stated, this connection can be directly traced to bivector, trivector, and *N*-vector structures, which is also the basis of entanglement. Changing either one can influence the other probabilistically, which is exactly how quantum algorithms evolve. We have also previously described in Chapter 6 on DNA, that DNA can be co-causal, as determined by morphic resonance. This is because survival of certain traits makes them more self-resonant, which affects the unfolding of other DNA.

Dr. Matzke: In addition, any answer state is equivalent to evolving the observer perspective in the hyperdimensional state space. But randomly arriving at a correct answer state for any possible question is unlikely, since we assume a very large and complex state space. Since the number of bit dimensions to support the entire multiverse is virtually infinite, the size of each mind can also be virtually without limit, i.e. the LOA idea of infinite intelligence. Psychics who can read auras report that our conscious mind is extremely small, like a snowflake on the tip of an iceberg, compared to the unconscious mind/aura. This means that the state space of overall mind is extremely large compared to the size of the neural correlate states. Also, from a representation and computing perspective, these mental states are outside conventional spacetime, making them maximally concurrent, space-like, and without limit to complexity.

This idea of a mind/body separation has been around for thousands of years, and that consciousness is fundamental and the physical world an illusion. Dean Radin does a great job in reviewing this history in his book *Supernormal*. His newest book *Real Magic* also equates the study of magic techniques and metaphysics, since both are ignored by mainstream scientists for similar reasons.[15] What is new about a source science discussion is that it combines these ideas with information science, hyperdimensional math, quantum physics, and metaphysics to describe how a nonphysical conscious mind can interact with the devices in the physical world, and especially the brain.

Our mind implemented with space-like states can tap into infinite intelligence. Also, there is the matter of God's book at the Pearly Gates that presumably contains complete information about everyone's life details. Most likely, the life review that can occur during a near-death experience or actual death uses this same outside-time information technology as does God's book.

Chapter Summary

We are not meat machines, but rather our minds are part of the source code that represents the quantum computer/OS that forms and runs our 3+1 spacetime universe. The essence of our quantum minds is the deep reality of vibratory bit dimensions that define everything in the universe. When two or three individual bit dimensions are concurrently combined, they respectively form the topology of the qubit and photon, meaning that our beings are literally the same source stuff as qubits and light. We perceive ourselves with halos, auras, aka cords, and as orbs because we are actually topological beings of light.

Chapter 9: We Are Meaning Beings

Human intelligence is derived from meaning and knowing, which are as mysterious as human self-awareness and consciousness. None of these topics are yet well understood by scientists. We believe that meaning is derived from the hyperdimensional mathematics that results from content correlational algorithm (correlithm) behaviors. Correlithms form a self-organizing meaning representation system that has orthogonal thought vectors, probabilities, and superposition, just like quantum systems. These source-bit dimensions represent the vibratory states from the Law of Attraction, which form the basis for meaning and, thus, real intelligence.

Space-Like Minds Are Exponentially Powerful

Dr. Matzke: The most important fact about these hyperdimensional correlithms is that they exist in a real hyperdimensional space and are not a simulated set of dimensions inside a computer embedded in 3D space. Computer architects have known since the dawn of mathematics and computers that the correct representation is critical for creating effective and efficient algorithms. For example, scientists can simulate up to 42-qubit quantum algorithms, but after that the simulator cannot be implemented at all in a classical computer; hence, quantum supremacy is predicted to be achieved at >50 qubits.[1] Quantum supremacy means that a quantum computer can solve a problem that no classical computer of any technology can ever solve.

Due to exponential growth in the number of quantum dimensions for a large numbers of qubits, it is impossible to simulate even 50 qubits, and to put that in perspective, 300 qubits contains 2^{300} states which is larger than the number of particles in the known universe. Simulating high-dimensional correlithms has the same efficiency/scaling restrictions as does simulating quantum algorithms. Usually the "answer" represents selecting the meaningful subspace out of an infinite number of possible projections.

Using correlithms, meaning is related to quantum physics and topology. The locality metric for detection of nearest neighbor clusters in a hyperdimensional space also cannot be simulated efficiently in three dimensions. For example, in a 3D space it is possible to use radar or sonar to detect a cluster of nearby objects without having to exhaustively search the entire space. There are reported to be billions of dimensions, thus the enumeration of all the subspaces becomes intractable (2^d subspaces for *d*-dimensions), which is called the "curse of dimensionality,"[2] but without it we would not be intelligent. Essentially, all effective clustering algorithms require heuristics or knowing which dimensions are included, and so are correlated, and which ones can be ignored. This is the power of the human Law of Attraction observer frame, where the correct dimensions are automatically added or ignored when computing the meaning cluster or rote, thereby creating the inclusion-based universe of Law of Attraction. This acts like an efficient high-dimensional radar finding nearby ideas.

Dr. Tiller: When the hyperdimensional space actually exists, then self-organizing meaning clustering, or rotes, are concurrent and fast, just like our 3D universe is massively parallel for all locality exhibited by photons, atoms, molecules, planets, stars, and galaxies. Self-organizational attraction of related rotes naturally happens concurrently in an actual hyperdimensional space, kind of like gravity attracts atoms near each other in 3+1 spacetime. It is a fact that the gravitational attraction of the almost uniform gas of hydrogen atoms in the early universe was how all suns in the universe were originally formed.

Dr. Matzke: Right, automatic clustering in rotes is important and must be part of the quantum simulator beneath our universe. Rotes are meaning clusters that must be a primitive hyperdimensional representation in order to support meaning, knowing, and telepathy. This representation must be self-organizing so like-attracts-like using a similarity metric. It is well understood from correlithm mathematics that two points near each other are highly unlikely, so when this occurs it represents an information content or source of negentropy. This is reasonable, since entropy only exists for metric spaces, and the hyperdimensional state space is a nonmetric spacetime. This self-organization generates the negentropy state because meaning clusters aggregate dimensions, which represents bits of information. Just as molecules are stable due to binding energy, so rotes are attractive and stable since they represent a kind of geometry and negentropy binding. Rotes bind/warp the hyperdimensional space, which Abraham calls a vortex, similar to how mass and gravity warp conventional spacetime.

The human mind uses attention and intention to control what dimensions are added or dropped during semantic clustering of rotes. Similar to how Lego blocks can be formed into many 3D shapes, rotes are constructed to include/exclude bit-dimensions and *N*-vectors to form specific meanings. Likewise, just as atom and molecules can be used to build other molecules, rotes can be constructed by combining with other rotes. Both of these Lego blocks and molecular metaphors are restrictive, since they exist only in 3D space, whereas rotes are assembled as collections of bit dimensions and *N*-vectors in *N*D space. Robert Monroe defined rotes as bundles of meaning, and humans do exactly that to create meaning by building on other established meaning. We would expect that this entire hyperdimensional process be isotropic and relativistic for all possible rotes, which can act as its own formal observer frames.

Computer data does not intrinsically contain meaning. An electronic library full of data does not "know" anything, even though it contains all that data. Any data that is spatially distributed when represented inside 3D books or disks is, therefore, not holistic. But with space-like rotes constructed in hyperdimensional spaces, each represents a special holistic observer frame. Since the number of dimensions can increase without limit, the complexity of meaning can also build without limit. In such a hyperspace, all meaningfully related ideas are very near each other, which easily allows for identifying the related perspectives and sequences.

Complex rotes are thus constructed with every possible meaning, each one representing a perspective or point (or an equivalent vector from some origin) in a hyperdimensional space using a collection of bit dimensions. We expect that even simple rotes with significant meaning would have millions to billions of bit-dimensions, plus structures such as bivectors, trivectors, and entanglement. Even though rotes have different complexity, they can be combined as first-class elements to form new rotes, since they are all constructed of maximally concurrent, orthogonal bit dimensions that exist outside classical spacetime.

For example, humans think of multiplication and addition as first-class ideas even though multiplication is defined using addition. The hierarchy of meaning make more complex structures but does not make those ideas bigger and slower. This ability to combine rotes to build other rotes could support infinite intelligence since this collection of bit dimensions is first-class, contains no mass, and is not distributed or limited by spacetime metrics. Also, complex space-like rotes would be extremely concurrent when finding similarity matches because rotes are verbnoun balanced and can act as both thoughts and as actions, plus a rote can be used as its own reference frame to compare similarity or nearness to other states.

We have used the idea from physics that rotes represent a hyperdimensional version of an observer frame, but with special properties. The rote dimensions represent an address, which essentially is a name. From many spiritual traditions, giving a name to something allows you to interact with and control it. For example, in some Jewish traditions you are not allowed to say the word for God because a name is not merely an arbitrary designation formed by combining sounds, but rather a name conveys the nature and essence of a thing. Spiritual names are complex enough to summon the spirit itself, and this idea is also used in Hermetic practices.[3] As a side note, in the Harry Potter books "He Who Must Not Be Named" was a warning to not attract the attention of Voldemort by speaking his name.

Dr. Tiller: Based on the mathematics of correlithms, meaning and hyperdimensional spaces are intricately tied together. Rotes represent meaning by clusters of bit dimensions and likewise other rotes. These rotes are defined by the address of the meaning, so are accessible "anywhere" and at "anytime." Meaning and telepathy are supported by this correlithm rote-addressing mechanism. Since rotes are outside of spacetime, the idea of a spiritual library (known as the Akashic Records of all knowledge of all time) that clairvoyants can access, is extremely possible.[4] Lucid dreamers report they can go to school in their dreams and learn every night, since learning is not part of the brain. This night school might represent a significant personal justification to learn how to lucid dream. But the question is, can humans really get smarter faster?

Complexity Building of Real Intelligence and Meaning

Dr. Matzke: Let us discuss further how thoughts and meaning can build in complexity by looking at single-cell creatures at the bottom of the life intelligence scale compared to humans with our roughly 100 billion neurons—thus we have at least 10^{11} more complexity and significantly more intelligence. Does this mean geniuses are ten times smarter than typical people? People with >160 IQ (>4 standard deviations) are less than 0.1% of the population. So, for the sake of a quantized conversation, let us assume each standard deviation is 1.5x smarter—then these geniuses would be $1.5^4=5$ times smarter than the average person. People exist who are documented super-geniuses (>190 IQ), that is 6 standard deviations or 11.4 times smarter than the average person.

What about infinite intelligence? Can we imagine mental beings that are orders of magnitude smarter than us because they can build and manage complexities of meaning that are hundreds or thousands of times larger than humans can? If someone could be about two hundred times smarter than humans, then by using the above metric, they would have an estimated IQ of 295. Some people who live now may be that smart, such as autistics and other savants, we just do not have any standard way to measure their IQ.

I am using the idea of quantized IQ as if we all agree what a scale of intelligence really means. In reality, IQ tests measure the ability of young people to learn, which is a measure of how intelligent they are but not how much they know. My simplistic approach to use IQ as a conversational way to discuss relative intelligence is not meant to be formal and does not reflect how much smart people actually know.

Spiritual Intelligence

Dr. Tiller: Human IQ models of intelligence might be totally the wrong metric. Dr. David Hawkins, the author of the book *Power vs Force,* created his Map of Consciousness as a metric that might be called a spiritual IQ.[5] The scale of this metric is 0 to 1,000, where the perfected Christ is 1,000 and typical humans are around 200. There is a simple test using kinesiology-based muscle testing to determine the Hawkins scale for anyone or anything. Beings with a Hawkins score above 500 are considered more complex and integrated from a spiritual and mind perspective. Table 13 shows the Hawkins scores and related emotional perspectives.

Table 13. Hawkins scale

God-View	Life-View	Level	Log	Emotion	Process	
Self	Is	Enlightenment	700-1000	Ineffable	Pure Consciousness	
All-Being	Perfect	Peace	600	Bliss	Illumination	
One	Complete	Joy	540	Serenity	Transfiguration	**P**
*Loving	Being	Love	500	Reverence	Revelation	**O**
Wise	Meaningful	Reason	400	Understanding	Abstraction	**W**
Merciful	Harmonious	Acceptance	350	Forgiveness	Transcendence	**E**
*Inspiring	Hopeful	Willingness	310	Optimism	Intention	**R**
Enabling	Satisfactory	Neutrality	250	Trust	Release	
*Permitting	Feasible	Courage	200	Affirmation	Empowerment	*
Indifferent	Demanding	Pride	175	Scorn	Inflation	
Vengeful	Antagonistic	Anger	150	Hate	Aggression	**F**
Denying	Disappointing	Desire	125	Craving	Enslavement	**O**
Punitive	Frightening	Fear	75	Anxiety	Withdrawal	**R**
Disdainful	Tragic	Grief	75	Regret	Despondency	**C**
Condemning	Hopeless	Apathy	50	Despair	Abdication	**E**
Vindictive	Evil	Guilt	30	Blame	Destruction	
Despise	Miserable	Shame	20	Humiliation	Elimination	

Just like traditional IQ, the Hawkins scale was originally thought to be fixed for each human. It is now known that spiritual events and other factors evident with the IHD can increase the Hawkins IQ of individuals. This is an extremely important idea since it means that, as a species, we can accelerate our mental cohesiveness, which is a sign of higher intelligence moving away from ego-based concerns and toward a more present-moment perspective. Humans' general ability to focus on the now and make complex socially conscious decisions is something that is hard to quantify, but Hawkins scale is a great start. Table 13 reminds me of Abraham's emotional ladder chart in Table 11.

Machine Intelligence

Dr. Matzke: Let's discuss machine intelligence. Can human geniuses be compared to other seemingly intelligent artificial systems? Human geniuses, such as world chess champions, also make complex decisions based on highly structured data and awareness of patterns. So how do computers compare with human champions? A useful example of human intelligence is when some world chess geniuses cannot only compute the chess moves, but also remember all the moves in many previous games they had played years before. IBM's Deep Blue chess computer, which contained thirty nodes, each with many processors and special custom chess-playing hardware, was able to beat the Russian world chess champion in 1997,[6] but that does not mean that the computer understood chess. IBM's Watson beat the world Jeopardy champion in 2011.[7] Likewise in 2016, Google DeepMind AlphaGo machines with generic hardware and software beat the world Go champion[8] using deep learning techniques. All of these machines had different architectures, and were the size of a refrigerator, compared to the size of the human brain.

Quantum speedup exists for Shor's algorithm, and likewise Grover's quantum search. This quantum speedup search algorithm, developed by Lov Grover, can significantly outperform insteps compared to any classical search algorithm.[9] Search is an interesting problem because classical algorithms generally take N steps to test all N data elements based on some specific search criteria. This is problematic when the size of *N* grows exponentially. Google solves this problem for finite but classically large data sets using *N* processors all running the same code in parallel (Google's original map-reduce system) required a specialized architecture, OS support, and a significant amount of parallel computing hardware and memory.[10]

Google also cannot achieve quantum speedup without actually using quantum systems, so even Google purchased a $10 million D-Wave quantum computer to run quantum optimization problems.[11] The travelling salesmen problem is a kind of optimization problem where the perfect solution is known to take exponential resources to solve, making it beyond the scope of purely classical computers. Content addressable memories using real hyperdimensional spaces, though, allow encoding of similarity to bypass traditional brute force search algorithms. Google is also building its own quantum computer with reported size of 72 qubits, which is exceeds the size of the quantum supremacy threshold.[12]

Google has also developed neural network programs for language translation that can be trained using large data sets. Each node in a neural network is a weight that represents the sum of all the data to meet some objective function. Google language translation is impressive considering that the program does all the translation as data without any meaning or manual heuristics. Each node in the neural net is somewhat equivalent to a point in our high-dimensional mind, except that humans appear to assign a label or meaning to their space-like address.

A neural net is not introspective so cannot assign a meaningful label to each node and the states are distributed. Some transcendent states from near-death experiences that humans relate do not have labels either, so sometimes it is hard for us to describe those memories into sequential language. Human meaning is distributed to be wave-like, space-like, and source-like, whereas computers really do not have meaning, knowing, or intelligence and only simulate high-dimensional spaces.[13] There are fundamental differences in simulating a correlithm, whereas human minds actually *are* a real correlithm infrastructure, supported by real high-dimensional spaces. Currently, there are no quantum AI machines that mimic the mind and meaning, except perhaps the real intelligence (RI) of humans.

Our minds naturally perform search through use of meaning based on content, since all the space-like states are represented concurrently using correlithms. Humans can also determine quickly that they do not know the answer. Search can be tricky, since it might require meaning to adapt the parameters, particularly if the goal of the search criteria is poorly specified or evolving. Searching, counting, probabilities, and other algorithms that must touch all data are not efficient computing problems when the data size is extremely large. Counting is required whenever probabilities are computed; however, simulating probabilities using exponentially large counts require infinite precision floating-point support, which is physically impossible. We do not know how quantum physics computes probabilities and normalizes with such extreme precision.

Some autistic savants can count extremely rapidly in a glance, which represents a concurrent counting algorithm.[14] All exceptional supernormal human behaviors should be reanalyzed for quantum algorithmic speedup. Out-of-time behaviors must also have a new metric, similar to Bell statistics. Space-like states may be self-normalizing, which removes the restriction of counting to create probabilities, while primitive qubit quantum states represent probabilities without counting.

Planning is another computational task that humans perform well due to meaning but is quite different from the well-defined scheduling of tasks that computers perform well. I know that designing a new piece of software requires understanding the meaning of the objectives and goals, breaking up the solution into manageable design patterns, actually writing the code plus test cases, and finally determining whether the goals are met by the written code and tests. None of these tasks can be performed by computers, since all entail meaning, which is why there is significant outsourcing for writing code going to countries such as India, with its large pool of English-speaking technology specialists. Once the code and tests have been written, computers can automatically run those tests to validate the code, but if something breaks, then a human must determine the root cause of the failure and fix it. Computers are not expected anytime soon to take over designing and writing new code. This is also true for any meaning-based jobs, such as law and medicine.

Planning and meaning are related to social understanding, and decisions about creating new laws for them are difficult. Even Isaac Asimov's "Three Laws of Robotics" (plus an additional 0th law) requires social understanding and planning to "not harm humans." Some early versions of these social awareness algorithms are being implemented in our autonomous vehicles to make choices that might minimize the loss of human life under certain circumstances. Of course, machines have no understanding of social consciousness ideas. A general solution of this social awareness is hard to imagine, except in science fiction. Even in the Asimov books, the robots could only accomplish the 0th law goal of "not harming humanity due to inaction" when the robots became telepathic, which is based on meaning.

Dr. Tiller: Thanks for that interesting summary of the various machine intelligence systems and their limitations compared to humans. Will machine intelligence ultimately outstrip humans?

Infinite Intelligence

Dr. Matzke: As long as machine intelligence is limited to spacetime, the answer is NO, because humans are not bound by spacetime. Other critics of AI also say this will not happen. Alternatively, it IS possible to imagine nonphysical beings such as Abraham that would be 1 million or 1 billion times smarter than the average human. Abraham reports that they represent infinite intelligence, which means they are like oracles, and know everything and can answer any question, even though we might not understand the answer. Let us assume that Abraham is at least 1 million times smarter than humans. Using the same metric as before, it would be 34 standard deviations and represent an IQ of 610. If Abraham had an IQ of 1,000, then that would represent 57 standard deviations, or

3.5 billion times smarter than humans; plus, they are telepathic. It might almost be like humans trying to talk with insects.

Over the past fifty years, computers have been scaling with each process generation, due to the de facto standard of Moore's law driving the semiconductor industry. We are used to getting more powerful computers that are two times smaller and faster every one-and-a-half to two years. Ordinary people during peak experiences such as NDEs, plus geniuses and savants, appear to have instant access to supercomputer-style computing boost to support advanced space-like awareness and meaning. The fact that humans can tap into superintelligence with the same hardware brain is one of the major justifications I use to describe why the brain cannot be a computer. The bad news is that Moore's law scaling will soon stop due to the costs and technology limits of building smaller features,[15] yet computers do not really exhibit general intelligence using common classical computer hardware.

The "supermind" is that ability to dial in any amount of computing resources just by letting go of spacetime, thereby switching from sequential computing to arbitrary amounts of concurrent meaning, space-like awareness, and parallel computing. Moving with a high velocity always slows the passage of time, due to relativity, so all computers also run slower, yet stepping out of spacetime is equivalent to accelerating the universe away from you, thereby speeding up your local time compared to the rest of the universe. This is a kind of reverse relativity—similar to how the Star Trek TV series computer cores ran in a stationary warp field to achieve faster computing. Quantum no-time and extreme concurrency gives unlimited speedup, whereas relativistic time warping due to time-dilation can only slow down the apparent passage of time.

Infinite Emotional Intelligence

Dr. Tiller: As we learned from earlier chapters, emotion is a dominant factor in organizing memory and meaning. Abraham talks about emotion as a key to building highly complex and robust vortices. Therefore, a large component of rote formation is the dimensions related to emotional context. Will you describe how emotion starts in the mind and not in the body?

Dr. Matzke: Extreme joy, love, compassion, and other responses represent a kind of infinite emotional intelligence. This is hard for many to understand because they think of emotions as being on a narrow scale (i.e., perhaps a linear scale from 1 to 10). Since emotional meaning is represented by using infinite hyperdimensional rotes, then imagining joy on an extended scale of 1 to 1,000 or 1 to 1 million seems far-fetched, yet this infinite joy, love, or compassion has been experienced and reported by many people. (Note: the linear joy scale is just for the purpose of this discussion and is not a real scale.)

Since the hyperdimensional nature of existence creates our multiverse, and these protodimensional properties are ubiquitous, we can expect the existence of other hyperintelligent and hyper-emotional beings such as Abraham. Assuming that hypercompassionate and hyperintelligent thought beings exist, they would be interested in humanity's evolution to awaken to our own supermind abilities, which is one reason why Abraham and other spirit guides work through channels to interact with and guide humanity. One of my friends communed with beings of Monroe's "the Gathering," which Robert Monroe labeled as Focus 35 state, where nonphysical intelligent beings gathered to watch Earth come of age. These nonphysical beings telepathically told my friend that they did not expect humans to be visiting "the Gathering" as of yet, which is a sign of our growth as individuals and as a species.

Supermind and Virtual Worlds

Dr. Tiller: The connection between meaning and infinite intelligence is important because as long as humans believe our brain is our mind, then we believe we are limited. Robert Monroe stated, "The greatest illusion is that we have limitations," and said that limitation is based on our belief of a brain-centric model of ourselves. As soon as we believe that intrinsic meaning is derived from hyperdimensional spaces and that building complex rotes is purely in the mind, then we can start applying techniques geared toward supermind.

Dr. Matzke: This increasing complexity is important because our dream worlds are entirely constructed as virtual worlds. Many people who have experienced lucid dreams, out-of-body experiences, and near-death phenomena have described them as extremely clear, memorable, joyous, and life-changing mentally-constructed virtual worlds. This would require some extremely complex information mechanism that is not possible within our limited brain.

In his book *Proof of Heaven*,[16] Dr. Eben Alexander eloquently describes elaborate colorful and alive virtual worlds, all envisioned while his brain was completely offline for a week due to an extreme case of bacterial meningitis. His memories of these worlds survived after he recovered and have changed his life focus ever since. Lucid dreamers construct whatever virtual worlds they desire. Some yogis reportedly create such a vivid virtual environment that all the nearby people share in their collective vision.

In fact, our entire physical world could be considered a dream running as a simulation in the ultimate quantum computer. This idea is important, since conventional extended 3D spaces can also be represented inside this hyperdimensional quantum ether. We showed with geometric algebra that we can simulate 3D rotations (quaternions) in both 4D and 5D spaces (tauquernions and tauquinions, respectively). Therefore, our dream worlds could present us with virtual 3D worlds.

These kinds of elaborate simulations of 3D extended virtual worlds are what drive the animation video and gaming industry, and virtual reality technology. It only takes computing relationships and our common sense about perspective, gravity, ray-tracing propagation of light, textures, etc., to create a virtual world. Geometric algebra scientist Chris Doran created a super-efficient real-time ray-tracing technology that is being built into next-generation gaming systems to control light sources and ray-tracing propagation. In our dreams and the Matrix movies, we realized that we can break the laws of gravity, velocity, and physicality of matter. Escher's artwork moved that to imagining even higher-dimensional thought worlds.

Spiritual people talk about downloads they receive, and how they instantly know stuff they could not have known using traditional means, as is the case with remote viewing. Much of what humans invent is really downloading from the Akashic Records, since all knowledge exists as downloadable rotes outside spacetime and we just have to address the records for retrieval. Archetypes and mathematics are part of these downloadable records. By understanding how rotes work along with the IHD, it should be possible to create advanced training tools to help people learn more quickly and maybe even download meaning into humans. This idea was also expressed in the Matrix movies. Imagine how this would radically and quickly change our world.

Dr. Tiller: According to Robert Monroe, after we die our mind is attracted to meaningful virtual locations based on our dominant beliefs, which contain the structures and knowledge of various highly individual spiritual and religious constructs. Monroe has defined fourteen different levels of consciousness with non-sequential numerical labels: Focus 10, Focus 12,…, etc. thru Focus 49, and he labels Focus 24 to 26 as the Belief System Territories. People get stuck in Focus 24–26 until they realize they are truly dead and then move on to Focus 27 and beyond.

Omniscient States

Dr. Matzke: Another aspect of infinite intelligence is the omniscient states reported during near-death experiences. In her book *Dying to Be Me*, Anita Moorjani eloquently describes this hyper-aware state during her NDE coma where spacetime was not a limit. While in the coma, she could tap into doctors' conversations down the hall about her condition and even into her brother's thoughts and emotions while he was flying in an airliner from another continent.[17] All of these memories were available to her after she awoke from her coma due to terminal cancer. She also represents an extremely important and documented case, because after awakening from her NDE she was healed from stage 4 cancer. These omniscient NDE states are the most concrete examples of requirements to support infinite intelligence. During Kundalini awakening, people also describe hyperaware states where they feel they have godlike omniscience.

All these seemingly unrelated phenomena are all built on the same omniscient, space-like, hyperdimensional attention and rote infrastructure. For example, during a lucid dream the aeronaut has complete control of the dream, so can switch their attention from the virtual world to the physical world. This choice turns their lucid dream into an out-of-body experience. Likewise, during an NDE, the person can switch their attention to other locations and people, thereby performing remote viewing or shared dreams. Psychometry is the ability to use an object as a map to a spacetime trail and find related meaning associated with that object. It is the same remote viewing technique where the act of remembering allows control of the mind's eye to the correlithm address of the desired meaning, no matter where in spacetime it exists. Early remote viewing experiments showed most people can navigate to abstract coordinates like latitudes and longitudes,[18] or use someone's name plus age as an address.

During NDEs, people often report going through a tunnel,[19] which I believe represents the experience of stepping out of time. In fact, the life review is an omniscient space-like state that occurs when our mind's eye is free of spacetime limits. In that panoramic time state, we simultaneously see all our memories from our whole life, but we still interpret that vision as a sequential life review. Our mind does not exist in normal spacetime and the supermind state allows us to instantly have access to the address of all our memories for this entire life, all our past lives, and anyone else's life. The act of "remembering" allows us to access any information using correlithm-style addressing.

Coincidences Intelligence

Dr. Tiller: A final topic for meaning is coincidences and whether they are just chance or whether there is something else at work. For example, many people might unexpectedly think of a friend or family member and then that person soon visits or calls. Rotes are defined as meaning that is not in the brain—when you think to call someone, they are connected to your thought by a rote. So, if your mind is paying attention, you connect with that external rote, just as remote viewers do. Another example might be that you get a presentient thought to drive slower and then you see a cop around the next bend. Essentially, this is an example of when your future self makes an emotional rote connection ("Yikes, there's a cop") with your slightly younger self.

Psychics who are healers or find lost people use the name and age of a person as an address to connect with that person. Once two people share the same rote correlithm dimensional address, they are sharing the thoughts and meanings from that common perspective in hyperdimensional space. These shared rote dimensions are implemented using correlithm dimensional structures, such as vectors, bivectors, trivectors, and entanglement. Perhaps the best label for these rote connections is "aka cords."

Dr. Matzke: The Law of Attraction literature states that cooperating components are attracted to whatever you focus on, and it might appear that many of these rendezvous are coincidences. As is the case with Bell statistics, impossible probabilities are due to underlying physics. Understand that clear intention creates hyperdimensional rotes that have meaning, and then similar meanings are naturally attracted. Meaning rotes are the mechanisms behind the Law of Attraction. The key is to expect and notice when these rendezvous occur, since they may be subtle, such as a thought to turn here, or stop and get a cup of coffee to meet someone, or notice some lost diamond laying in your path. Insights are telepathic rotes that allow cooperating meaning matching components to be noticed, but they are not coincidences.

Chapter Summary

Real intelligence in humans is due to the fact we are meaning beings and meaning is not in the brain, but rather is embedded in the correlithm capabilities of hyperdimensional spaces. Rotes are clusters of meaning dimensions that can grow to arbitrary complexity. With the existence of real hyperdimensional spaces, humans are much smarter than would be possible with only brain-based computing. We can envision a time in the future when humans are collectively much smarter, more emotionally mature, and perhaps also wiser by using those capabilities to help mankind have a more loving and meaningful existence.

Meaning is the sum total of all dimensions associated with individual, physical/quantum unconscious, as well as collective states such as anima/animus, archetypes, and morphogenesis. Meaning is formed by the hyperdimensional structure of rotes. These are not part of the physical brain, which strongly suggests that our memories and meaning survive the loss of the physical body/brain.

Chapter 10: We Are Eternal Beings

There is a saying, "Think outside the box." In this case, the box is the universe defined by spacetime itself. Most likely the more accurate statement is: "Thoughts exist outside the spacetime box." This idea of anything existing outside of the spacetime box of our universe of space and also time is hard to comprehend, especially when the box is defined by spacetime itself. Conventional physicists also have a lot to say about time.[1]

John Wheeler is attributed as saying,[2] "Time is nature's way to keep everything from happening all at once," and equivalently, "Space keeps everything from happening all at the same place." As big as our universe is, the spacetime address of any event could still be cataloged as an address in the larger hyperdimensional structure of the universe. In that context, we can think of time as just an additional part of the dimensional address. In fact, most computer systems store time-dependent data as spatial dimensional data.[3] Even Jeff Hawkins hierarchical temporal memory (HTM)[4] is looking for patterns through time as if they were patterns through space. Since quantum bit dimensions are infinite, there is a large enough address space to define a spacetime address for all events for all time and for all space, thereby defining an infinite quantum oracle.

Mind Outside Time

Dr. Tiller: This big idea that we are eternal beings comes as a natural extension of the hyperdimensional infrastructure that supports quantum mechanics, thoughts, and meaning. Since hyperdimensionality must exist due to quantum mechanics, our mind experiences most likely exist outside our brain, which means that our sense of self must survive the death of our physical brain and body. The brain is a quantum antenna with self-regulating controls for our bio-body suit.

Einstein's relativity theory proved that space and time are intimately connected, such that together they form a spacetime continuum. You cannot talk about time without talking about space. Gravity is also more related to warping of time rather than of space. Quantum mechanics and meaning both naturally arise out of the topological properties of hyperdimensional protodimensional bitvectors. Time as we know it (continuous and relativistic) only exists in our 3+1 spacetime universe, which is simulated within the bigger hyperspacetime of bit dimensions. A derivative is a measure of the change in either spatial or temporal dimensions. So, along with these primitive bit dimensions come primitive concepts of prototime, or simply change. Can you expound upon the idea of change?

Remembering Is Time Traveling

Dr. Matzke: Change of states comes in two major flavors, reversible and irreversible. Time comes as a result of irreversible change that destroys information, such as noise, irreversible logic gates, the measurement of a quantum state, or wait-signal ordering. We know from universal quantum reversible Toffoli gates (that can reversibly compute any Boolean logic expression) that if you increase the dimensionality large enough so no information is erased, then most computations are reversible. So, if an infinite number of dimensions exist, this means there is an infinite amount of states and addresses, which means there a great deal of room for all thoughts and none are ever lost. This is related to multiverse theories.

With that idea, thoughts can be remembered from anywhere and at any time, not just from the past. It is like how looking up a book requires you to know the title and shelf in the physical library or URL/ISPN of the book in your electronic library. Each thought rote represents its own address. Remembering is the process of using the meaning of something as the address of that information, which means you can remember the past (a memory) or the future (a precognition and retrocausation), and from anywhere in space (a remote viewing). Telepathy, though, is just remembering the meaning address of the other person's thoughts. The temporal properties are primarily determined by the hyperdimensional concurrent spatial infrastructure.

Since time is another dimension, just like we can see the change in elevation in a landscape, so changes in time values can be shown spatially as variations on a spatial plot. For instance, I have personally built and patented a logic simulator that can efficiently and instantly move to any point in the past and see the computed values. Likewise, Datomic database written in Clojure[5] is a modern functional language database that never erases information and maintains a time context for all old transaction values. Datomic is a side-effect-free database that naturally allows temporal-related logic expressions and a more general parallel computing environment. Both of these examples use space to manage time values.

Generally, our single perspective represents a focus on the meaning related with a single point in spacetime. Remote viewing research demonstrated that virtually any human can naturally place their attention at any abstract coordinate in spacetime, since we use this ability to remember.[6]

It is possible to go above our timeline and interact with multiple past lives simultaneously, just like a marionette does with several puppets. NLP timeline therapy describes a process for healing yourself in the past of this life and also in past lives. Robert Monroe's "Inspec" (short for Intelligent Species) was his future self that interacted with his younger self, similar to timeline therapy.[7] Another example is Jenna Catherine's book *Conversing with the Future: Visions of the Year 2020,* in which she describes her present-day self, talking with her future self, using a combination of precognitive telepathy.[8]

Our minds eye can also simultaneously observe and aggregate multiple observer space-like points concurrently, which give us a sense of gestalt wholeness. This is the kind of space-like state where NDE omniscience is possible. When we step outside of time, our mind's eye sees all of time simultaneously as a kind of panoramic time perspective. The true nature of hyperdimensional mind is that hyperdimensional bit dimensions are mathematically orthogonal and naturally give rise to concurrent thoughts. Our sequential language and single time-like focus keep our mind in time limited to a small number of short-term memories at once.[9] Humans are believed to be limited to processing seven pieces of information (plus or minus two) in short-term memory at once, but this is not true for savants and geniuses. Also, if you manipulate your apparent perceived rate of time, then there is no limit.

There are many other examples of nonordinary experiences of time. Athletes develop this concurrent awareness of their environments in what is often called "being in the zone,"[10] which activates our concurrent mind by getting outside of sequential time. For example, while in the zone state experience many sports players can think extremely clear and quickly, such that everyone around them appears to be moving in slow-motion. They step out of time and tap into concurrent thought computing. Related to this zone state, some people report that during a car accident they experience the trigger event as happening in slow-motion, which we believe is directly due to stepping out of time and presentience.

All events in the present moment are concurrent. The power of now can be enhanced by extending your present moment, thereby creating more and more mental concurrency and clarity.[11] Most people believe they have to drink caffeine to think quickly, but meditation predisposes you to concurrent thinking, which creates much better clarity and lucidity, with larger and more complex amounts of thoughts and heart intelligence. Meditation supports outside-of-time concurrent thinking, which maximizes integration of information. Many brain-centric thinkers say that dreaming and meditation act like a garbage-collection process, but from a source science approach, they suggest integration and concurrency. We call this "gestalt" or "holistic" thinking, which is not possible with classical spacetime-segregated representations of information.

To use a golf example, think of extending the size of your present moment to be as long as the time it takes for your ball to drop in the hole during a putt. In this time state, you are essentially looking through time and lining up the putt to create an arc of the ball's path that ends in the hole. This example was illustrated in the movie *The Legend of Bagger Vance,* where all the states of the golf ball through time were shown simultaneously, such that the white ball formed a white lighted track showing the path the ball would take.[12] No computation is required, just look through time while lining up the end of the putt with the hole and take the shot. In the book *Time for a Change,* NLP legend Richard Bandler introduces his favorite hypnotic techniques for time and space distortion using hyperesthesia.[13] He discusses how to "hit a fast ball" or beat a "fifth-degree black belt" by "speeding up" your perception and time rate. Hitting the fast ball is also helped by making the ball appear bigger, due to distortion of space perception.

From a computational and physics perspective, the only way to have the perception of time slowing down is to step outside of time and obtain the supercomputing boost of space-like concurrent information states and awareness. Source science states that the mind is not in time, so we experience a sequential world because we just pay too much attention to our brain in time and our dominant use of sequential language. Mystics are most likely people who live their lives slightly out of time. Their mind is in heaven and still connected to their body on Earth. Shamans have used these techniques to keep their tribe safe from external enemies for thousands of years.

There are meditation and yoga exercises that also train us to pay attention concurrently.[14] Bill, you are a long-term meditator, can you describe how meditation helps us disconnect from the brain and step out of time?

Time and Meditation

Dr. Tiller: From my experience, meditation has three key outcomes:

- Slows down the rate of your thoughts, which
- Changes the mind from sequential thinking to concurrent states of being, which
- Integrates thoughts and emotions holistically.

The instruction for beginning meditators is to think just one thought, such as focusing on breathing or a mantra. This is harder than it seems because our mind races through an average of 20,000 to 60,000 thoughts per day, assuming one to two seconds per thought, while some estimates are ten times that amount. So just observe when your mind strays and gently bring it back to a single thought. When you can hold a single thought for ten seconds, you have just slowed down your rate of thoughts by three to ten times.

When you can hold a single thought for a minute or an hour, you eventually experience the state of the void, which is the formless state of no-time and no-thought. Beginners say meditation is boring, yet that is exactly the process to stop thought and step out of time. These dualistic mind states are fundamental ways of being, where sequential thoughts are inside time and space-like concurrent thoughts are outside time.

Dr. Matzke: Controlling the rate of our thoughts changes our experience of how time passes. My original motivation to study quantum computing was to understand how to use quantum states to represent concurrent computing. As in any good fast algorithm, the data representation is primary. We also know from Shor's algorithm that some choice of states performs concurrent computation, which is faster than any possible sequential computing. Meditation does several things to our brain/mind system related to time and concurrent computing:

- Lowers the brain wave frequency
- Manipulates the size of our present moment

- Expands observer frame into many more space-like states

Our psychological present moment is typically a window of about one to three seconds—where everything else is either past or future.[15] So all things in the moment are concurrent and chained together by sequences of each following present moment. This sequence of present moments acts like a clock for the human mind. The traditional conventional wisdom is that faster is better for computation, but this is counter-intuitive for meditation, where slower is better, because more space-like concurrency occurs as each present moment gets longer.

Since each mental thought is its own set of concurrent thought vectors, they can be organized either sequentially or concurrently. Mediation allows people to switch from sequential time (in time) to concurrent quantum time (outside time) where more emotional and mental states are simultaneous or concurrent. The change of our present moment is actually a manipulation of external time from less sequential to more concurrent, making us more intelligent and more like savants. My experience is that when thoughts occur concurrently, it is hard to remember in which order they occurred.

Time and Gravity

Dr. Tiller: Manipulating our sense of time is a concurrent informational effect as well as potentially a gravitational one. Gravity pulls in the direction where time slows down the most. Could this be because time and gravity are connected? So, if the mind can manipulate its sense of time, and also warp space with rotes, then perhaps it can affect the physical world with levitation effects. Levitating small objects might be possible, but levitating large objects, such as a person, would require a huge time bubble to counteract the force of gravity.

Dr. Matzke: According to mainstream science, there is no credible proof of levitation or telekinesis, but if it is possible it would use this kind of spacetime-warping technology. Many anecdotal examples of levitation exist, including personal stories and hopping and poltergeist cases, but no controlled research has occurred on telekinesis for levitation. In the book *Real Magic*, Dean Radin reports on many historical events where sacred people levitated on command in front of large audiences.[16] Despite the skepticism, American, Russian, and Chinese governments have expressed research interest in levitation and anti-gravity research.

In February 2017, some researchers at the University of Chicago found that they could levitate a variety of small objects using a temperature gradient between a warm plate and very cold plate in a vacuum chamber. They first noticed this effect when a piece of lint accidently got trapped in the chamber. What this result says is that hour-long stable thermodynamic gradients[17] can counteract the effect of gravity for nonmagnetic generic objects, such as ceramic and polyethylene spheres, glass bubbles, ice particles, lint strands, and thistle seeds. Since the mind can affect entropy, perhaps this platform may also be useful for studying telekinesis for levitation.

I have met several people who have reported that they have accidently teleported themselves, which also represents a kind of spacetime warping.[18] The Bible is also full of accounts of bilocation of Jesus and many saints. This bilocation may be some combination of out-of-body experience or actually be a moving of the body to a new address, which is equivalent to moving the assemblage point.

Another historical context is the aborigine, who introduced the term "Dreamtime" to describe dreaming and represent their concepts of "time out of time."[19] Other translations of Dreamtime also attach the meaning of "eternal and uncreated." Yet another explains that Dreamtime is hard to conceptualize in English since it is not related to a specific time or place, but rather is simultaneous in the past, the present, and the future (similar to our panoramic time). This is a rich and sacred topic, because in Dreamtime an individual's entire ancestry exists as one, culminating in the idea that all knowledge is acquired through one's ancestors. This is similar to the concepts of the Akashic Records and life review reported during near death experiences. Dreamtime also represents the sacred creation myth where "once upon a time" time out of time, The Creation was formed by ancestral Totemic Spirit Beings.[20]

Time and Eternal Self

Dr. Tiller: There is significant overlap between Dreamtime ideas and source science. It is clear from this discussion that our mind is extremely powerful due to its hyperdimensional nature, and therefore survives the physical death of the body. Due to our capacity for hyper-intelligence, concurrent thought requires a nonclassical bit representation. This same infrastructure means that our mind transcends classical time. Just as quantum states existed before and are the cause of the formation of our classical universe, so our quantum mind also precedes our physical bodies and the universe. Remembering past lives is real, since all these states are part of the primordial hyperdimensional supermind outside of classical spacetime. Timeline therapy utilizes this ability.

Our magnificent minds are infinite and eternal, and are not restricted to any brain structure. Our true eternal self does not die, but instead we interact with multiple bodies through multiple lifetimes. Our true mental self is androgynous, yet our memories and emotions over many lifetimes give us our feminine and masculine experiences and mixtures. Once our physical body dies, we initially connect with all of our departed family members. Later, our mind either connects with another body or we leave to explore the rest of the mental virtual multiverse.[21]

According to Monroe, in the future year 3000 we will connect and disconnect from bodies at will and be able to enjoy physical experiences or nonphysical astral travel. We can also imagine that we could build your ghostbrain-based machine that souls could interact with when visiting the physical world. Now, let's discuss the idea of eternity.

Dr. Matzke: Our eternal nature is due to our hyperdimensional framework. Eternity is an infinite temporal concept that is as hard to comprehend as is infinity as a spatial concept. What does it mean to be eternal? The physical universe is about 13.8 billion years old, yet that is an instant compared to the eternity of time or no time. From the perspective of eternity, normal time scales have very little significance. We know already that changes of mental states can happen independent of any classical world time scale.

Thus, on one extreme we have the present moment and on the other eternity. Yet both are the same thing from an outside-of-time perspective. When we take our infinite and eternal self and focus it all on the present moment, this allows us to be fully present and to have the best space-like awareness and make the best impeccable decisions from moment to moment. We have very limited experience, concepts, and language patterns about an abnormal time, so I hope this chapter helped with exploring those ideas.

Chapter Summary

The human mind is eternal because it is not within our brain. With practice, we can remember anywhere and anywhen. We can step out of time and, due to concurrent thoughts, can experience the world with arbitrary detail. For instance, we can slow down thoughts and replay them. We are more than our physical bodies, which means we are eternal beings. One of the mantras repeated in some spiritual practices is: "I always have been, I always will be, I am." The "I" is eternal in the state of "I am."

Chapter 11: We Are Lucid and Transcendent Beings

The words "lucid" and "lucidity" relate to human thought during both waking hours and color dreams. The primary meanings of these two words are "mental clarity," "able to think clearly," "easy to understand," "ability to see things clearly; rationality; sanity," and "having full use of one's faculties." Interestingly in the context of source science's beings of light perspective, another definition applies: "suffused with light." Lucid thought requires an interesting balance of awareness, meaning, consciousness, intention, and knowing. This may sound repetitive, but all of those properties differentiate human space-like thoughts/being from computers and computer information.

To anyone who has experienced touching-the-divine moments, lucidity is an advanced state of being in which the person is aware of the awareness, conscious of the consciousness, knows that she knows everything has deep meaning, feels strong emotions, and intends to intend. The degrees of lucidity range from low autopilot (almost unconscious or low awareness) to extreme lucidity (direct knowing and hyperesthesia plus directing the flow). These extreme lucid cases naturally happen during lucid dreams, in the zone experiences, Kundalini awakenings, nirvana (transcendent state in which there is neither suffering, desire, nor sense of self, and represents the final goal of Buddhism), and near-death experiences. Being lucid is like being conscious, since everyone can identify those states even though they are hard to describe and not always able to replicate.

Extreme Lucid States

Dr. Matzke: People who regularly attain lucid dreams know that this intimately connected state is quite special. Many people also experience these very lucid moments during emotional firsts, such as holding a newborn child or being sexually intimate. I have experienced a few lucid dreams where I was aware of and knew something special was occurring. At times, my meditations can be very lucid, with clear insight, understanding, and direction.

My most extreme lucid experiences occurred during one of my visits to the Monroe Institute for a weeklong meditation camp using Monroe's hemi-sync sound technology. About halfway through the week, we had a scheduled no-talking morning. I experienced an extremely lucid and profound session where I interacted for the first time with one of my spirit guides and later talked with six four-leaf clovers, where they also talked to me.[1] The lucidity was profound during this period and I could easily remember these interactions, even twenty-five years later. That lucid state was definitely outside time, since I later could not place an order to these events because there were no markers to define a global time sequence. The deep meditative states switched my thought process from sequential to concurrent thinking. This change in time perception is possible due to the concurrent thought vector representation and shows up in people's direct experience.

After returning home, I continued to meditate all weekend to keep this state alive. On Monday, I went to my normal job as computer programmer and started interacting with people and going to meetings. I then became aware that I was exhibiting hyperesthesia about my surroundings, including telepathic connection with people's thoughts and emotions. In this hyperaware lucid state, making complex decisions seemed obvious to me. In Bandler's book *Time for a Change*, he also discusses techniques to aid with hyperesthesia so that it is possible to savor everyday events at a very deep level, like a smile, a sunset, a symphony, or a massage.[2]

People who report Kundalini awakenings[3] (described as the abrupt rising of prana up the spine) also speak of hyperesthesia of light, sounds, emotions, thoughts, body, spasms, energy patterns in the body, and supreme bliss, plus feelings of infinite love, universal connectivity, and transcendent awareness.[4] When this Kundalini awakening happens unexpectedly, people do not know how to handle the physical sensations, so they can get freaked out.[5] As result of these Kundalini crises, a Kundalini hotline became available for many years, though it closed in 2005. It served an important role because conventional medical personnel misdiagnose these events as psychological trauma, rather than as blissful events.[6] For example, the Physio-Kundalini Syndrome Index contains nineteen experiential manifestations in three major categories of motor manifestations, sensory manifestations, and psychological manifestations.[7] These same categories are almost identical to the near-death experiences reported by Kenneth Ring's The Omega Project.[8]

Various techniques can be used to encourage a Kundalini rising (and awakening), including spiritual transmission by a guru or teacher, or by spiritual practices such as yoga or meditation. It is recommended that you work with a trained master when attempting to awaken the Kundalini, since most people do not have the control of focus to deal with such hyperawareness and hyperprana flows. Significant historical background, research, practices, books, and online information exists on Kundalini.[9]

Extreme Omniscient States

Dr. Tiller: Because of the lucid and intimate nature of these experiences, it would seem that everyone would want to live in such a hyperaware state. Usually, this state of omniscience accompanies the high lucidity and deep knowing. The warning about these states is that due to an inflated human ego, increased omniscience does not automatically invoke deep wisdom and high moral values. In the grand infinite scheme of things, power, wealth, and control do not have much meaning for an omniscient being. This ego inflation of "feeling like god" though does eventually subside with the feeling of humility about the nature of reality and deep compassion.

These highly lucid states are hard to explain in words that people understand. This is particularly true if you are trying to explain this event in the moment, to friends, medical personnel, or police officers. Generally, people in these states avoid other people, since the strong emotions and discordant thoughts that people emit are overwhelming to the awakened person.

People are drawn to these lucid states because they are highly intimate and blissful. This is a common theme for all such hyperlucid events, because the person feels connected to everything and everyone, so it feels like being at home in the spirit world. This connection is due to the dissolution of spatial boundaries, due to our mind being disconnected from normal spacetime limits, and due to the unbounded intimacy, joy, bliss, and knowing in these hyperaware expanded states. People would call this the state of grace. Touching the divine state of grace usually, but not always, changes people for the rest of their lives to be more meditative, contemplative, compassionate, humane, and spiritually focused.

Extreme Transcendent States

Dr. Matzke: Also, lucidity appears to be strongly related to the sense of transcendence. Some people use the word "transcendent" as a common description for hyperaware lucid states. People know when they are transcendent, yet it is a word that very few have an appreciation for its meaning. The dictionary definitions of transcendence include (with my preferred order):

- (of God) Existing apart from and not subject to the limitations of the material universe
- Beyond or above the range of normal or merely physical human experience
- The search for a transcendent level of knowledge
- Synonyms include "spiritual," "mystical," "divine," "without equal," and "beyond compare"
- Surpassing the ordinary; exceptional

Most of the hyperaware states would be classified as transpersonal experiences, which is defined as events "extending or going beyond the personal or individual," especially with regard to esoteric and formless mental experiences beyond the usual limits of ego and personality. Transpersonal experiences happen because we are transcendent beings. Computers are defined purely by the hardware and software and cannot exist outside that hardware or be transcendent. They do not have access to space-like states, which is why computers will never be truly intelligent or conscious.

My favorite books are ones about peoples' transcendent experiences, because their descriptions are about states that are extremely hard to put in words. Infinite knowing, infinite awareness, infinite joy, infinite love, and infinite compassion are common themes that people want to communicate, yet many of those feelings and concepts do not have suitable words. Trying to describe a single highly concurrent and emotional experience in a few short sequential sentences is like to trying to capture the magnificence of the Grand Canyon in a postcard. The saying "Wish you were here" is wholly inadequate.

Blissfulness is another state that is hard to convey. Some of my most blissful experiences were the thirty or more times I attended breathwork classes at Unity Church in Dallas in 2001.[10] The breathwork process involves lying comfortably on the ground with eyes closed for an hour, while performing slow balanced breathing, deeply in and out. The balanced breathing keeps you from hyperventilating. The idea is that source prana captured in the air accumulates in the body faster than usual during breathwork, until your whole body feels like it is glowing. In a group setting, sometimes people start sobbing or laughing uncontrollably as they release stuck emotions.

At the peak of the breathwork session after about forty-five minutes, my palms would start glowing and I would start doing energetic self-scanning and self-healing with my hands. At some point, I would no longer feel the urge to breathe, but rather want to just lie there blissfully glowing. Then the final step was when the breath would start breathing me. Yoga traditions have advanced breath control techniques, known as pranayama, yet many yoga instructors believe the breath *is* prana.[11] Based on my experience, prana is independent of air, yet air can convey prana as well as other objects, like food, water, body, and nature. Concentrating on prana using breathwork, visualization, meditation, yoga, or chakra work can be a steppingstone to blissful, lucid, and transcendent experiences. Most people who have touched the divine want to routinely return to that state of grace, bliss, lucidity, and transcendence.

Dr. Tiller: The vibratory source reality defined by the vibratory bit-vectors states can best describe us as space-like beings of light. Our wave-like source nature means we are everywhere and nowhere. We represent oneness that is omniscient, connected, holistic, and transcendent with extreme lucidity, direct knowing, and meaning without words. The Buddhists have the Tibetan term "Pramāṇa," which is often translated as valid cognition or instrument of knowledge, and refers to epistemic ways of knowing (act of acquiring knowledge itself). We are infinite and eternal source beings with source-like vibrational modes that can connect and interact with all other levels of source reality.

Chapter Summary

Extreme levels of lucidity are an important state to acknowledge. As scientists, we want to understand how it is possible to be lucid, transcendent, aware, and conscious. It would be hard to imagine a machine intelligence being lucid, since the time-like data has no meaning, since it is not space-like. Consequently, there is no knowing and nothing is holistically connected in traditional computers. An artificial intelligence can observe but not connect to telepathically merge with an intimate event and its emotions. Humans can become highly lucid about their own intimate and blissful states. Alternatively, intimate and blissful states can enhance lucidity due to the expansion of the present-moment window.

Emotions are a big part of lucidity, because the blissful and intimate nature of connecting is normal for source beings.

Hyperesthesia intensifies all emotions, so people tend to choose positive emotions, since amplified negative ones would be too much to bear. Grounding, along with breathing and appreciation, opens the heart chakra to allow hyperawareness of the beauty of nature, music, dance, laughter, food, friends, and all of life. The state of awe is synergistic with this expanded awareness. Basking in the state of extreme emotional bliss is a divine transcendent experience that we can imagine represents what heaven would feel like. Only living things can experience meaningful, intimate, hyperemotional states with corresponding meaning that comes with transcendent hyperawareness and lucidity.

Part III: Source Science And The Future

Futurists, scientists, and mystics tap into their vision of the future and give us glimpses of what the future might be like. Unfortunately, most of the time, scientists, futurists, and Hollywood are using the outdated classical paradigm to make and interpret those visions. This section provides a set of predictions using the source science perspective that our sacred minds are separate from our bodies and powerful beyond our individual and collective beliefs.

A common theme we discuss is that current advancements in technology sometimes take fifty to one hundred years, as was the case with computers, much of physics, quantum technology, space technology, biotechnology, and medical technology. However, any time investments in basic and applied research increase, then progress can be made more quickly. We hope this section inspires researchers and businesses to accelerate the development of these advanced technologies.

One case in point is what is happening with artificial intelligence (AI) using deep learning and also quantum computing. Some companies, such as Google, IBM, Intel, and Microsoft and many others, are working on both AI and quantum computing because they understand that both are fundamental technologies, and that quantum computing could, they hope, ultimately give the computational leverage needed to make AI extremely efficient.

My perspective on how humans' real intelligence and quantum computing converge is based on source science being the model that human intelligence is built on, meaning derived from deep reality of quantum computing bit physics fundamentals. So, ultimately, the business investments into source science research and development would also lead to much broader understanding of human intelligence and how we might leverage truly aware, meaning-based and real-intelligence systems much differently than can be envisioned from using only conventional quantum AI models. The following chapters explore what the future would look like based on source science ideas.

Chapter 12: Future of Technology Due to Source Science

Humans have control over technology related to meaning, so that we can learn by ourselves, as demonstrated by any young child. This smart intelligence is the dominant factor that is transforming our world and society. Humans are meaning machines—or more accurately meaning minds—based on some universal mechanism that must be supported by modern science and physics. AI proponents would argue that neural networks do the same thing, so meaning is an illusion as long as the patterns can be matched after training data. We remind classical AI researchers that the simulation of a hyperdimensional spaces is different than actually having a real space-like hyperdimensional space. Essentially, this is the same argument supported by the quantum supremacy goal. We believe that this meaning mechanism uses the infinite hyperdimensional concurrent states that must exist for quantum computing, all known properties of quantum physics, and all known phenomena of metaphysics.

The main approach by engineers for building machine intelligence is to construct training sets using deep learning with large amounts of data. Some people argue that that kind of information processing will allow computers to outstrip human information abilities.[1] Humans excel more than computers with big *meaning* sets, while computers appear to excel more than humans with big *data* sets. It might be hard to quantify, but we believe that each human manages many more quantum bits than the largest classical systems' data bits, and the reason for this is that the source-like mind has no limits to complexity. People with eidetic and photographic memory represent the supermind example, where they have arbitrary access to both meaning and detailed data.

As a society we depend on our communication, computer, internet, utilities, and power systems to the degree that our modern society would stop working without them. We also rely heavily on human intelligence to imagine, design, build, and maintain these complex systems. Our society is codependent between human intelligence and machine data processing with AI. Much of the source science technology trends focus on accelerating the human intelligence side of this equation rather than the machine intelligence side. These predictions are widely different from traditional AI forecasts because they are based on the concept that understanding the true deep reality nature of our quantum mind intelligence is rooted in more than the classical, physical, and neurological. As an example, AI did go astray in 2010 when left to run unchecked stock trading programs, resulting in a rapid negative spiral and was eventual shut down manually.[2] Now, automatic limits are in place to stop trading during large declines.

Developing Source Science Technology

Dr. Matzke: Source science intimately connects the math and physics of hyperdimensional bit dimensions to that of meaning and mind. Most physicists know that quantum principles are more fundamental and thus give rise to the classical universe, including spacetime itself at Planck's dimensions. *Exactly how* the discrete quantum realm gives rise to the apparent continuous classical universe is still a mystery, but they know it must be true or else bits, qubits, ebits, black holes, superconductivity, gravity, etc., would not exist. Bits and information are fundamental to physics and give rise to all consistency laws of physics. This powerful "it from bit" and quantum-source matrix infrastructure is information based, which gives further rise to quantum phenomena, plus the emergence of energy, mass, and spacetime. Something as primitive and powerful as this can, and most likely does, support mind and metaphysics. The challenge is to build a model to understand how this is possible and then make predictions based on that understanding.

The future of technology is to continue investing in and researching the quantum model of the universe, but adding the belief/knowledge that mind, thought, meaning, awareness, and consciousness are fundamentally part of the same source science backdrop. Many ordinary people, saints, sages, seers, gurus, kahunas, and yogis have been saying this for millennia. Now it is time to add the ordinary and conservative people, such as physicists, engineers, and business associates, to that choir. As with most technology, this intersection may take fifty to a hundred years, but could be a lot faster with the correct models, focus, education, and investments. You and I have already been working on these topics for fifty years, so what is different now?

Dr. Tiller: We are talking about more than just consciousness research. This hyperdimensional source science model essentially makes all systems open, which thermodynamically means isolated systems were never truly possible. We can train our minds to connect, observe, and influence all physical and quantum systems at any level. Our minds are the ultimate source-code tool for observing, thinking, and meaning, but also for direct interaction with any level of physics, including transcending locality in both space and time. The challenge will be to continue designing experiments that illustrate these ideas and reality and improve human abilities in these areas. These experiments are not for the proof, but rather for individual experience and technology development, and then applying this new understanding for mass consumption. Any scientists who put their collective heads in the ground will just slow down the process of understanding the true nature of our hyperdimensional quantum reality. For them to do so would be the moral and intellectual equivalent of ignoring quantum theory. As I know from my own research funding, it takes R&D investments to make this happen.

Supermind and Superheart Technologies

Dr. Matzke: I agree and here is the proposed focus. Space-like concurrent information systems represent the hyperdimensional computing infrastructure and operating system of the multiverse. This is also the same infrastructure that supports our minds, including thoughts, meaning, feelings, attention, consciousness, intention, and supermind. I am going to focus on supermind and superheart first, since from a technological perspective that is the metaphorical tide that raises all boats.

With the model that infinite heart intelligence is possible, the technology to evolve our individual intelligence comes in many forms. When we become more heart intelligent, we can accelerate the growth and integration process even faster. Intelligence with heart seems to be a common theme from many sources, including meditation, HeartMath, Abraham, Suzy Miller, Buddha, Christ, and many others.

But what does it really mean to raise your intelligence? From a source science perspective, it means you increase the number of simultaneous bit dimensions as part of your being and integrate them by creating superpositions of individually separate thoughts and emotions. An integrated whole is more space-like and thus more intelligent since you can deal with wider ranges of meaningful emotional experiences and decisions with grace and composure. From this perspective you can make better decisions for the good of all involved, which leads to fewer polarizing states. Like the current climate of extreme polarization in politics, immigration, religion, the economy, and more, people tend to take sides, which leads to conflict and fighting. We believe there is a better way.

All thoughts and emotional states are not opposites but rather mathematically orthogonal thought vectors, so that we can have superposition mixtures of apparently opposing viewpoints in any domain. They do not truly exclude each other and this new mixture of thought and emotional focuses on compromise rather than on polarization. Most people focus on polarization because they believe topics are mutually exclusive, but this is mathematically not true. This kind of standoff is also an emotionally immature state, since those people believe fighting is required over compromise. The Law of Attraction says you can only attract states and cannot push them away or exclude them. Do not fight against what you do not want else you will attract more, but rather focus on what you do want with heart.

Advanced heart intelligence contains a balance of thoughts and emotions. Most of the dimensional content complexities for our beliefs are due to the significant number of emotional attribute dimensions. Focusing on thoughts based only on logic is less complex than those with emotional states, as evidenced by lower scores on Dr. David Hawkins scale of consciousness. For example, assume two "sides" believe in the logic of their perspective, but one side is based on anger while the other is based on joy, then Hawkins score for joyful solution will be higher. Negative emotions tend to shut down the chakras and corresponding emotional body, which also contains fewer bit dimensions and less complexity. According to Hawkins, a score of 200 is the level of integrity: below 200, the person lives with deception; above 200, they live with truth.[3] According to Hawkins, a score of 400 is the level of logic and a score of 500 is the level of love.

A similar goal is presented by Suzy Miller on her website:[4] "From her vantage point the story of autism is the story of a vibrationally evolved population, who cannot be fully present in their bodies. The reason for this is that the vibration of their bodies and the planet, in general, cannot currently support the full embodiment of the love that they came here to be." We know from working with these kids they are love centric, and also demonstrate telepathy and/or orb behaviors. Plus, many exhibit savant intelligence.

This leads us to two kinds of vibrational complexity of being: individual and collective. These two influences affect each other since we are all connected at the quantum mind level and there are ways to accelerate heart intelligence.

Dr. Tiller: Exactly and here is a summary of many of these ways:

- Meditation and prayer: Integrates being with more superposition by expanding thought
- Grounding, earthing, and breathing: builds available prana by increasing flow and connection
- Open heart chakra: Awe, laughter, appreciation, joy, love, compassion, song, dance, art
- Integration: massage, yoga, martial arts, acupuncture, reiki, healers, psychologists, etc.
- Advanced education: Improves ability to focus, memory, use logic, and control emotions
- Spiritual classes: Monroe Institute, HeartMath, NLP, remote viewing, dreaming, Abraham, etc.
- Touch the Divine: intimacy, the zone, remote viewing, lucid dreams, telepathy, OBE, NDE, Kundalini, prayer, tantric, nirvana, etc.
- IHD broadcast: Increases Hawkins score of groups of people

This list is not comprehensive, so please consider other classes, techniques, groups, and individuals that are reputable and offer spiritual benefits that match your goals. All of these practices, though, build on the complexity and integration of our vibrational states, which allows us to be more like light and to experience space-like states. Sometimes the expanded prana states can be accidental, but with more exposure to them, the more adept you will become to stay with them, motivated by the fact that it simply feels good.

Dr. Matzke: Let us continue on with the main topic of supermind technology. The processes listed above get individuals in the space-like supermind state, where awareness, intimacy, emotions, clarity, consciousness, and knowing are significantly amplified compared to the old normal.[5]

Historically, people studying under a master would serve as an apprentice for decades to learn the skills to transcend the everyday mind and life. Now, it is possible to learn those skills relatively quickly. The primary obstacle is our own beliefs, disbeliefs, and lack of appropriate models with the corresponding language.

In the transcendental meditation (TM) community, initiates who achieve a *siddhi* (a paranormal capability) are instructed to ignore that ability.[6] In TM, achieving an enlightened state is the goal, not to gain the abilities possible from that state. In Indian religions and culture, a Siddha is a person who is accomplished. This term refers to perfected masters who have achieved a high degree of physical as well as spiritual perfection or enlightenment. I would paraphrase that from these refined vibrations, a Siddha loses the mundane ego focus of humanity and achieves a divine state.

This refined vibrational state of a Siddha is the extreme state, yet glimpses of those abilities come relatively earlier and quickly in the following manner:

1. Ability to stay lucid and focused for long periods of time
2. Clarity in thoughts and emotions
3. Very good memory and integration of complex amounts of interrelated information
4. Precise communication due to deep understanding of the meaning of concepts and words
5. Insights and intuition from higher self about passions, work, and decisions
6. Joyful and compassionate with others
7. Telepathic with others' thoughts and emotions
8. Sense of sacredness about life and the world
9. Sense of everything always working itself out

These early signs indicate the correct balance of positive emotions and tapping into the supermind.

Dr. Tiller: The flip side is also possible when the balanced emotions are missing. These show up as:

1. Distractions
2. Confusion in thinking and a wide range of negative emotions
3. Trouble with memory and complex information
4. Difficulty with words and meaning

5. Few insights or intuition
6. General negative outlook on life
7. Projection of paranoid intentions and actions onto others
8. Sense of anger, hatred, and contempt
9. Things are difficult, even with significant amounts of effort

As is apparent, these two lists are parallel, except the first is a space-like state of being with positive emotions so there is significant supermind technology lift. This is what LOA teachers also report. The second list describes in-time thinking with negative emotions and with little or no lift due to complex prana states. Each perspective attracts what they believe due to the Law of Attraction processes.

Mind and Consciousness Are Outside the Brain

Dr. Matzke: Those are great contrasting lists. Discussing other more long-term predictions due to source science model of supermind is an especially important topic, since most of the traditional Western and AI researchers assume that the brain is a classical neural computer. This thinking leads to a false world view. We review these false beliefs and the reason why they are misguided and the alternative better model, direction, and insight. These false world views lead to many false directions, and so we present the following source science alternative perspective:

1. **Belief we are meat machines.** Transcendent, supermind, and quantum mind phenomena are not supported by purely classical brain modes, yet these phenomena exist. Real intelligence that supports mind, thoughts, meaning, emotions, consciousness, transcendence, and space-like states is more than classical neurology.
2. **Belief that thoughts are in the brain.** Near-death and out-of-body reports about extraordinary experiences and memory when the brain is medically offline suggest that thoughts are not in the brain. Hyperdimensional space-like states cannot

exist in a purely classical brain, or only in microtubules. The research from IHD, shared dreams, telepathy, rotes, meaning, emotional superposition, near-death experiences, and precognition all indicate meaning without neurons. Any kind of psychokinesis affect shows that some fundamental relationship with entropy must exist to allow the mind to influence so many different kinds of systems, especially quantum, random, atomic, and temporal ones. The science of PK and ultimately controlled manifestation is fundamental research that ought to attract investors, just as big physics particle accelerators, space flight, AI, and quantum computing do today.

3. **Belief we can someday download our mind into a computer and become immortal digital avatars.** Since we are already immortal, this is not a valid reason. Also, since our hyperdimensional quantum mind is *not contained* in the 3D brain, we cannot really measure or clone it (quantum no cloning). Instead, we can construct electronic ehostbrains and train our minds to directly interact with them to support telepresence and virtualization.
4. **Belief that neural interfaces can be built to control the external world.** Neurons firing are not the cause of thought, but are a byproduct of thought. Quantum states are not directly observable by machines, yet are accessible with telepathy. Instead, build a high-gain REG and train people to interact with it using biofeedback training. This is the beginning of electronic ehostbrain technology.
5. **Belief in the "singularity" when machine intelligence transcends human intelligence.** Lack of meaning, emotions, and space-like states makes this impossible. AI may be useful, but does not support general intelligence, meaning, emotions, transcendent states, and superminds. Machine intelligence is limited to narrow areas where open-ended meaning is not required, and big human constructed training data sets exist. Accelerating supermind capabilities is

the new perspective, such that we use more and more of the quantum mind concurrency, meaning, and transcendence beyond the limits of the physical brain.

6. **Belief we can model emotions and feelings.** The meaning of love, hate, joy, fear, and other emotions are felt in a deep meaning and gestalt manner by living systems. Computers might be able to recognize these emotions on peoples' faces, but can never experience them, since that requires space-like meaning.
7. **Belief that traditional educational practices are best.** The school curriculum is set by educators with classical Western world views and policy-makers forbidding spiritual/religious topics. Direct knowing, dreaming university, and downloads without the traditional learning process proves that there are alternatives. Also, the traditional view is not true, as evidenced by the lack of success of the mainstreaming of special needs and autistic children. Just as kids take classes on 3Rs, science, cooking, economics, sex education, art, music, and private driving classes in high school, we would be better off including classes on alternate world views, including meditation, emotions, lucid dreaming, remote viewing, and telepathy. Most likely, magnet schools could work but not those associated with religious organizations. This approach might also be useful to naturally initiate and awaken instant savant supermind abilities without trauma.
8. **Belief that IQs are fixed.** The supermind and IHD ideas demonstrate that IQs and Hawkins score can be changed by advanced supermind training. Tapping into space-like states and especially lucid-dreaming night schools and shared dreams may allow rapid learning compared to traditional methods. Understanding how downloads and emotional superposition work would allow for more rapid and holistic learning processes that support verbnoun-balanced states of being and not just doing.

9. **Belief that science only advances with investments in new large machines.** Since the mind can tap into any information from the Akashic Records, innovation and invention can occur at a highly accelerated rate. Advanced insight, intuition, and direct knowing are possible without large capital investments to advance physical theories. Using cooperative spirit guides would also allow for efficient and allowable mining of the Akashic Records for new technology. I know that some groups have historically done this, without disclosing it. Most intuitive innovation already comes from here.
10. **Belief that consciousness is an illusion.** With our space-like model of awareness and consciousness, it is clear that limited classical models can never exhibit those wave-like phenomena. Awareness, consciousness, and knowing can now be understood in the context of information and noncomputability by looking at space-like states.
11. **Belief it is possible to build truly secure environments.** Truly secure environments are a demonstrably false idea. For example, the United States used remote viewing experts to spy on the Russians for decades, and vice versa. Also, since the mind is an open hyperdimensional information structure, it can focus on any location (remote viewing), at any time (precognition), and at any scale (quark, atomic, or semiconductor levels).
12. **Belief that thought does not directly affect the physical world.** This Descartes assumption is now known to be a dramatic misconception. In the future, semiconductors, DNA, and many highly-sensitive, deeply-shielded, big-science projects will be affected by individual and mass consciousness. Failing to study this could cause future failures in our infrastructure, systems, or utilities. Embracing this idea, though, will lead to benefits from IHD-related projects, such as systematically reducing crime, as demonstrated by the TM studies and using IHDs. There are endless opportunities to understand and employ this concept and IHD technology.

13. **Belief that we will always depend on fossil fuel, nuclear, wind, or solar for our energy sources.** Thought can control the order in systems, acting like a negative entropy source. It is still not clear at this time if any of this energy from the quantum foam infrastructure of empty space can be converted into useful commercial energy.

Dr. Tiller: This list is impressive and certainly makes many unexpected predictions. Challenging traditional beliefs leads to many new opportunities.

Source Science and Healing:

Dr. Matzke: Modern medical science practices and technology also do not have as many answers as they could, due to:

1. **Belief that Western medical science is the only authorized healing approach.** Worldwide, many cultures have their own indigenous medical science, such as acupuncture, chi, prana, homeopathy, and traditional Indian Ayurvedic medicine. Also, Western medicine cannot account for spontaneous healing or the effect of prayer or even the placebo effect. Significantly more research in conjunction with medical intuitives and spiritual guides could lead to significant novel healing technology that is beyond the scope of allopathic Western medicine. Current medical laws have been established to keep ineffective technology from harming or deceiving patients, but those laws should still allow for evidence-based medicine to be based on the models that go beyond Western approaches and include thought, intent, prayer, and prana.
2. **Belief in current diagnostic machines, drugs, and surgery are the only acceptable science-based medical industries.** The idea of alternative medical techniques, such as medical intuition, balancing, reiki, NLP, acupuncture, and other prana-based treatments, can be used to diagnosis and treat disease even before traditional medical techniques can

detect the ailment. For example, IHD technology could improve the health of whole groups of people.

3. **Disbeliefs about intercessory prayer for healing.** In 1986, Dr. Larry Dossey conducted a medical study on the positive effects of intercessory prayer because "he felt he was ethically obliged to pray for his patients," since he believed that withholding prayer would constitute not be applying the best-known medical practices.[7] He prayed by entering a meditative state and asking the Absolute that his patients achieve the best possible outcome. In his book *Healing Words,* Dossey writes that prayer "is the Universe's affirmation that we are immortal and eternal, that we are not alone."[8] All of this agrees with the nonlocality of mind, intention, and the effect on entropy we present in source science.
4. **Disbeliefs on spontaneous healing.** Prayer, acupuncture, balancing, and prana work can affect healing in ways we do not understand. Exactly how the body knows to heal itself under placebo, prayer, or spontaneous healing conditions is the mystery and miracle of healing. Somehow the body returns to homeostasis, which is an increase in order of the specific body systems that have a medical malfunctioning. Most healers do not attribute the healing to them personally, but rather call on a higher power to intercede on their request. The mind can increase order.

Dr. Tiller: I have been proposing for a new information medicine approach for a very long time. My colleague Nisha Manek, MD, also has written extensively about this expanded perspective in her new book: *Bridging Science and Spirit: The Genius of William A. Tiller's Physics and the Promise of Information Medicine.*[9]

Source Science and Hyperdimensional Spacetime Technology

Dr. Matzke: Since our quantum mind exists outside of our brain and outside of spacetime, we have the ability to control spacetime itself in unexpected ways. But Western thinking holds us back, due to:

1. **Belief that faster means smarter.** Smaller and smaller computers have used faster and faster clocks to drive the computing industry along Moore's law until they will soon reach the limits of semiconductor scaling. Shrinking semiconductor wires and transistors also make the chip area reachable per clock cycle smaller with each process generation.[10] Humans using relatively slow neurons are much smarter than our largest and fastest machines. In the human mind, everything during one present moment clock happens in parallel, so by slowing the mental wavelength we actually have more space-like parallelism. This only works because our supermind is not classical—it can tap into zero-mass infinite intelligence space-like states, which supports intimacy and meaning.
2. **Belief in relying on electronic communication systems.** People can be telepathic, exhibit remote viewing, astral travel, and share dreams. Thus, we are drawn to our modern electronic communications systems because we have the same native abilities to communicate with anyone, anywhere. In the future, we might be able to rely on our innate direct communication abilities rather than electronic facsimiles, and in the process change our world view and make our emotional guidance system more powerful.
3. **Belief in current trends in augmented reality technology.** We are drawn to virtual and augmented reality computer systems because our minds are part of the ultimate virtual reality bio-body suit that simulates the entire universe. Training our mind to gain control of this native quantum-matrix ability can be accomplished by mastering meditation, lucid dreaming, and astral travel. Creating shared holodeck-style virtual mental environments during shared dreams may be the boost we need to stimulate our cultural beliefs.

4. **Belief that matter is physical.** In reality, every "thing" and even the "nothing" of spacetime are just bits and probability waves running inside an infinite quantum supercomputer. Even the empty nothingness of spacetime quantum foam is made of quantum fields, Higgs bosons, dark matter, and dark energy, which we propose are all entangled 4D or 5D constructs. Teleportation might not require a high-energy wormhole, but rather a flip to the other side of entanglement. This could work like a hidden hyperdimensional doorway. People have reported first-hand thought-based teleportation experiences, which ought to be a strong impetus to start funding research in these areas.
5. **Belief in limits.** If thought can directly manipulate the universe, then we can directly manifest quanta, magnetism, electricity, light, matter, and gravity. Using Abraham's words: "We can use the energy that creates worlds to attract and create whatever we can imagine." This secret can transform the world if we can tap into our all-loving, all-knowing, and all-powerful godlike capabilities.

Over the last hundreds of years, research has been performed for both quantum and metaphysical phenomena. The focus for metaphysical research has been targeted toward proving it was real, whereas the quantum experiments focused on the nature of these phenomena. Imagine if churches or fundamentalists had declared it wrong or the devil's work to study quantum physics?

Actually, the first air-conditioners in 1840s were labeled as the devils work in a smear campaign by the established ice industries. If this anti-science perspective had happened more widely, then our modern world might be without engines, air-conditioners, electronics, laser-driven internet, cell phones, satellites, and too many other advancements.

This is what can happen with metaphysical research where there are disbeliefs and stigmas associated with working on these models and research. The trend ought to be to explore the nature of these source science phenomena while still applying inventive scientific practices.

A friend of mine said he did not want to believe that any of this source science technology would be possible, because "there's no proof." Yet esoteric technologies, such as chemistry, plastics, immunology, engines, transportation, quantum mechanics, semiconductors, lasers, relativity, manufacturing, superconductivity, space flight, GPS systems, and AI, have transformed our world over the last century without anyone except the technologists understanding just how important each piece of technology was. That same story will be said about source science technology in thirty to fifty years when a new generation of quantum-minded technology leads to significant transformations of both individuals and our society.

Dr. Tiller: These kinds of source science predictions are definitely different from traditional futurists' models. Just like any other kind of advanced technology can be used for good or bad, and our predictions require great responsibility to use them for good. Therefore, we must encourage more loving, contemplative, intimate, lucid, and sacred lives and nurture our individual and collective change away from the false and negative emotional world views. Experiencing the sacred and connected nature of our deep reality will allow knowing and, thus, believing.

Chapter Summary

Our beliefs and models of ourselves affect how we fit in the universe, which affects everything we do, imagine, and build. Just like physicists built consistent models of weird quantum and relativistic phenomena, going forward we need source scientists to standardize the accepted models to include quantum, hyperdimensional spacetime, thought, lucidity, meaning, and consciousness.

And just like current technology investments are being made in semiconductors, space technology, AI, and quantum computing, it is now time to also start investing in source science-based technologies, companies, and projects. This should also include the entertainment industry, where informative and uplifting movies can be made about source science concepts. These investments can lead us to much richer technology and more-meaningful human experiences, and tie the sacredness of humans to the sacredness of reality. We call this next level the "source science age," where quantum consciousness is the Standard Model.

Chapter 13: Future of Spirituality Due to Source Science

An important part of humanity's view of itself depends on the nature of our spiritual beliefs. Our spiritual worldviews depend on our beliefs about whether the brain and mind are separate. In the source science model of quantum information science, thoughts and mind connect our science models with topics that historically fall in the spiritual domain. For example, what would religious leaders say if science could prove that our mind is separate from our brain and could survive physical death? How would people change their moral outlooks if more humans were competent at telepathy? What if we had IHD technology that would enable intention-based healing? Notice we are talking about spiritual ideals independent of any religious organization.

Source science truly could lead to a set of universal spiritual models based on quantum thought and scientific models of mind and consciousness. These spiritual models would contain the intersection of many of today's common spiritual beliefs and practices, but cast in a modern new common consensus language. Source science spiritual models would also be based on scientific fact, plus experiences of extreme lucidity, intense feelings, direct knowing, and deep meaning. We explicitly do not propose that there be a universal religion, but rather that these universal science-based spiritual models might be similar to the kind of models, beliefs, and practices developed by enlightened Buddhists[1] or the Hindu-based Theosophical Society.[2] Even the Buddha himself rejected metaphysical speculations, and put aside certain questions which he named the unanswerables. Some of those unanswerables though can now be addressed.

Intersection of Science and Spirit

Dr. Matzke: Source science spiritual models could represent a balanced intersection of Western scientific method and Eastern Pramāṇa, which is a Buddhist term for valid cognition or instrument of knowledge. Pramāṇa refers to epistemic ways of knowing based on perception and inference. For example, Buddha's injunction in the Kalama Sutta was not to accept anything on mere tradition or scripture. The Buddhist logico-epistemology represented the science of their time, but Western and Eastern logic systems are NOT mutually exclusive or incompatible. Indian logic is influenced by the study of grammar, whereas Classical logic, which is principally informed by modern Western logic and scientific method, is influenced by the study of mathematics and physics. The statement "critical and systematic analysis of the diverse means of correct cognition that we use practically in our quest for knowledge" is used to describe Eastern epistemology and also can be naturally applied to Western scientific methods.

Western science is focused on the study of things that are temporally impermanent and so are labeled as illusions, from the Eastern perspective. Buddhism focuses on true permanence, which excludes all appearances perceived during the whole life of an individual, through all senses, including sounds, smells, tastes, and tactile sensations in their totality. Enlightened Buddhist adepts would state that dharma (the eternal and inherent nature of reality) is, therefore, reality as-it-is, and that their practices involve developing an awareness of this deep reality. According to Eastern adepts, the mental world is real and the physical world is an illusion, which is the reverse of the Western perspective. The Eastern adepts also appear to have directly connected into the true nature of quantum permanence outside the apparent transience of spacetime, matter, and energy.

These two views of reality are directly related to our spiritual models and the interaction between physical and quantum perspectives. Both ideologies purport that one side of the coin is real and the other side is the illusion. As we know from correlithms, nothing is mutually exclusive, so if we could have the best of both worlds it would be called heaven on Earth. Imagine a rich comfortable physical reality and a meaningful lucid mental world. This is the world of the year 3000 AD that Robert Monroe describes in his third book *Ultimate Journey*.[3] Monroe also describes how the cloud of negative emotional energy surrounding the Earth will be gone in the future—the heaviness of our negative thoughts will be gone.

> He also reported on a dialog with his higher self. Monroe asked if they were his guardian angels and they replied: "We aren't your anything. You and we are the same. You have been helping yourself all the time. We are just the part that helps you remember."

Monroe later added, "Your Guardian Angel is no more than the true self that lives outside of time," which is based on the experience of approximately 2,000 previous lives. For Bob:

> "It is you yourself, the part of you that possesses the memory and experience of your previous lives. This group of previous lives contains considerable power and knowledge thanks to the combined set of experiences."[4]

Understanding many of these experiences is hard because the concepts and meaning being conveyed have no common context. It is like trying to talk to physicists without using the language of mathematics.

Dr. Tiller: It is important to understand that each specialty of science ultimately develops their own language, and mathematics, which is usually common among all the sciences. The deep understanding of concepts requires deep understanding of the corresponding language. Spiritual ideas also have their own language, some of which overlap with source science terminologies.

Source Science and Spiritual Ideas Are Compatible

Dr. Matzke: Descartes used Western critical thinking to separate knowledge from doubt, where "knowledge is conviction based on a reason so strong that it can never be shaken by any stronger reason." Much of modern quantum physics can be only indirectly measured, but represents fact and knowledge. Experience with Buddhist-style direct knowing may also fall into this scientific method based on Descartes critical thinking. We also call this source science mixture of science and spirit as "sacred science" or "spirited science."

Most religious ideas are usually built on specific stories that are documented as a set of experiences, beliefs, and ceremonies. Many religious leaders received these insights due to touching the divine. Spiritual ideas represent the common ideas that would support many religious beliefs, such as prayer, miracles, auras, creation stories, the afterlife, goodness, morals, higher beings, and souls. Science itself also has beliefs that overlap with these common beliefs, such as creation stories, intelligence models, and the concept of eternity. The goal is to present these ideas in a simple manner without offending the strict beliefs that various religions or groups may have. Some more common spiritual-related topics that intersect with source science ideas include:

1. **Belief that science excludes spiritual topics.** Related to Descartes assumption "that those things that could be weighed, measured, and counted were truer than those that could not be quantified. If it could not be counted, in other words, it did not count." With science now including many things that can only be indirectly or statistically measured, the realm of science is expanding to count statistically, but many scientists still do not comprehend this transition.

Likewise, one of the definitions of "scientism" is possible dangers of excessive reductionism in all fields of human knowledge. Scientific reductionist processes ultimately reached the quantum world, where all the rules drastically changed due primarily to topics such as quantization, superposition, entanglement, probabilities, hyperdimensionality, complementarity, and uncertainty. Source science naturally includes spiritual topics that are related to the hyperdimensional nature of deep reality, which includes quantum-related consciousness as part of everything at all levels.

2. **Belief that we are meat machines and that spiritual ideas are irrelevant.** Source science supports the big idea that we are spiritual beings interacting in 3D reality with a physical bio-body suit. Extreme lucidity, direct knowing, telepathy, experiencing omnipotence, transcendence, grace, sacredness, life review, extreme joy, extreme love, time warp, miracles, siddhis, and many others are all documented examples of humans touching the divine nature of deep reality. Scientists can and ought to continue to explore these topics, since source science connects the science and spiritual ideas with critical thinking. The systematic study of mind and reality is an ancient endeavor, so source science is simply a modern restatement that includes information and quantum models.
3. **Belief in a God or gods.** An infinite God is extremely hard to imagine, so we must rely on belief, yet a 2016 poll showed that 90 percent of Americans believe in the existence of God.[5] Atheists, for many reasons, believe that God does not exist, and the largest numbers of atheists are found in communist or formerly communist countries. Agnostics believe that nothing is known or can be known of the existence or nature of God and they outnumber atheists (officially they are also atheists). Nontheists state that believing in a creator deity is a false view, so officially include atheists but some religions also are nontheistic. Nontheistic religions include

Hinduism, Buddhism, and Jainism. Proving God exists is like proving love exists—knowing the existence of love is a belief about the existence of an immeasurable emotion. From a source science perspective, we are all made of hyperdimensional bits, which is a powerful quantum informational infrastructure with meaning. Using alternative language, we are made of the same stuff as the all-knowing God, so therefore we are all godlike and made in God's image using god-stuff. In either case, we can experience transcendence and knowing by touching the divine. This is a big responsibility, knowing that we are more powerful than we can imagine, whether we choose to label these omniscient space-like states as godlike or not.

4. **Belief in holy men, adepts, and saints**. Most likely anyone who connects with their full higher self while still being connected with their body can experience a sacred life. This is a supermind and space-like lifestyle that is omniscient and hyperemotional, resulting in deep compassion for all the suffering that is around them. This sacred life can be experienced independent of religious beliefs, but once it happens there is no going back. From that point onward, your life takes dedication to fostering these states. A partial list of holy people who exemplified this include the expected names, such as Muhammad, Buddha, Krishna, Jesus, Dalai Lama, and Moses, and unexpected others, such as Confucius, Mary Baker Eddy, Helena Blavatsky, Joseph Smith Jr., and Martin Luther.[6] Anyone can live a divine and sacred existence.
5. **Belief that humans are sinners.** In the grand scheme of cosmic beings, our morals and values might seem arbitrary. The Ten Commandments, Five Precepts, emotional ladder, and many other religious laws can be viewed as rules to lift humanity beyond basic survival and toward enlightenment. Abraham's messages seem to have a moral compass based on an understanding of how the Law of Attraction works. Are we born sinners? I never felt that way nor felt at all driven

by guilt. Does karma exist? Most likely yes, since karma is the sum of our individual and collective source lives. The good news is that karma can be reprogrammed, since our minds represent the source-code of the universe. Choose to live your life with love rather than hate.

6. **Belief that sacredness requires suffering or poverty.** Buddha said, "We are the cause of our own suffering." According to many philosophies, we cause our own suffering by the sinful and violent thoughts and choices we make. This is true for many topics, so choose positive emotions and thoughts, and amplify the prana while letting go of attachments that cause you angst. Buddhism espouses this kind of thinking. With the belief that everything is sacred, we can stop suffering through better choices and physical, mental, and spiritual balance. We do not have to denounce the physical world to be sacred, and we can even experience sacredness while not believing in God.
7. **Belief that each person's religion is the only true one.** If we assume that there exist multiple infinite heart intelligent nonphysical cosmic beings, then we might classify them as gods. If we assume that positive emotions win out over negative ones, then hopefully they are benevolent gods. This line of reasoning makes more sense than do vengeful gods or holy wars, which are more likely human negative emotions projected onto our deities. Religious polarization assumes that only true opposites exist, which is also false. It might be impossible to prove the existence or nonexistence of God, but we can look at superposition that supports the commonality among spiritual practices, as is the case with intercessory prayer studies, mediation, transcendent experiences, and many other topics. Source science opens the door for science-based spiritual models, but not to another religious institution.
8. **Belief in prayer.** A recent 2011 US study reported that 80 percent of people polled believe in the power of prayer.[7] There

are many consequences of this belief, including both positive and negative intentions. Intercessory prayer is an example of positive intentions, and collective hate is an example of negative intentions. We are all also telepathic to varying degrees, so we all can collectively police our thoughts to send positive intentions, if for no other reason than to counteract all the negative thoughts from the haters. We have a responsibility to build a collective worldwide positive vortex.

9. **Belief about when life begins.** We live in a time when peoples' religious beliefs still affect local and national laws. The question on when life begins becomes even trickier with the idea that our mental being attaches to the brain at some point. That eternal being may have lived many past reincarnated lives. Also, once a baby is born, that infant's mind can release from that brain to give permission for a walk-in (another spiritual being) to occupy the vacated brain. According to the recent book by Robert Shapiro, *Are You a Walk-In?*, 17 percent of the US population in 2016 are walk-ins.[8] These topics can be more readily discussed now that idea of mind is distinct from the brain has gained some acceptance.
10. **Beliefs about death.** Abraham irreverently talks about death as "croaking." Yes, it is hard on the people left behind because they might believe the mind *is* the brain and will also obviously miss that person. People with near-death experiences report that death is a transcendent state without pain. We need to rethink all of the death-related topics, including assisted suicide and rituals associated with death, from a new perspective to help reduce the fear and pain associated with dying.
11. **Belief about what happens after we die.** Americans have been polled for seventy years and the belief in an afterlife is consistently higher than 70 percent (see Figure 39).[9] In similar studies, however, only 20–25 percent of people believe in reincarnation.[10] Research on near-death experiences and past-life accounts show that people know a lot of information

that is classically not otherwise accessible. For example, source science's open systems and models of our mind and soul is a collection of hyperdimensional bits, suggesting that the focal point of ourselves survives our connection with the brain. Since these states cannot be directly measured, this kind of research will still be human reported and thus be anecdotal or subjective.

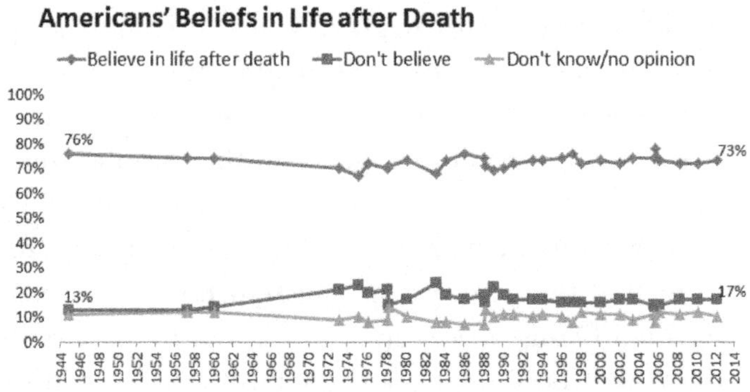

Figure 39. Americans' beliefs in life after death

12. **Belief in heaven and hell.** Due to the Law of Attraction and the virtual nature of the mind, I point to the Focus 24–26 Belief Systems Territories of Robert Monroe.[11] The dominant thought patterns from each life attract that person to "other like-minded patterns of thought." So, people with similar thoughts associated with religious beliefs might have their assemblage of minds labeled as "heaven." Those who assemble with like-minded hate-filled beliefs might have their assemblage labeled as "hell." Notice there is no judgment to those labels, but merely a label for like-minded individuals. The individual life review naturally occurs for everyone when spacetime focus is released, so the amplification of emotions during that process will show up as extreme compassion toward all. There is no Judgment Day and self-judgment only occurs by stepping out of time.

13. **The goal is to leave Earth and ascend to heaven.** According to Abraham, our physical existence is the leading edge of thought, and we use the energy that creates worlds (see top twelve LOA principles).[12] Another approach is to enjoy the miracle that is life and strive for heaven on Earth with perfect balance between the physical and mental planes.
14. **Belief in the meaning of life.** If meaning does truly exist and we are eternal, then life has eternal meaning. The deep transcendent experiences of emotional, joy, love, sacredness, intimacy, omniscience, and eternity also show the validity of the meaning, and thus sacredness, of mind and living beings. Even though we are each an eternal being separate from our body, each physical life is still sacred. The first precept of Buddha is "to abstain from taking life" because life is sacred—which when consistently applied means not killing animals for food and living a vegetarian lifestyle.
15. **Belief in miracles.** The definition of "miracle" is "a surprising and welcome event that is not explicable by natural or scientific laws and is therefore considered to be the work of a divine agency." Sometimes a miracle occurs as spontaneous healing, as we discussed with Anita Moorjani.[13] As a scientist, I say the human body is so intricate and complicated that it is amazing it works at all, not to mention understanding how it self-developed from a single cell or theoretically evolved from a chemical soup. Life itself is technologically a miracle, because mankind has no clue how DNA really works or how to build a system as complicated. Technologists do not know how to build groups of cells to work together or how they form brains using collections of neurons. But prana knows.

Dr. Tiller: The idea that everything is both sacred and conscious extends science to include topics historically associated with the spiritual domain. Can this extended science still be labeled as science, or is it something else? Buddhist and Hindu adepts used thought as their primary instrument of science, whereas Western scientists used models, logic, and measurement as focal points. However, using the mind as the ultimate instrument to directly observe and change the universe, source science has just added the mind as the next instrument upgrade, to work with even broader scientific models. I assert this is still science, just being applied to a broader set of topics and tools, similar to the revolution that occurred with relativity, quantum mechanics, and information science. Essentially, source science is the intersection of these domains knowing that the mind is a space-like information system and part of the source-code of the universe.

Chapter Summary

Extending physics to create deep-reality models of the universe that include quantum mind and hyperdimensional information realms allows science to begin investigating topics that historically fall into the spiritual realm. This is partially due to the fact that science has already been including such topics as the Big Bang and models of time. One of the benefits of having these topics included as a part of science is to change the discussion from beliefs to experimentally testable and agreed-upon models. Creating consensus is what science is about, and building consensus models for spiritual ideas allows use of a common language and concepts. The experiments that include the mind as an instrument might blur the line between objective and subjective nature of reality, however they will also lead to unified spiritual models based on source science concepts.

Chapter 14: Future of Humanity and Earth Due to Source Science

Many people believe that humanity is all alone in the universe and that belief is key to how life evolves. But astrophysicists now know that there exist more than 200 billion stars in our Milky Way galaxy. In addition, the estimated number of galaxies in the universe is also more than 200 billion, each with their own billions of stars and planets. These numbers are so large that the Drake equation was created to estimate the number of communicative extraterrestrial civilizations in our Milky Way galaxy alone:[1]

$$N = R_* \cdot f_p \cdot n_e \cdot f_l \cdot f_i \cdot f_c \cdot L$$

where:

N = the number of civilizations in our galaxy with which communication might be possible and
R_* = the average rate of star formations in our galaxy
f_p = the fraction of those stars that have planets
n_e = the average number of planets that can potentially support life per star that has planets
f_l = the fraction of planets that could support life that actually develop life at some point
f_i = the fraction of planets with life that actually go on to develop "intelligent life" (civilizations)

f_c = the fraction of civilizations that develop a technology that releases detectable signs of their existence into space
L = the length of time for which such civilizations release detectable signals into space

The original estimate by Dr. Frank Drake predicted that 3,500 civilizations exist in our galaxy, and newer estimates predict that range to be as many as 4,500. Other statistical models employing the standard variation concept suggest an upper bound to be 15,785 civilizations. With such large numbers of possible civilizations in our galaxy, this prompted the famous scientist Enrico Fermi to question: "Where is everybody?"[2] We ask the same.

The L term in the Drake equation is considered the most important one, which is extremely dependent on the lifetime that a civilization remains electromagnetically communicative. We have no idea how long a technological civilization can last. Even if only one extraterrestrial civilization lasts for billions of years, or becomes immortal, then the L factor would be enough to reduce Drake's equation to $N = L$. Actually, Drake recognizes this in his license plate: "NEQLSL" (N equals L). It is important to realize that there are alternatives to physical civilizations using only electromagnetic communication, since, based on source science concepts, advanced races would most likely be using telepathy and hyperdimensional travel.

The Reality of Other Cosmic Beings

Dr. Matzke: Now if we consider the much larger quantum-based multiverse and the *highly likely reality* of the existence of other intelligent beings, then the multiverse is most likely teaming with both physical and nonphysical beings and societies. For example, Lissette Larkins reports telepathically interacting with extraterrestrials in her three-book series, beginning with *Talking to Extraterrestrials.*[3] Another colleague of mine reports that he has been interacting telepathically with highly advanced fifth-dimensional aliens over many years and that our negative thoughts are polluting their world.[4] The big conclusion is—we are not alone in the multiverse—and this is directly related to the idea that our brain and mind are separate as part of a hyperdimensional nature of reality. There most likely exists an intergalactic organization from multiple planets and species.

There are many individuals and indications that prove daily we are not alone in the universe. For example, walk-ins and those astral traveling orbs represent another kind of evidence that hyperdimensional intelligent beings abound in the multiverse. Likewise, Monroe's "Gathering" is yet another example where interested nonphysical intelligent beings are watching what is happening on Earth. I know many Monroe Institute students who have visited the Gathering and describe the telepathic interactions with the zoo of nonphysical extraterrestrials. According to Monroe, the research at the Monroe Institute has encountered hundreds, if not thousands, of intelligent beings of all types, just a phase-shift away from our reality. Astral projection and lucid dreams are other ways to visit faraway cities, continents, planets, galaxies, and realities in the blink of an eye, without any big-science technology.

Dr. Tiller: The bigger question to ask is: How can humans become part of the galactic and hyperdimensional communities of beings? Can Earth and humanity develop a utopian society in the future, in spite of the negative emotion-based influences of the fear peddlers and power brokers? The context driving this question is based on the source science premise that we are eternal spiritual beings having a physical experience. What are your thoughts, Doug?

The Utopian Future of Planet Earth

Dr. Matzke: I keep going back to my hero, Robert Monroe, because he represented an engineer with an inquisitive mind and spiritually oriented skill set. He was called a "planetary pioneer" and his book *Far Journey* discussed the future planet Earth on around 3000 CE:[5]

> There were no cities or evidence of any mechanized civilization on the surface of the planet. The air was clean, clear, and ecological balance of the planet was restored. He questioned the entity accompanying him about the environment, and it was said that the ecological balance was restored by design, not by virtue of a disaster followed by random rebound back to health. There were no people at all living en masse on the planet, and this was also by design. In fact, the whole planet was at a different frequency level.
>
> Monroe eventually came across entities on the planet, but they were nonphysical and used nonverbal communication. They told him that they did "use" physical bodies on occasion, and that they kept the bodies, which they referred to as "containers" manifested from thought patterns using any mass at hand, in "ecology cocoons" to keep them preserved, ready for use and in good condition. These entities, even while occupying a body, could transmute matter. One of them materialized a piece of fruit, and gave it to Monroe, who consumed it with relish. They told Monroe he could experience "compressed learning modes," which they defined as being able to experience "Earth consciousness" from the viewpoint of every species—they could, in essence, integrate their consciousness at will with any life form, experience that life form, and disengage the consciousness from it. There was no need for "sleep," and they could draw energy from ambient space, whether they used a body or not.

This utopian description sounds like a cross between the Garden of Eden and a holodeck world. Monroe is not the only predictor of a future utopian Earth. The most famous is Nostradamus (1503–1566), who predicted that after "the time of troubles" in the 1990s and after the turn of the century there would be one thousand years of peace.[6] This era would be defined where people would learn how to raise their consciousness en masse and there would be no limit to what was possible. Nostradamus said this would occur because people have underestimated the power of their minds and would start utilizing the full power of their psychic minds.

As discussed earlier, in *Conversing with the Future, Visions of the Year 2020,* Jenna Catherine talks telepathically with future humans about a similar future utopia where people make different collective decisions to create a better world.[7] In the introduction to the same book, Dolores Cannon also echoes these same ideas, because she is a hypnotherapist who creates doorways she calls "time tunnels" to study reincarnation. I have also met other people who routinely telepathically talk with their future selves.[8] In addition, precognition research and experiences are common, even though people tend to keep these experiences to themselves.

The ability to predict the future is dependent on our models of both mind and time. The first important understanding is that our mind is outside time, because it is associated with hyperdimensional space-like quantum states rather than the brain. Therefore, we learned from earlier chapters that humans can also tap into the future through precognition and retrocausation. Most thoughts from remote viewing and precognition arrive as submodalities and probabilities. So just like Nostradamus, we can visit all possible probabilities and describe the most likely scenarios based on current Law of Attraction principles and our collective vortex. Telepathy can also be described in exactly the same manner as our model of meaning and probability clouds.

Based on the probabilistic geometries, the future is not deterministic, but is simply a set of possible futures. Even Nostradamus predictions were sometimes negative, with much doom and gloom. He said, "If I tell you the most horrible things man can do to himself, will you do something to stop it?" Dolores Cannon summarizes her understanding of Nostradamus as:[9]

> He said: "You have created everything that is within your life. You may not want to admit that, because much in our

> lives is far from ideal. But once you realize that you do create your own reality, then you can just as easily uncreate the unpleasant things in your life. If you create your life, then you create the future you will live in." He said "if you realize that your mind can create a world of peace and harmony, then all you have to do is focus and concentrate on creating that reality. He also said that if the power of one person's mind is that powerful, imagine the power of group mind. Our energy is so scattered, but once we learn to focus it the power of group concentration is tremendous. This is because the power is not only multiplied it is squared, and this power can truly create miracles.

Cannon's insightfulness is amazing, because it is the same language of Abraham and the same we have consistently used in this book. What else can we do to accomplish a loving utopian society when we set an inspired vision of the future?

Accessing Our Probabilistic Future

Dr. Tiller: The relationship between the probabilistic hyperdimensional nature of mind and how those probabilities show up in time is a very important step in our acceptance that these future predictions could be real. Without a mental model that supports tapping into the probabilistic futures, these predictions are relegated to just wishful thinking, even though the ability to tap into the Akashic Records and future probabilities is one of our innate abilities.

Dr. Matzke: Many seers attach actual dates to predictions of the future, but remember dates are manmade and, thus, arbitrary. Just like thoughts, dates are also probabilistic, so do not take future dates literally, especially when they are twenty to forty years in the future. Even though humanity has made great progress, only bits and pieces of space travel or computer technology science fiction predictions have been realized today.

Can humanity collectively tap into the superior knowledge from these more advanced races, not only for technology but also for social order? For example, some stories about communication with extraterrestrials state they live to be more than a thousand years old and gain the equivalent knowledge of ten PhDs by the time they reach one hundred years old. How do we learn and choose wisely to head toward that utopia rather than dystopia?

Other people and groups have been formally thinking about these topics.[10] To the uninformed, there are many pitfalls on the road to a utopian society, if it is even possible at all. Organizational intelligence is not well understood or agreed upon in the world either, which is why there are so many competing and conflicting political ideologies, monetary policies, value systems, and spiritual organizations. Transparency, truth, trust, telepathy, and supermind will most likely significantly help in making good decisions on the road to a better future. In particular, using telepathy to uncover the true motives behind peoples' actions would help minimize the manipulation and polarization that is rampant these days.

The goal is to apply heart-based thinking and decisions to technology development, business practices, legal matters, social matters, monetary measures, spiritual models, and religious debates. Many of the problems with our society are the result from people making greedy, hateful, fearful, or controlling decisions. Making heart-based decisions in all matters will lead to a better way of compassionate living. If money is the problem, then imagine the good that would happen if the resources of the industrial war machines were used for other purposes.

Buddhism teaches that we each have our individual propensity and impulses for violent thoughts. For example, if someone does something you disagree with, do you mentally call them an idiot and plot for revenge? Similarly, disagreements can act as a justification for controlling another person's behaviors. Probably more important, if you judge your own actions negatively, then you are being violent to yourself. Choosing to be peaceful and accepting of yourself and others is important for erasing judgmental, violent, fearful, and angry thoughts. These behaviors are so unconscious that most of us are not aware of our own violent tendencies. The simple yet powerful four-step Hawaiian Ho'oponopono forgiveness ritual ("I am sorry. Please forgive me. I love you. Thank you.") is a great tool for erasing these tendencies, because by forgiving yourself, you are erasing your own violent impulses, which are not mirrored anymore in outside world.

Another simple example of heart-based thinking can be applied to a legal concept, such as patents. Some prana technology we present here could never be patented because a lack of traditional measurement protocols, this means it is impossible to determine measurable effects and thus whether someone is illegally infringing. But patents are about controlling other people's access to inventions, and most spiritual people do not want to control what is already free.

Hawaiians and Native American Indians also historically do not believe in ownership of land. Patents are a kind of ownership contract, and most business contracts take on a completely different form when spirited business meets spirited science. The structure of spirited organizations and corporations take on a completely different focus other than money, greed, control, competition, and winning at all costs. Spirited governments also focus on supporting people rather than supporting the power brokers of the world. Perhaps new spirited governments will evolve from this kind of thinking, which is compatible with the spirited science, spirited business, and spirited theology ways of heart-based thinking.

This all may seem farfetched. Jenna Catherine states in her vision of the future that there is no greed, no fear, no lying, no money, no control, no lawyers, no prisons, and one world political party in which everyone is simply learning, has compassion, has love, and responds instantly to the telepathic needs of the community. This is only possible by using heart-based thinking at all levels of society, plus by relying on telepathy and supermind to make optimal heart-based decisions that are good for all involved. As a society, we must develop knowledge of what love, compassion, and empathy can do to naturally transform our society where truth and justice are automatic. The uncompassionate power brokers of the world will also have to be dismantled, because their money and power comes from controlling and manipulating people and politics for their own agendas. On the flipside, there can be heart-based billionaires.

In ancient Rome, sport was watching gladiators fighting to the death. For example, today, football and wrestling are manufactured excitement labeled as entertainment, just as the running of the bulls in Spain is entertainment. Since we know we have the ability for extreme lucidity, joy, intimacy, and other deep emotions, it seems possible to be able to tap into this rush of energy from entertainment using lucid dreaming and astral travel. This positive future is only possible if we avoid the worst aspects of humanity and focus on the sacred side of our spiritual beings. Winners and losers are historically thought to be mutually exclusive, but win–win scenarios are really opportunities for superposition of ideas. Superposition looks like compromise compared to polarized viewpoints.

For many years, I have been talking with others about how to combine spirit, science, and business ideas into a coherent heart-based methodology. Capitalism and traditional business law are not necessarily heart-based processes, and in the worst case their exploitative goals represent the antithesis of justice and compassion. This is most obvious through the ages, with overseas governments and companies having colonized or exploited indigenous populations and resources. Nonprofit organizations and open-source projects are positive examples of compassionate people with compassionate goals. Our collective goal for the next ten years might be: Create a more compassionate planet by 2030, perhaps by using IHD technology to change competition into cooperation. I know you have been thinking along these lines as well.

How to Build a Better Future

Dr. Tiller: We have discussed several examples where groups of people and/or IHD technology could amplify a thought that is more desirable than some other. If this could be done on a large scale, ridding the world of greed, anger, hate, and fear in a decade, then we could create the peaceful times predicted by seers. We must choose to change our collective emotional patterns, or else our society will be stuck in a negative emotional loop of suspicion, conflict, greed, fear, anger, hatred, revenge, and violence. This negative vortex represents the dark side of the force our society is currently immersed in and heavily sustained by the conservative media.

Even Hollywood blockbusters tend to use this formula, since excitement comes from conflict. What is weird about this idea is that emotions do not really exist if humans are merely meat machines. In reality, emotions have deep meaning that is only possible because humans are quantum-meaning machines. Let us choose to program the positive meaning of our own emotional minds and our collective society mind by focusing on humans, not on machines. The goal is to deprogram the worst parts and amplify the best parts of humanity, a kind of compassion-based spiritual intervention. This could become a whole new trend in Hollywood.

Another idea is to use IHD and group-thought technology to build connections, telepathy, and intimacy between people. This would also be a transformational process, since many humans feel alone in the world. Eradicating loneliness by showing how connected we all are would be wonderfully healing. Experiencing deep lucidity and intimacy would allow people to touch their own divinity, which could be a transformative process in itself. Enabling people to experience the omniscience of supermind is another sacred experience. All of these experiential processes can lead to hope and excitement about the future because we can individually know and viscerally prove to ourselves that we are spiritual beings having a physical experience.[11]

Dr. Matzke: I like those ideas. The Bible states, "The truth will set you free," which can apply to many situations besides Christian ideals. From a source science perspective, our mind is formed of quantum states organized in space-like fashion outside spacetime. The truth can be stated as follows:

1. Mind is separate from brain
2. Mind is a quantum-meaning machine
3. Mind can directly interact with and influence the physical world
4. We are spiritual beings having a physical experience
5. We are nonphysical and immortal beings
6. We are more powerful than we can imagine
7. Holistic heart-based intelligence is our true power
8. The multiverse is teaming with other mental beings like us

This deep reality is the source science truth and the freedom we seek is to understand this birthright. This kind of source science thinking changes everything because it invalidates the untruths propagated by traditional scientists and mainstream media who want to maintain the status quo for the current power brokers.

Every hundred years, society seems to become less savage than in the previous century—for example, slavery. In another hundred years, what will we say about the savagery going on today? Like people starving, or burning oil, or polluting our Earth, or deforestation, or fighting holy wars, or subjugating minorities, or promoting extreme hatred, or ignoring loneliness, or fearing death, or denying the existence of extraterrestrial life, or many others? Understanding the nature of our self in the universe is our birthright, and choosing heart-based intelligent solutions can break through polarized thinking. We can choose this utopian direction without being labeled naive. This was the same kind of freedom sought by the early America settlers who came to the New World, and now we, their beneficiaries, are heading into a new world in which we can use source science energy that *creates* worlds. Others predicted this future, so let us make it a reality.

Chapter Summary

Humans are eternal spiritual beings living a physical experience supported by the quantum infrastructure that creates our universe and worlds. By understanding how the universe is really constructed and how conscious intelligence is naturally a part of everything, we can then interact with planet Earth as a playground for experiencing this reality. Meanwhile, understanding that we are part of a much bigger multiverse and galactic society of beings means that we can experience how magnificent we are and simultaneously comprehend what a small part of the galaxy we live in.

With an entire multiverse out there with thousands of species, we could travel for many lifetimes to experience all of this wonderment. Let us not waste our rich emotional abilities with violent video games, movies, books, and more when we have so many other choices for entertainment. Where is our copy of the *Hitchhiker's Guide to the Galaxy*?

Chapter 15: Final Thoughts on Source Science

As we stated earlier, we live in a special time in history when scientists and physicists are learning more than ever before about the structure of the universe. This understanding can be broken into three domains: (1) the nature of the very small using quantum laws; (2) the very large using gravitational laws; and (3) the very intelligent using informational laws. The convergence of these three big areas helps us to understand our universe and how we humans fit in. This is ultimately coming full circle to the ancient understanding of the shamans, sages, and monks.

During each epic of science, we imagined humans using our current scientific models. With the invention of machines, we understood human muscles as levers and pulleys. With the invention of engines, we understood human hearts as pumping engines. Once we understood computer science, we began to believe that human mental functionings were like computer functionings. Now that we understand quantum computing, we believe it is time to see humans as having quantum minds, since purely classical solutions are no longer enough to explain either physics or all of human behavior.

The model of a quantum brain is very different from that of a quantum mind too, since a quantum brain takes the perspective that matter is dominant. Our quantum mind takes the approach that the mind is independent and dominant, and that the brain is a very specialized antenna. Our quantum mind model touches the reality that meaning, emotions, lucidity, and supermind are intimately connected with quantum bit physics, so could be paraphrased as a spiritual beings model connecting with a consciousness is the primal model of the universe.

Quantum physics and quantum computational models outstrip anything that a purely classical world view supports, so it should be no surprise that quantum-based mind models also support behaviors not possible with only classical physics. Infinite bit dimensions, no time computational models, and Law of Attraction mathematical models remove the limits set by a classical world view. Our model of humans goes hand in hand with our model of the universe, such that we limit ourselves by the limits of our models of mind.

Source Science Is the Root of Miracles

Dr. Matzke: The single biggest mistaken model many scientists and the public still believe in is that our brains are neurological classical computers. This gaffe is the lynch pin for imposing limits on humanity, since it denies the most miraculous spiritual and sacred parts of humanity. Life itself is an unknown miracle. In fact, no scientist has every *created* life in a test tube (using nonliving chemicals). The next most miraculous part about life is how meaning has allowed living species to survive and become as intelligent as the smartest species on Earth today. I believe that both of these two miracles are due to interlocking principles: there exists some natural mechanism that brings life and meaning into biological systems, and we can call that mechanism "source."

Fundamentally, source is the same quantum bit dimensions that creates the entire physical universe supporting a quantum simulation and operating system infrastructure. This infinite quantum simulator is so powerful that all multiverses are supported by its probabilistic informational infrastructure, such that even spacetime and energy emerges from its properties. We do not use the term "infinite" lightly, since we know that Shor's algorithm and ebit behaviors require an exponential number of orthogonal bit dimensions. These bit dimensions also support qubits and ebits, which mean they support concurrent space-like states, which are responsible for all the non-computable transcendent states observed in human behaviors, including infinite intelligence and omniscient experiences.

Dr. Tiller: My work and that of other physicists, such as Sir Roger Penrose, all point to the idea that purely classical physics and accepted computability theory does not account for meaning, lucidity, supermind, and consciousness capabilities. Penrose uses the term "non-computable"[1] to describe consciousness, and I have always believed that quantum physics based solely on an energy-focused Schrodinger wave equation was incomplete. The reason for this is now clear, since most of quantum physics and quantum computing is typically approached as if embedded in 3+1 spacetime. We now know this is not the case, since it is impossible to embed the 4D topology associated with *each ebit* as fitting inside three dimensions, which gives rise to the apparent nonlocality. Ebits are not separable states, so become space-like and not comprehensible using the Schrodinger wave equation. The apparent nonlocality is due to the hyperdimensional structure of ebits.

Dr. Matzke: Each physical bit is its own orthonormal protodimension, where two bits form a 2D qubit and two qubits form a 4D ebit. Landauer stated that bits are physical, so they are a mechanism supported directly in physics, not just mathematical constructs used by mathematicians and computer scientists. Also, due to entropy metrics and Landauer's principle, bits have an effective energy and, thus, an effective mass. Since direct support exists for protodimensional bits in physics where they can be maximally concurrent in a space-like manner, there also exists a natural representation for thoughts directly supported at that level of protophysics. We believe the collection of thoughts we call mind is directly supported in the same source protophysics that created the universe at the Big Bit Bang. Similarly, Abraham states we have the source "energy that creates worlds" at our disposal.

This powerful quantum information is the ultimate quantum computer and quantum operating system supporting the entire multiverse. These infinite numbers of bit dimensions exist outside spacetime and, in fact, represent the quantum ether responsible for forming spacetime quantum-foam mechanisms. We propose that only *one* all-powerful quantum information source mechanism is required to support all observed behaviors in the universe. We invoke Occam's razor that the hyperdimensional bit dimensions are powerful enough to support all of quantum state behaviors and also that the quantum correlithms are powerful enough to support mind, supermind, meaning, and consciousness.

Information can be naturally created in two identified ways in this nonmetric hyperdimensional spacetime using non-Shannon bits of the coin demo and the self-organizing meaning mechanism of correlithms. Order is created without using energy by grouping sets of bit dimensions together to form clustering or warping in hyperdimensional protospace. We would call this grouping a "vortex," since it acts similarly to how gravity warps conventional spacetime. Both information-creating systems become more ordered and, therefore, represent a source of negentropy, and may even represent the source of information and subsequent energy states of the Big Bang.

Dr. Tiller: This is an important idea—that energy can be created due to information. This relationship between space, time, energy, and bits is important because energy metrics only emerges in the metric space formed by spacetime. Hyperdimensional bit dimensions are outside this metric space, where informational topology is supreme, so energy, matter, space, and time do not yet exist. From this broader hyperdimensional perspective, all nonmetric spaces are open, since no distance or time metrics exist. This means that thought, attention, and intention made of these same bit dimensions can directly interact with and affect any part of physics. This is exactly what is seen by the remote viewing and PK research that I and others have performed.

Even black holes emit Hawking radiation due to entangled states. Traditionally closed systems appear to be open when entanglement occurs or the hyperdimensional mind is interacting. This is due to space-like interactions through both space and/or time. Nonmetric spaces and ebits make systems appear to be open, and we sometimes describe those systems with holographic properties. R-space and deltrons were my early attempt to understand how to define open systems, and I find your approach interesting, using hyperspace and ebits to support the open properties of nonmetric spacetime, plus have all the forms of computational completeness. Your approach is intriguing, that frequencies and wavelengths inside spacetime emerge from concurrent quantum states.

Source Science Is Space-Like

Dr. Matzke: I propose that your deltron requirements can be met using space-like bit dimensions. Nonmetric hyperdimensional protospacetime is a very important topic because spacetime, energy, and matter do not yet exist. Most importantly, mass does not exist either; therefore, quantum states and thought can be accumulated to arbitrary levels of concurrency and complexity without reaching a black hole density limit. Consequently, the infinity of bit dimensions can build in complexity without limit, which can translate to lucidity, emotional states, omniscient awareness, infinite intelligence, and consciousness. These space-like and wave-like states are everywhere, nowhere, and nowhen and so represent the missing non-computable mechanism needed to represent all experienced human mental states. This space-like state representation cannot be supported by classical information systems using either energy or matter representations. This unlimited complexity building supports Monroe's idea that "we are more powerful than we can imagine," Nostradamus declaration that "people have underestimated the power of their minds," and Abraham's statement that they are "infinite intelligence."

Even though these protodimensional quantum states exist, they are not directly observable using any known measurement technology except direct awareness, and most of these states are not directly linked to our physical universe. These unobservable bit dimensions are independent of the bits supporting quantum states of energy and matter of our universe, similar to how quantum states support the quantum foam and zero-point energy of the empty vacuum of space. We would call our individual sets of quantum states "quantum mind" or "higher self" or "spiritual beings" or "angels" or "aliens" or "gods." Intelligent beings such as Abraham, the LOA unseen helpers, and mental beings at the "Gathering" exist using these states. Also, we all are actually mental-meaning machines independent of and interacting with our brains.

A critic of this approach might ask, "Does the source science model of quantum mind seem technologically extravagant? Isn't there a simpler mechanism to support mind?" The simple answer is no, because any model that does not include all the requirements of general real intelligence, meaning, lucidity, emotions, consciousness, attention, intention, transcendence, omniscience, supermind, telepathy, precognition, PK, and other metaphysics phenomena is an incomplete model. Our approach actually takes the simplest approach by using Occam's razor, which is to use the default deep reality of the source science protophysical infrastructure that must exist to support quantum computation and state that it is also powerful enough to support all the quantum mind requirements. Any model that is less inclusive would most likely be using a subset of these overall real requirements and might not really solve the hard problems of unlimited mental states. Any other model that meets all these requirements would also be a potential alternative model. Excluding any of these requirements is denying the reality of who we really are.

Notice that the metaphysical components are a small part of the overall requirements, but they are very important, since they need a key transcendent representation of information/thought that is outside space and outside time and, thus, not related to classical energy or matter. The hyperdimensional bit-level bit dimensions are the representation that supports this protophysics. Once the nonmetric hyperspace requirements are met using bit dimensions, then the emergent properties of space-like states, such as infinite complexity and Law of Attraction mathematics, naturally solve the hard problems of consciousness, meaning, general intelligence, transcendent states, omniscience, and infinite intelligence.

Source Science in Simplest Terms

Dr. Tiller: As a material scientist, it is sometimes hard for me to completely understand your areas of expertise in information, computation, quantum computation, and hyperdimensional math. Yet I do agree that the out-of-the-box thinking requirements entail a transcendent solution that is beyond classical physics and even beyond the typical approach of Schrodinger wave equations that presuppose the spacetime and energy framework. The properties of entanglement and hyperdimensional protophysics could be that solution, since protospace and prototime give the emergent properties needed to bootstrap the universe as the Big Bit Bang, plus support space-like states.

To describe this model in the simplest manner possible, we use the terms "quantum mind" and "spiritual beings" because they focus on the dualistic model that gives the mind and brain separate properties. Here is my simple summary list of properties separated for both mind and brain, where both are important and work together to give our current control of our bodies at the speed of thought. We do not focus here on the impact of thought on DNA but do include the overall auric field and auric bodies as part of the mental higher self:

- The mind is the quantum computer in the cloud that supports meaning, all thought, and even nonthought. This meaning is possible due to the Law of Attraction capabilities of the hyperdimensional states representing our mind. These states are not classical (not in the brain), so are eternal and include all experiences from all timeline lives and our higher self. These mental states attach to the brain/body near birth or during a walk-in and become the remote control for the bio-body suit. Our conscious mind attached in time to the antenna brain and can only interact with the 3D neural interface, whereas our unconscious mind contains a near-infinite number of dimensions that are all space-like concurrent and outside time and outside the brain. The mind states do not fit in the brain and did not begin with the brain.

- Since our mind contains meaning due to correlithms supporting the Law of Attraction principles, all learning happens in the mental domain. Telepathy and rotes are examples of meaning that are directly available to the mind, but without using the brain. During meditation, the brain waves slow down to longer alpha, theta, or delta states that are due to the mind detaching from the brain. Meditation allows the mind to become less sequential by switching from in time and become more concurrent by being outside time. The near-death experience of life review occurs when stepping out of time at near-death or actual death.
- The brain is an antenna that maps the hyperdimensional mind into three dimensions. Since the neurons are folded and interlaced, within the skull the effective dimensionality of the brain is most likely higher than three dimensions, similar to fractal geometry. For example, the cerebral cortex by itself is a 2D sheet and has a measured fractal dimension of from 2.6 to 2.8.
- The brain, along with the extended brain stem and central nervous system, has many autonomous controls over the body and is a marvel of engineering. If the brain is damaged, then the mind has trouble interacting with the brain/body. The pyramidal cells in the motor cortex are the starting point for all motion in the body, so there must be a reliable mechanism for the mind to interact with those cells; most likely it is through injecting order into the brain. Anesthetics can rapidly cause the mind to disconnect from the brain and, thus, cause unconsciousness. Dreaming also allows the body to release from the brain and even paralyze muscles during active REM sleep, except for the eyes. During near-death

experiences, survivors later report they were able to see the scene as if watching from the ceiling. All of the brain and neural research is fascinating—we just have to remember to interpret these kinds of research results knowing that the mind is not equivalent to the brain. DNA is also an open system, allowing higher-level influence on how the cells grow and evolve into complex living systems. This model should affect how people view reality and, subsequently, how they live their lives.

Source Science Challenge

Dr. Matzke: Thanks for that concise summary, Bill. The dualistic brain/mind model is supported by all the hyperdimensional states of mind. These maximally concurrent states outside time give us the sense of stability of observation of the external world. We can even peek slightly into the future using precognition and retrocausation, and in faraway locations using remote viewing. Since thoughts are not in the brain, then telepathy is not only possible but, in fact, we rely on it all of the time. We just have to quiet the mind to connect with the insights of our higher self.

I am a firm believer that very young children learn meaning by using telepathy, and then add language labels. Children learn emotions the same way, since emotions are deep in meaning. Are you one of those people who interrupt others before they are finished talking? That may be because you already received their entire thought and are ready to respond. Insight about this will help you to be more patient with others until they finish speaking.

The greater the number of meaning and positive emotions we integrate into a cohesive whole thought pattern, the smarter we will become. Meditation, dreaming, and anchoring help integrate, through superposition of thought vectors, thereby creating states that are non-polarizing thoughts and emotional states. Emphasizing positive emotions allows for a larger flow of prana states of the mental body to interact and become aligned with the physical body, thus making the body feel better. Laughter, appreciation, joy, compassion, gratitude, passion, love, and humor should all be amplified, since many of these positive emotional states open the heart chakra. Grounding and breathing also boosts the prana connection with the body. Amplifying these emotional and prana states makes our bodies feel great. Having a larger set of prana states means more complexity of the mind and higher heart intelligence. It would be wonderful if our mental coherence grew such that we could all exhibit telepathy and experience orb consciousness, like some awesomism kids do.

Humans and everything else are all connected in the mental space and it is a colossal illusion that we are separate due to the apparent reality of our physical bodies. We are all connected spiritual beings, connected with mental quantum strands that show up as feelings, intuition, insights, coincidences, direct knowing, telepathy, and visions. These communications tend to appear as submodalities, which is the symbolic meaning language of the Law of Attraction, because words and sentences are not the nature of the mind. Language and words are mostly sequential, but our true mind is massively parallel and symbolic, which is why some people can speed read whole pages at a glance. Most computer programmers know it would be impossible to take an arbitrary algorithm and make is massively parallel, yet the mind can do this with any information, since it has infinity of state dimensions at its disposal and works outside time. Evolutionarily, quantum minds have made us alive and kept us alive.

The source science model naturally supports the Law of Attraction. Protodimensional bits as vectors represent the vibrations of LOA. Those bits form *N*-vector structures of thought/meaning called rotes, and those affect the physical world through probabilistic entropy changes, including by directly affecting the brain. These thought vectors represent vortices of like-minded thoughts that actually form a growing rote complexity structure. Quantum thoughts turn into things in the physical world using this process, because the correlithms bootstraps how the brain and mind interacts using hyperdimensional codes.

Our thoughts are massively parallel vibrational states outside the brain, so thoughts are really quantum things. These massively parallel quantum states form our auric bodies, including all meaning, especially emotional meaning. Moving up the emotional ladder is about moving to more positive emotional states, which naturally allows for more prana to flow due to an opened heart chakra and results in more quantum states and greater emotional intelligence. These massive quantum states intersect with like-minded helpers and show up as insights, rendezvous, and coincidences.

Daily meditation helps us align and integrate the orthogonal quantum thought vectors, so they represent the higher vantage point of superposition of separate rote vortices into a single unified supermind vortex. This massive complexity rote is self-consistent and aligned with all aspects of your higher self. This combines many smaller inconsistent vortices into a single unified supermind vortex. From this higher alignment, you are actually more intelligent by being able to tap into infinite intelligence since all concurrent quantum states combine to a single more-complex and consistent spiritual you. This focused and aligned consistency allows manifestations to naturally and easily occur. Choose only positive emotional states, since exclusion is not possible in quantum LOA. These superposition principles for supermind are supported directly with the mathematics of correlithms applied to quantum thought domain. These protophysical mechanisms are why the Law of Attraction works like any other physical law.

Since our quantum thoughts exist outside the brain, our individuality survives physical death or, as Abraham calls it, croaking. Fear is a counterproductive emotional state—in particular, fear of death. Choose positive emotions over any fears by aligning your open heart, grounding, breathing, and living life with greater attention, appreciation, laughter, intimacy, joy, love, lucidity, consciousness, and sacredness. Create an immense vortex of positive emotions and life will become much more alive and meaningful.

We truly are infinite heart intelligence spiritual beings of light—and simply need to understand and know that in order to experience our true spiritual and sacred nature. Meditation and conviction in this model allows the proof to show up every day as insights, positive emotional experiences of life, intimacy, emotional resilience, coincidences, shared thoughts, telepathy, precognition, sacredness, and direct knowing. On the flipside, believing that we are merely meat machines can dampen each day with a resounding thud. This is the power of the Law of Attraction. If we know we are supermind, we will experience the magically transcendent zone states and strive for a contemplative lifestyle to reinforce those sacred life-fulling experiences.

The source science model gives us hope about humanity and our place in the universe. Source science truly represents the next human quantum information age that will lead to amazing new technology and world changes. Each of us can individually turn the fundamental nature of this deep reality into our own reality. Collectively, we can also invest in business and government support for this class of source science technology and make the changes appear even faster on a worldwide level.

I did not write this book as a how-to manual on expanded consciousness, but focused on the research and concepts for the source science model that supports those states of being. By changing our model of how the universe is structured, we change our models of our self. We can do so much with this knowledge—so let us collectively get started!

Glossary

3+1 spacetime: Denotes the three dimensions of space and one dimension of time that are considered a unified 4D spacetime according to Einstein's relativity theory.

Abraham: The name of a group consciousness from the nonphysical dimension who communicate via channeling through Esther Hicks regarding the Law of Attraction (LOA). Esther describes Abraham as infinite intelligence.

acausal: Not involving causation or arising from a cause.

adepts: A person who is skilled or proficient at something. Eastern adepts are those skilled in Eastern esoteric phenomena.

adjacency: A relationship of being adjacent to something, or near enough so as to touch.

agency: Action or intervention, especially such as to produce a particular effect.

agnostic: Belief that nothing is known or can be known of the existence or nature of God.

AI (artificial intelligence): The theory and development of computer systems able to perform tasks that normally require human intelligence, such as visual perception, speech recognition, decision-making, and translation between languages.

AI theory: Traditional AI theory is predicated on the assumption that the brain is a classical computer, so therefore it is generally assumed that engineers can build a classical computer that is as intelligent as humans using the theories of how neurons work.

aka cords: Prana connections that pervasively connect everything. Clairvoyants can see these connections as bands of light.

Akasha: In Hinduism, means base and the essence behind all that is manifested; the primal source from where everything originated from another dimension.

Akashic Records: A cosmic library that contains records of all events, thoughts, words, emotions, and intent ever to have occurred in the past, present, or future.

allopathic: Refers to science-based modern Western medicine, such as the use of medications or surgery to treat or suppress symptoms or the ill effects of disease.

amplitude: The maximum extent of a vibration or oscillation, measured from the position of equilibrium.

anchoring: The NLP process of associating an internal response with some external or internal trigger so that the response may be quickly, and sometimes covertly, re-accessed.

AND logic: The logical conjunction; the AND of a set of operands is true if, and only if, all of its operands are true.

androgynous: Someone who has both male and female characteristics, and therefore appears to be of indeterminate sex.

anima: Carl Jung's term for the inner feminine side of men.

animus: Carl Jung's term for the inner masculine side of women.

anticommutative: A noncommutative operation where the sign is reversed when the order is reversed. For example, in GALG: $\mathbf{a}*\mathbf{b} = -\mathbf{b}*\mathbf{a}$.

antineutrino: The antiparticles of neutrinos. The antineutrino is an elementary subatomic particle with infinitesimal mass and with no electric charge.

antiparticle: Subatomic particle having the same mass as a given particle but opposite electric or magnetic properties. Every kind of subatomic particle has a corresponding antiparticle.

antiquarks: The antiparticles of quarks. Quarks and antiquarks combine to form protons and neutrons (and other particles), which form the nucleus of atoms.

anu: Of Sanskrit origin, it means atom or molecule.

archetypes: Carl Jung defined archetypes as universal, archaic patterns and images that derive from the collective unconscious and are the psychic counterpart of instinct. Archetypes are highly developed elements of the collective unconscious.

Argand diagram: A planar diagram on which complex numbers are represented geometrically using Cartesian axes, the horizontal coordinate representing the real part of the number and the vertical coordinate the complex part.

artificial intelligence (AI) theory: *See* AI (artificial intelligence) and AI theory.

Asperger's syndrome: An Autism Spectrum Disorder (ASD) and part of a unique group of neurodevelopmental disorders. Asperger's is often called the "genius gene," and many with ASD are, in fact, geniuses.

astral projection: A term used in esotericism to describe an intentional out-of-body experience.

astral travel: *See* **astral projection**.

atheist: A person who disbelieves or lacks belief in the existence or possibility of God or gods.

attractors: An attractor is a set of numerical values toward which a system tends to evolve, for a wide variety of starting conditions of the system. Used by Rupert Sheldrake, attractors are the ends or goals toward which morphic fields attract the systems under their influence.

aura: A supposed emanation surrounding the body of a living creature and regarded as an essential part of the individual.

aura balls: Free-floating balls of auric light that show up on photographs or can be seen by sensitives.

auric bodies: The seven (or more) layers of auric light around our physical bodies.

auric eyesight: Synonymous with auric vision.

auric light: The apparent glow that is not traditional light, but is seen as light by sensitives.

auric vision: The ability of certain sensitive people to be able to perceive auras as auric light.

auric-sensitive: People who are able to perceive auras using some modality of vision or feeling.

awareness: The knowledge or perception of a situation or fact.

Awesomism: Suzy Miller's term to describe a new way to understand the diagnosis of autism.

axon structure: An axon is a long, slender projection of a nerve cell, or neuron, that typically conducts electrical impulses away from the neuron's cell body to the axon terminals.

Ayurvedic medicine: One of the world's oldest holistic ("whole-body") healing systems with historical roots in the Indian subcontinent. It is based on the belief that health and wellness depend on a delicate balance between the mind, body, and spirit.

baryons: Heavy subatomic particles that are made up of three quarks. Protons and neutrons, as well as other particles, are baryons. *Also see* hadrons.

belief system territories: Robert Monroe's name for the locations where souls visit after death, based on the afterlife beliefs they held while physically alive. The area is for those who know that they are dead but who are unable to transcend particular thought-patterns. Also known as Focus 24-26.

Bell operator: In Hilbert spaces, a sequence of quantum operators (Hadamard gate and a CNOT gate) that produces the entangled Bell states. In geometric algebra, the Bell operator is the simultaneous sum of qubit spinors, $B = (\mathbf{S}_A + \mathbf{S}_B)$ for qubits **A** and **B**. *Also see* Magic operator.

Bell states: Four specific quantum states of two qubits that represent the simplest (and maximal) examples of quantum entanglement. Bell states are either symmetric or antisymmetric with respect to the individual qubits. They are named after quantum researcher John Bell. *Also see* Magic states.

Bell's statistics: The results of measuring both entangled qubits show they are perfectly correlated with each other (or anti-correlated) even though each looks random. John Bell was the first to prove that the measurement correlations in the Bell state are stronger than could ever exist between classical systems.

Bell's theorem: Developed by quantum researcher John Bell and states that no physical theory of local hidden variables can ever reproduce all of the predictions of quantum mechanics.

Big Bang: The rapid expansion of matter from a state of extremely high density and temperature that according to current cosmological theories marked the origin of the universe. Explosively rapid inflation of spacetime itself caused the temperature to drop from the initial conditions.

big data sets: The term applied to extremely large collections of data all related to a specific topic. Sometimes these data sets are useful for training machine learning algorithms.

bio-body suit: All the layers of uniquely different kinds of substance needed to allow our own kernel of spirit to meaningfully interface with our outer spacetime reality using the body and brain.

bioelectromagnetism: The study of the interaction between electromagnetic fields and biological entities. Areas of study include electrical or electromagnetic fields produced by living cells, tissues, or organisms, including bioluminescent bacteria, and the electric currents that flow in nerves and muscles. Not to be confused with prana.

biofeedback: A process whereby electronic monitoring of a normally automatic bodily function is used to train someone to acquire voluntary control of that function.

biofield: Proportional to the spatial gradient of the sum total of all the types of different vibrations associated with a human or other living system. Clairvoyants describe these vibrations as a halo or aura. Is not a classical field.

bit: A primitive binary distinction used in physics and computer science related to information theory, communications, and entropy. These two state values are most commonly represented as either 0 or 1, but other representations such as true/false, yes/no, +/–, or on/off are possible. This book uses an orthonormal bit-vector representation using noncommutative geometric algebra conventions.

Bit Bang: Our relabeling of the Big Bang as the specialized low entropy quantum states that preceded the appearance of the physical universe.

bit dimensions: Our label for the primitive dimensions that build quantum mechanics are actually bits that can be expressed using geometric algebra in mathematical manner consistent with physics.

bit physics: The idea that bits are part of physics, due to the "it from bit" model used in black hole physics and Landauer's principle.

bivector: A 2D planar object with right-hand orientation formed by taking the outer product of two orthonormal vectors. *Also see* vector and trivector.

black holes: A region of spacetime exhibiting gravitational attraction so strong that nothing—no particles or even electromagnetic radiation, such as light—can escape from it. Usually formed when a massive sun collapses under its own weight after all the hydrogen is burned out.

black hole mechanics: Black hole thermodynamics is the area of study that seeks to reconcile the laws of thermodynamics with the existence of black hole event horizons.

Boltzmann constant: This constant (*k*), named after its discoverer, Ludwig Boltzmann, is a physical constant that relates the average relative kinetic energy of particles in a gas with the temperature of the gas. In 2019, Boltzmann constant is one of the seven "defining constants" that have been given exact definitions.

Boolean logic: A form of algebra that is centered on three simple Boolean operators: "Or," "And," and "Not." At the heart of Boolean logic is the idea that all values have only binary values of either True or False.

Bose information measure: After identifying the number of distinguishable states, then use –log2 of count to determine the Bose measure. For example, for a classical pair of coins, there are four possible states (HH, TT, HT, and TH), giving 1/4 probabilities. For quantum coins, there are only three unique states (HH, TT, XY where X!=Y) since two are indistinguishable, giving 1/3 probabilities. Likewise, for quantum dice only twenty-one distinguishable states exist rather than thirty-six for classical dice.

Bose statistics: Synonymous with Bose–Einstein statistics.

Bose–Einstein statistics: The Bose–Einstein statistics apply only to those particles not limited to single occupancy of the same state—that is, particles that do not obey the Pauli Exclusion Principle restrictions. Such particles have integer values of spin and are named "bosons," after the statistics that correctly describe their behavior. There must also be no significant interaction between the particles. The reason Bose produced accurate results was that since photons are indistinguishable from each other, one cannot treat any two photons having equal energy as being two distinct identifiable photons.

bosonic signatures: In GALG, bosons are defined as nilpotent, where expression **B*B** = 0.

boson: A subatomic particle, such as a photon, that has zero or integral spin and follows the statistical description given by Bose and Einstein.

Buddha: Indian religious leader from circa 500 BC who founded Buddhism.

causality: The principle that there is a relationship between cause and effect.

central processing unit (CPU): The part of a computer in which operations are controlled and executed by running stored programs.

chakras: From Indian thought, chakras are the primary centers of spiritual power in the human body located along the spine. There are seven major chakras and many more minor chakras. Chakras are viewed by clairvoyants as colored vortices projecting to the front and from the back.

channeling: To allow (that some person or entity) communication through a psychic connection or to receive a message in this manner.

chi: Chinese word meaning aliveness, life force energy, or life breath. Prana is also known as Ki, Qi, or Prana. Chi is a subtle energy that is held to animate the body internally and is of central importance in some Eastern systems of medical treatment, exercise, or self-defense.

chirality variations: Asymmetric in such a way that the structure and its mirror image are not equivalent.

chreodes: Represents the developmental pathway followed by a cell as it grows to form part of a specialized organ. Sheldrake also defines these as canalized pathways of change within a morphic field.

clairaudience: The ability of a human to cognitively hear information that is not accessible by our normal sound sensory system.

clairsentience: The ability of a human to cognitively feel information that is not accessible by our normal emotional or physical sensory systems.

clairvoyance: The ability of a human to cognitively see information that is not accessible by our normal sight sensory system.

classical logic: Is a branch of mathematics and a branch of philosophy. Philosophically, logic is at least closely related to the study of correct reasoning. Reasoning is an epistemic, mental activity so logic is at least closely allied with epistemology. Logic is also a central branch of computer science, due, in part, to interesting computational relations in Boolean logical systems and, in part, to the close connection between formal deductive argumentation and reasoning.

classical waves: In classical physics, where energy is transmitted through a medium.

Clojure: Is a modern, dynamic, and functional dialect of the Lisp programming language on the Java virtual machine platform that limits side effects and supports Lisp-style macros.

co-exclusion: Two states that are related to each other by the inverse operator (using multiplication). These states cannot exist simultaneously because they represent an operator that switches between these states. For example, the classical coin states of head and tails are co-exclusion states, since they exclude each other, where H+T = 0, or H = –T. This represents the prototime primitive which is expressed as multiplication in GALG. *Also see* co-occurrence.

co-occurrence: The sum of multiple orthogonal states (using addition) which represents pure concurrency of those states, because it is impossible to distinguish between (or count) two identical tokens unless they are presented exactly concurrently (exact simultaneity, since it is not relativistic). For example, a qubit is a co-occurrence of two state vectors, **A** = **a0** + **a1**. This represents the protospace building primitive due to the exact concurrency in time, which is expressed as addition in GALG. *Also see* co-exclusion.

coherence: The quality of being logical and consistent or of forming a unified whole. In quantum theory, coherence describes all properties of the correlation between physical quantities of a single wave, or between several waves or wave packets, as in the case of lasers.

coincidences: A remarkable concurrence of events or circumstances without apparent causal connection with one another.

complementarity: The concept that two contrasted theories, such as the wave and particle theories of light, may be able to explain a set of phenomena, although each separately only accounts for some aspects.

concurrent states: Any states that can occur simultaneously are concurrent, and typically they are orthogonal, as is the case of the two qubit states.

Confucius: A Chinese philosopher and politician who created a philosophy that emphasized personal and governmental morality, correctness of social relationships, justice, kindness, and sincerity.

consciousness: The state of being awake and aware of one's surroundings.

consciousness studies: The scientific study of how humans can be conscious or aware.

constructive/destructive interference: Wave emission from multiple sources separated in spacetime, or scattered from multiple and similar objects separated in spacetime, to produce a superposed wave envelope that has a greatly increased amplitude when all the wavelets are in phase with each other and they add constructively, but a greatly decreased amplitude when they are out of phase with each other and add destructively.

content-addressable memory (CAM): A term associated with Pentti Kanerva's model of neural networks that describes how the address of data points in a hyperdimensional model actually represents the data.

correlation: A mutual statistical relationship or connection between two or more things.

correlithm: The contraction of terms "correlational algorithm" associated with Nick Lawrence's neural network model is mathematically related to content-addressable memories (CAMs).

correlithm math: The central idea that randomly generated points in a high-dimensional space are a "standard distance" apart from all other such points and a "standard radius" from the midpoint of the data set. These points act like tokens that are nearly orthogonal, so can represent vector spaces and phase relationships.

Coulomb's constant: The electric force constant (*k*), or the electrostatic constant that is the constant of proportionality in Coulomb's law that quantifies the amount of force between two stationary, electrically charged particles.

Coulomb's law: States that the force where the magnitude of the electrostatic force of attraction or repulsion between two point charges is directly proportional to the product of the magnitudes of charges and inversely proportional to the square of the distance between them.

coupled systems: Any systems are coupled that have correlations in their states. Mathematically, the systems can be defined using dependent and independent variables.

curse of dimensionality: Refers to various phenomena that arise when analyzing and organizing data in high-dimensional spaces (often with hundreds or thousands of dimensions) that do not occur in low-dimensional settings. The common theme of these problems is that when the dimensionality increases, the volume of the space increases so fast that the available data become sparse.

Dalai Lama: Title given by the Tibetan people to the foremost spiritual leader of the Gelug or "Yellow Hat" school of Tibetan Buddhism, the newest of the classical schools of Tibetan Buddhism. The 14th and current Dalai Lama is Tenzin Gyatso, who lives as a refugee in India.

dark energy: A theoretical repulsive force that counteracts gravity and causes the universe to expand at an accelerating rate.

dark matter: Material that cannot be seen directly because it does not absorb, reflect, or emit light, so it cannot be detected by observing electromagnetic radiation. We know that dark matter exists because of the gravitational effect it has on objects that we can observe directly, such as galaxy formation and gravitational lensing around galaxies.

Datomic: An operational database management system—designed for transactional, domain-specific data. It is, by definition, not designed to be a data warehouse because it accumulates immutable facts over time, so new values do not overwrite the older ones.

decoherence: In quantum physics, the process in which a system's behavior changes from that which can be explained by quantum mechanics to that which can be explained by classical mechanics. Usually noise causes quantum states to become decoherent.

deep learning: A broader family of machine learning methods based on artificial neural networks with representation learning. Learning can be supervised, semi-supervised, or unsupervised and typically uses large data sets.

deep reality: Describes the quantum informational reality behind the extraordinary human behaviors, which cannot be defined by using only classical physics.

deltron: Tiller's name for a type of substance from the emotion domain of reality that can travel both slower than EM light in a vacuum and thus interact with D-space substance, and faster than such EM light and thus interact with R-space substance. This allows D-space substance to interact with R-space substance via deltron/deltron interactions without violating Einstein's relativity theory constraints.

deltron agency: The behavior of deltrons that forms the bridge between conventional spacetime (D-space) and reciprocal space (R-space).

dentrite structure: Projections of a neuron (nerve cell) that receive signals (information) from other neurons via synapse connections.

derivative: A fundamental tool of calculus that measures the sensitivity to change of the function value with respect to a change in its arguments.

Descartes assumption: Descartes proposed that no human qualities of consciousness, intention, emotion, mind, or spirit can significantly influence a well-designed target experiment in physical reality. We stipulate this is an invalid assumption and not a law.

destructive interference: When the crest of one wave meets the trough of another wave, then the amplitudes destructively cancels each other.

determinism: The doctrine that all events, including human action, are ultimately determined by causes external to the will. Some philosophers have taken determinism to imply that individual human beings have no free will and cannot be held morally responsible for their actions. Due to uncertainty in initial conditions, even "simple" three-body physics models are not deterministic.

dharma: The eternal and inherent nature of reality, regarded in Hinduism as a cosmic law underlying right behavior and social order.

dimensionality (D) of space: Informally defined as the minimum number of coordinates needed to specify any point within the space.

direct-knowing: Knowing or knowledge acquired through directly perceiving something in the moment. This may be using the normal senses or thru paranormal senses.

discrete: Individually separate and distinct.

disorder: Disruption of the systematic functioning or neat arrangement of some system. Entropy is always increasing to the state of more disorder in a closed system.

divine: Connecting to or relating to a god, especially the Supreme Being.

Drake equation: A probabilistic formula used to estimate the number of active, communicative extraterrestrial civilizations in the Milky Way galaxy.

Dreamtime: The dreamtime is the key to all the encoded mythology teachings about existence of the Australian Aboriginal peoples. These are the stories that explain the Aboriginal world view, which originated in the "golden age" when the first ancestors were created.

earthing: The process of transferring the immediate discharge of the electrical energy directly to the Earth by the help of the low-resistance wire. Also, the name of a company that sells grounding equipment.

ebit: The smallest discrete example of an entangled state, which represents Bell's statistics. An ebit is formed from two 2D qubits and so represents a 4D state space.

ebit agency: The behavior of ebits that forms the apparent nonlocal connection between two entangled qubits.

ebit locality: Expresses how, for an ebit, even though two constituent qubits are extremely far apart, the measurement of either qubit affects the mate instantaneously, as if local to each other.

ebit-complete: New term for the requirement to support ebit entanglement states and operators.

ehostbrain: Matzke's term for a proposed electronic device that can act like a high bit-rate PK device, such that humans could control it (using biofeedback techniques) like our own brains.

ehostbrain technology: The technology and design of an ehostbrain, such that it mimics the technology connecting our minds and brains.

eidetic memory: The ability to recall an image from memory with high precision for a brief period after seeing it only once, and without using a mnemonic device.

electric primitives: Any charged particles, such as electrons, positrons, protons, etc., that have the smallest amount of discrete charge.

electromagnetic (EM) fields: A classical field produced by moving electric charges.

electromagnetic waves: Refers to the waves of the electromagnetic field, propagating through space, carrying electromagnetic radiant energy, which includes radio waves, microwaves, infrared, light, ultraviolet, X-rays, and gamma rays.

electromagnetism: The interaction of electric currents or fields and magnetic fields.

electromyography (EMG): The recording of the electrical activity of muscle tissue using electrodes attached to the skin or inserted into the muscle (or its representation as a visual display or audible signal).

emotional ladder: Defined by Abraham as the twenty-two steps of emotions from the most negative to most positive. The goal is to move up the ladder to more positive emotional states.

empty space: The regions of the universe that is essentially empty of any matter or energy.

energy combing: An energy-balancing technique to imagine the energy from your fingers to comb the aura of another person.

entanglement: The physical quantum phenomenon that occurs when a pair or group of particles is generated, interact, or share spatial proximity in a way such that the quantum state of each particle of the pair or group cannot be described independently of the quantum state of the others, even when the particles are separated by a large distance.

entropy: A thermodynamic quantity representing the unavailability of a system's thermal energy for conversion into mechanical work, often interpreted as the degree of disorder or randomness in the system.

epistemic: Relating to knowledge or to the degree of its validation.

equihedron: Matzke's term for a high-dimensional version of a 2D equilateral triangle or 3D equilateral tetrahedron, where all the points are equal distance from all other points.

equilateral triangle: A triangle, where the three sides are all the same length.

ether: (Sanskrit *akasha*). Though not considered a factor in present scientific theory on the nature of the material universe, ether has for millenniums been so referred to by India's sages. Paramahansa Yogananda spoke of ether as the background on which God projects the cosmic motion picture of creation. Space gives dimension to objects; ether separates the images. This "background," a creative force that coordinates all spatial vibrations, is a necessary factor when considering the subtler forces—thought and life energy (*prana*)—and the nature of space and the origin of material forces and matter. Modern physics now understands that empty space is formed by quantum wave potential that manifests as zero-point energy, which is the modern Lorentz invariant version of the ether.

etheric bodies: The etheric bodies are clairvoyantly seen as a double or a twin of the physical body and may be the source of the structure of the physical body.

Faraday cage: A grounded metal screen surrounding an object to exclude electrostatic and electromagnetic influences.

fermions: The twelve fundamental subatomic particles, which have half-integral spin and follows the statistical description given by Fermi and Dirac. Each fermion has a corresponding antiparticle. Six quarks and six leptons (either three electrons or three neutrino generations) and their antiparticles are fermions.

field: A physical quantity, represented by a number (or tensor) that has a value for each point in spacetime. Usually, in this region, each point is affected by a force due to the field strength.

first-class elements: Both physics and computer science share this term, where an entity supports all the operations generally available to other entities in a formal manner that leads to generalization by removing restrictions.

Five Precepts: These rules of training are the most important system of morality for Buddhist lay people. They constitute the basic code of ethics to be undertaken by lay followers of Buddhism. The precepts are commitments to abstain from killing living beings, stealing, sexual misconduct, lying, and intoxication.

Focus 24–26: *See* **Belief System Territories**.

Focus 27: Robert Monroe's definition for the edge of human thought capacity. This is the site of a way-station (not a terminus) for rest and recovery from the trauma of physical death.

Fourier transform: A unique mathematical operation that decomposes a series of values from the time domain into its constituent frequency domain representation.

frame: A framework that is used for the observation and mathematical description of physical phenomena and the formulation of physical laws, usually consisting of an observer, a coordinate system, and a clock or clocks assigning times at positions with respect to the coordinate system.

free will: The ability to choose between different possible courses of action unimpeded; this assumes that we are free to choose our behavior, in other words, we are self-determined.

frequency: The rate at which a vibration occurs that constitutes a wave, either in a material (as in sound waves), or in an electromagnetic field (as in radio waves and light), usually measured at a rate of cycles per second.

FSMs: A finite state machine is an abstract machine that can be in exactly one of a finite number of states at any given time, so has limited memory. The FSM can change from one state to another in response to some inputs; the change from one state to another is called a transition. Used in computer technology to control elevators, stop lights, vending machines, and etc.

GALG: *See* geometric algebra.

galvanic skin response (GSR): A change in the electrical resistance of the skin caused by emotional stress, measurable with a sensitive galvanometer, e.g. in lie-detector tests.

gas discharge device: A system made up of a gas, electrodes, and an enclosing wall in which an electric current is carried by charged particles in response to an electric field, the gradient of the electric potential, or the voltage between two surfaces.

gauge invariance: The lack of change in the measurable quantities, despite the field being transformed by a gauge transform. Gauge invariance is recognized as the physical principle governing the fundamental forces between all elementary particles. Such invariance must be satisfied for all observable quantum quantities in order to ensure that any arbitrariness in A and B do not affect the field strength. Gauge invariance is also known as gauge symmetry.

gauge symmetry: *See* gauge invariance.

gauge theory: The word "gauge" means a measurement, and sometimes the fundamental fields cannot be directly measured; however, some associated quantities can be measured, and this transformation is called a "gauge transformation."

general relativity: Einstein's law of gravitation and its relation to other forces of nature.

genius: A person who is exceptionally intelligent or creative, either generally or in some particular respect.

geometric algebra (GALG): The geometric algebra of a vector space is an algebra over a field, noted for its multiplication operation called the geometric product on a space of elements called multivectors, which contains both the scalars, vectors, bivectors, N-vectors and the vector space.

gestalt: An organized whole that is perceived as more than the sum of its parts.

god-stuff: If we presumed that God exists, what is God made of that makes it all knowing and all powerful. This is a highly technical term.

Google's MapReduce system: A programming model introduced by Google for processing and generating large data sets on clusters of computers. Google first formulated the framework for the purpose of serving Google's Web page indexing, and the new framework replaced earlier indexing algorithms. By 2014, Google was no longer using MapReduce as their primary big data processing model.

gravitons: The hypothetical quantum of gravity, an elementary particle that mediates the force of gravity. There is no complete quantum field theory of gravitons due to an outstanding mathematical problem with renormalization in general relativity.

gravity waves: An energy-carrying wave propagating through a gravitational field, produced when a massive body is accelerated or otherwise disturbed. Gravitational waves were first postulated by Einstein in 1916 and were first observed directly in September 2015.

gravity well: A gravity well is the pull of gravity exerted by a large body in space. The Sun has a large (or deep) gravity well that people can visualize as a ball making a dent on a rubber sheet, but the well is mostly due to the bending of time rather than of space.

grounding: Refers to contact with the Earth's surface electrons by electrically connecting to the Earth. This can occur walking barefoot outside or sitting, working, or sleeping indoors connected to conductive systems that have an electrical connection with the Earth. *Also see* earthing.

Grover's quantum search: A quantum algorithm devised by Lov Grover in 1996 that finds with high probability the unique input to a black-box function that produces a particular output value, using just $O(\sqrt{N})$ evaluations of the function, where N is the size of the function's domain. The same search problem in classical computation cannot be solved in fewer than O(N) evaluations.

gurus: In Hinduism and Buddhism, a spiritual teacher, especially one who imparts initiation.

H-space: *See* hyperdimensional space.

hadron: A subatomic composite particle made of two or more quarks held together by strong force in a way similar way to how molecules are held together by the electromagnetic force. Baryons and mesons are examples of hadrons. Most of the mass of ordinary matter comes from two hadrons (baryons with three quarks), the proton, and the neutron. *Also see* hadron class.

hadron class: Several classes of hadrons are: mesons having two quarks, baryons having three quarks, plus exotic hadrons consisting of tetraquarks with four quarks, and pentaquarks with five quarks.

Hawaiian Ho'oponopono forgiveness ritual: The Hawaiian practice of reconciliation and forgiveness. Promotes self-healing by just repeating the phrase: "I love you. I am sorry. Forgive me. Thank you." over and over again.

Hawkins scale: The scale of consciousness, as discussed in the book *Power vs Force* by Dr. David Hawkins, spanning from 0–1000. Having a scale of 500 or above indicates pure unconditional love, and it is in this state that we are in complete harmony with our body and our environment.

heart intelligence: According to the HeartMath organization, this is the flow of awareness, understanding, and intuition that we experience when the mind and emotions are brought into coherent alignment with the heart.

HeartMath: According to the HeartMath organization, this is a unique system of rigorous scientific research, validated techniques, leading-edge products, programs, and advanced technologies for people interested in personal development and improved emotional, mental, and physical health. *Also see* heart intelligence.

Heisenberg uncertainty principle: In quantum mechanics, any of a variety of mathematical inequalities asserting a fundamental limit to the precision with which the values for certain pairs of physical quantities of a particle, such as position *x* and momentum *p*, which are known as complementary variables.

Hermetics: A religious, philosophical, and esoteric tradition based primarily on writings attributed to Hermes Trismegistus. These writings have greatly influenced the Western esoteric tradition and were considered to be of great importance during both the Renaissance and the Reformation.

hierarchical temporal memories (HTM): A biologically constrained theory of intelligence, originally described in the 2004 book *On Intelligence* by Jeff Hawkins with Sandra Blakeslee. At the core of HTM are learning algorithms that can store, learn, infer, and recall high-order sequences.

Higgs boson: An elementary force (or particle) in the Standard Model of particle physics, produced by the quantum excitation of the Higgs field (named after Peter Higgs), one of the fields in particle physics theory that is responsible for the unexpected mass of the gauge bosons (Z/W bosons). Bosons should have zero mass but the Higgs field breaks some symmetry laws of the electroweak interaction.

Higgs field: A scalar field (and scalar particle) that has a non-zero value (or vacuum expectation) everywhere because it would take less energy for the field to have a non-zero value than a zero value.

high-dimensional mathematics: *See* hyperdimensional mathematics.

high-energy physics: The branch of physics that studies fundamental particles that do not occur under normal circumstances in nature, but can be created and detected during energetic collisions of other particles, as is done in particle accelerators.

high-κ dielectrics: Refers to any material with a high dielectric constant (κ, kappa), as compared to silicon dioxide. The implementation of high-κ gate dielectrics is one of several strategies developed to allow further miniaturization of microelectronic components, colloquially referred to as extending Moore's law.

Hilbert space: The mathematical concept of a Hilbert space, named after David Hilbert, generalizes the notion of Euclidean space.

It extends the methods of vector algebra and calculus from the two-dimensional Euclidean plane and three-dimensional space to spaces with any finite or infinite number of dimensions.

holarchy: A holarchy is a connection between holons, where a holon is both a part and a whole. Generally, one can say that holons at one level are "made up of, or make up" the holons or parts of another level. This can be demonstrated in the holarchic relationships (subatomic particles ↔ atoms ↔ molecules ↔ etc., through all levels up to societies) where each holon is a "level" of organization. *Also see* holons.

holistic: Characterized by comprehension of the parts of something as intimately interconnected and explicable only by reference to the whole.

holodeck: A fictional device from the television franchise Star Trek. It is a chamber or stage where participants may engage with different virtual reality environments.

hologram: A 2D photograph of an interference pattern which, when suitably illuminated with a laser, produces a 3D image.

holons: Something that is simultaneously a whole and a part. Arthur Koestler proposed the word holon to describe the hybrid nature of sub-wholes and parts within *in vivo* systems, because although it is easy to identify sub-wholes or parts, wholes and parts in an absolute sense do not exist anywhere. A holon is maintained by the throughput of matter—energy and information—entropy connected to other holons and is simultaneously a whole in itself and at the same time is nested within another holon, and so is a part of something much larger than itself. *Also see* holarchy.

HTM: *See* hierarchical temporal memories.

human aura: The "biofield" pattern around the human body that can be seen by one with developed clairvoyant sight. This does not assume the pattern is electromagnetic in origin.

hyperawareness: The ability to awaken your internal awareness to become hyperaware of your surroundings using physical and nonphysical senses.

hypercube: A geometric figure in four or more dimensions that is analogous to a cube in three dimensions. A tesseract is a 4D hypercube.

hyperdimensional address: Represents the coordinates of a point in a hyperdimensional space.

hyperdimensional mathematics: The set of mathematical techniques and geometric understanding of models that express more than three dimensions. If some of these are related to quantum theory or neural theory, then they may have to comprehend complex concepts and properties, such as: noncommutative, graded vectors, superposition, unitary, nilpotent, idempotent, entanglement, standard distance, standard radius, etc.

hyperdimensional space (H-space): *See* Hilbert space.

hyperesthesia: A condition that involves an abnormal increase in sensitivity to stimuli of the senses.

hyper-intelligence: Above the level of intelligence even compared to other human geniuses and savants in general or specific areas. This term is specifically used to evoke the idea that there might exist intelligence far beyond what we can comprehend, such as the idea of an all-knowing God.

hyper-hypotenuse: Assuming there is a hyperdimensional cube or rectangle, then the diagonal between two opposite corner is the hyper-hypotenuse, whose length grows with respect with the number of dimensions.

idempotent: An element that is equal to itself when raised to a power $n \geq 2$. This means that multiple applications of this operator I have the same effect as applying it once.

immutable: Unchanging over time or unable to be changed.

Indian logic: Indian logic stands as one of the three original traditions of logic, alongside the Greek and the Chinese logic. One of schools of India logic asserts that there are four valid means of knowledge: perception, inference, comparison, and sound, or testimony. Invalid knowledge involves memory, doubt, error, and hypothetical argument. Indian logic's ultimate concern is bringing an end to human suffering, which results from ignorance of reality. Liberation is brought about through right knowledge using these principles.

inertial frame: From special relativity, all inertial frames are in a state of constant, rectilinear motion with respect to one another; an accelerometer moving with any of them would detect zero acceleration.

infinite: Limitless or endless in space, extent, or size; impossible to measure or calculate.

infinite intelligence: The term used by Abraham to describe itself. *See* hyper-intelligence.

information theory: Information theory studies the quantification, storage, and communication of information. It was originally proposed by Claude Shannon in 1948 to find fundamental limits on signal processing and communication operations, such as data compression.

inseparable: In entanglement, one constituent cannot be fully described without considering the other(s). Mathematically, this is defined where a quantum state cannot be factored as a product of states of its local constituents; that is to say, they are not individual particles but are an inseparable whole.

Inspec (intelligent species): The term Robert Monroe used to identify his future self that was interacting with and helping his younger self. This is conceptually similar to timeline therapy.

instant savants: An acquired savant syndrome where astonishing new abilities—typically in music, art, or mathematics—appear unexpectedly in ordinary persons after a head injury, stroke, or other central nervous system (CNS) incident and where no such abilities or interests were present pre-incident.

intention: An idea that you plan or intend to carry out. Your goal, purpose, or aim is your intention.

intentionality: The Oxford Dictionary defines this as "the quality or fact of being intentional; of or pertaining to purpose, pertaining to operation of the mind." As such, it represents the quality of one's conscious purpose, often thought of as self-directed mind.

intention host device (IHD): An electronic device used at the Tiller Institute that encodes intention imprinted during a meditation session. These imprinted IHDs have been shown to have an effect on a variety of physical systems in a laboratory setting.

intercessory prayer: The act of praying to a deity on behalf of others.

interferometer: An instrument in which the interference of two beams of light is employed to make precise measurements.

intimacy: Deeply knowing another person (or thing or place) and feeling deeply known. Deep intimacy can feel like a transpersonal connection.

introspection: The examination or observation of one's own conscious thoughts, feelings, mental states, and emotional processes.

intuitive: Someone who senses things about people and their surroundings and their experiences that are not so evident to "normal" people. They may see, hear, feel, and know things others do not experience. When their intuition is really strong, we may call them psychic.

irreversible: Some action or state that is not able to be undone or altered. Quantum measurement is an example of an irreversible quantum computing operation. *Also see* singular.

isotropic: Uniformity of some property independent of the orientations or with no preferred direction. An isotropic medium is one such that the permittivity, ε, and permeability, μ, of the medium are uniform in all directions of the medium, the simplest instance being free space.

Jesus: A first-century Jewish preacher and religious leader. He is the central figure of Christianity, which is the most practiced religion on the Earth. For Christians, he is the Son of God, preexisting with God and the Holy Spirit.

kahuna: In Hawaii, a wise man or shaman.

karma: In Hinduism and Buddhism, the sum of a person's actions in this and previous states of existence, viewed as deciding their fate in future existences. It also refers to the spiritual principle of cause and effect where intent and actions of an individual influence the future life and lives of that individual.

Karnaugh map: A diagram consisting of a rectangular array of squares, each representing a different combination of the variables of a Boolean function and is used as a pictorial method of simplifying Boolean algebra expressions.

knowing: The state of having knowledge or being aware, usually applied to humans. In this book, we stipulate that computers might have access to data, but they do not *know* anything.

Krishna: This is the name of a Hindu god believed to be an incarnation of the god Vishnu. In some Hindu traditions, Krishna is regarded as the Supreme Deity.

Kundalini: In Hinduism, a form of divine feminine energy believed to be located at the base of the spine.

Kundalini awakening: Described as rising up from the root chakra, through the central energy channel inside or alongside the spine, reaching the top of the head. An event where the Kundalini is awakened through regular practice of Mantra, Tantra, Yantra, Asanas, or Meditation, or it can be awakened by a guru. This can happen when one is either prepared or unprepared.

Kundalini rising: *See* Kundalini awakening.

Landauer's principle: A physical principle pertaining to the lower theoretical limit of energy consumption of computation when a bit of information is irreversibly erased.

Law of Attraction (LOA): A New Age principle that thoughts can directly attract other like-minded people and events related to the meaning of that thought. Abraham proposes LOA is a real law of the universe (like gravity) and influences our life, whether we believe in it or not. *Also see* Abraham.

law of entropy: *See* entropy.

law of increasing disorder: *See* entropy.

learning-without-a-brain: The term that describes the ability for organisms to learn even though they do not contain neurons or a brain.

leptons: An elementary particle of half-integer spin that does not undergo strong force interactions. Two main classes of leptons exist, charged leptons (electron generations), and neutral leptons (neutrino generations).

levitation: The ability (of a human) to cause an object to lift in space against the normal downward gravitational force.

life force: Is a concept of spiritualism, the energy and source of all life. *See* prana.

life review: A life review is a phenomenon widely reported as occurring during near-death experiences, in which a person rapidly sees much or the totality of their life history. Referred to as having their life "flash before their eyes."

light cone: The path that a flash of light, emanating from a single event and traveling in all directions, would take through spacetime. This is defined as the surface of a cone in 3D space-time. *See* light-like.

light-like: Description of region of spacetime that is ON the cone connected by traveling at the speed of light. Essentially these are regions of spacetime that are casually connected by light. An example of this is all telecommunication systems (microwaves, satellites, and radar) that use EM light or radio waves.

logic gate: An idealized or physical electronic device implementing a Boolean function, a logical operation performed on one or more binary inputs that produces a single binary output. Examples are NOT logic, AND logic, NAND logic, OR Logic, NOR logic, and XNOR logic.

Lorentz invariant: Property of a system that is invariant under the transformation relating the spacetime coordinates of one frame of reference to another in special relativity.

lucid dreaming: A dream during which the dreamer is aware that they are dreaming. During a lucid dream, the dreamer may gain some amount of control over the dream characters, narrative, and environment; however, this is not actually necessary for a dream to be described as lucid.

lucidity: The ability to see and understand things clearly. *See* lucid dreaming.

machine intelligence: In computer science, artificial intelligence is sometimes called "machine intelligence," which is intelligence demonstrated by machines, in contrast to the natural intelligence displayed by humans and animals.

Magic operator: In Hilbert spaces, a sequence of quantum operators that produces the entangled Magic states, which are complex conjugates of Bell states. In geometric algebra, the Magic operator is the simultaneous subtraction of the qubit spinors, $M = (\mathbf{S}_A - \mathbf{S}_B)$ for qubits **A** and **B**. *Also see* Bell operator.

Magic states: Four specific quantum states of two qubits that are the complex conjugates of the Bell states. *Also see* Bell states.

magnetic monopole: A hypothetical isolated particle with a single magnetic pole analogous to how electrons define the single-pole electric charge.

Maharishi Effect: In the 1960s, Maharishi Mahesh Yogi described a paranormal effect claiming a significant number of individuals (of the people in a given area) practicing the Transcendental Meditation technique (TM) could have a positive effect on the local environment.

manifestations: A perceptible, outward, or visible expression of some underlying process.

Map of Consciousness: The book *Map of Consciousness Explained* is a compilation of Dr. David R. Hawkins lectures on human consciousness and their associated energy fields.

mass primitive: *See* graviton.

Mathematica: A modern technical symbolic mathematical computing system spanning most areas of technical computing—including neural networks, machine learning, image processing, geometry, data science, visualizations, and others. The system is used in many technical, scientific, engineering, mathematical, and computing fields.

matter waves: A central part of the theory of quantum mechanics, being an example of wave–particle duality. All matter exhibits wave-like behavior, since electrons can experience interference patterns just like photons.

medical intuitive: An alternative medicine practitioner who can use their intuitive abilities to find the cause of a physical or emotional condition through the use of insight rather than traditional medical diagnostics.

memristor: In addition to the resistor, capacitor, and inductor, a fourth primitive electronic device proposed in 1971 by Leon Chua, which is a nonlinear passive two-terminal electrical component. As the name implies, this device is a programmable resistor that acts like a two-terminal nonvolatile memory. Memristors were actually built in 2008 by Hewlett-Packard.

meson: Any member of a family of subatomic particles (such as the pion or kaon) composed of a quark and an antiquark. Mesons are sensitive to the strong force, the fundamental interaction that binds the components of the nucleus by governing the behavior of their constituent quarks. *Also see* hadron.

metaphysics: The branch of philosophy that examines the fundamental nature of reality, including the relationship between mind and matter, between substance and attribute, and between potentiality and actuality.

miracle: A surprising and welcome event that is not explicable by natural or scientific laws and is therefore considered to be the work of a divine agency.

misalignment: The term used by Abraham that describes when your higher self and thoughts do not agree, resulting in your not feeling well. When you feel good about a subject, you are aligned with that topic.

modality: From NLP, refers to our internal representations of thoughts, which relate to the five senses (visual, auditory, kinesthetic, olfactory, and gustatory) plus our internal dialogue. *Also see* neuro linguistic programming (NLP) and submodalities.

modes: A concept from quantum theory that implies a number of discrete wavelengths in a quantum well. We use the term in this book to talk about vibratory modes, similar to knot theory or string theory, without implying a frequency exists.

moieties: Each of two parts into which a thing is or can be divided.

monopole: A single electric charge or magnetic pole, especially a hypothetical isolated magnetic pole.

Monroe Institute: The world's leading education center for the study of human consciousness, founded in 1974 by Robert Monroe.

Moore's law: The principle that the speed and capability of computers can be expected to double every two years, as a result of decreases in transistor size, and resultant increases in the number of transistors a microchip can contain due to each new semiconductor process generation.

morphogenesis: The biological process that causes an organism to develop its shape. It is one of three fundamental aspects of developmental biology, along with the control of cell growth and cellular differentiation, unified in evolutionary developmental biology.

Moses: The most important prophet in Judaism and also an important prophet in Christianity, Islam, the Baha'i Faith, and a number of other Abrahamic religions.

multi-being: The term applied to Abraham, since they are a blending of many separate beings.

multiplicative cancellation: When the product of two terms cause some or all of the terms to become zero, since the product produces sub-terms of opposite signs that add and cancel. For example, in GALG: $(\mathbf{a} + \mathbf{a}\wedge\mathbf{b})^2 = (\mathbf{a} + \mathbf{a}\wedge\mathbf{b})*\mathbf{a} + (\mathbf{a} + \mathbf{a}\wedge\mathbf{b})*\ \mathbf{a}\wedge\mathbf{b} = (1 - \mathbf{b}) + (-1 + \mathbf{b}) = 0$.

multivector: The sum of any number of unique set of a scalar and graded *N*-vectors in geometric algebra.

multiverse: A hypothetical group of multiple universes. Together, these universes comprise everything that exists: the entirety of space, time, matter, energy, information, and the physical laws and constants that describe them.

***N*-vector**: Generic geometric algebra term for an oriented arbitrary dimensional hyper volume. For example, a bivector is an oriented 2D plane (**a^b**), a trivector is an oriented 3D volume (**a^b^c**), etc.

NAND logic: The not both; the NAND of a set of operands is true if, and only if, at least one of its operands is false. NAND gates (and NOR gates) are so-called "universal gates" since they can be combined to mimic all other logic gates.

NDEs: *See* near-death experiences.

near-death experiences (NDEs): An unusual experience taking place on the brink of death and recounted by a person after recovery, typically an out-of-body experience or a vision of a tunnel of light followed by a life review.

negative-entropy: Negative entropy means that something is becoming less disordered. In order for something to become less disordered, energy must be used, because the second law of thermodynamics states that a closed system is always in a state of increasing entropy (or disorder).

negentropy: *See* negative-entropy.

nested hierarchy: A well-defined (super)set that contains and consists of other specified (sub)sets. An analogy would be a set of Russian nested dolls.

neural: Relating to a nerve or the nervous system.

neural computing: The hypothetical information processing performed by networks of neurons. Neural computation is affiliated with the philosophical tradition known as "computational theory of mind," which advances the thesis that neural computation explains intelligence and cognition.

neural network: A series of computer algorithms that endeavors to recognize underlying relationships in a set of data through a process that mimics the apparent way the human brain operates.

neuro-linguistic programming (NLP): An approach to communication, personal development, and psychotherapy created by

Richard Bandler and John Grinder in California in the 1970s. (Not associated with Natural Language Processing, which also uses the initials of NLP.)

neutrinos: A fermion that interacts only via the weak subatomic force and gravity. The neutrino is so named because it is electrically neutral and because its rest mass is so small.

Newtonian spectrum: Isaac Newton published a paper in 1672 where he explained how the rainbow—created by refracting white light with a prism, resolving it into its component colors: red, orange, yellow, green, blue, indigo, and violet.

nilpotent: An element that is equal to zero when raised to a power where $n \geq 2$.

nirvana: Buddhism defines this transcendent state in which there is neither suffering, desire, nor sense of self, and the subject is released from the effects of karma and the cycle of death and rebirth. It represents the final goal of Buddhism.

noise immunity: The ability of an apparatus or system to perform its functions when interference (noise) is present.

non-Shannon information: In 1948, Claude Shannon defined "information theory" as the study the quantification, storage, and communication of information, which is based on the statistical relations between tokens, so related to entropy. Mike Manthey described how the coin demo creates information using simultaneity of tokens, so represents a non-statistical form of information.

noncommutative: Informally, this means that "order matters." More formally, the result obtained using any two elements of the set where the operation results differs with the order in which the elements are used. Typically, common operations, such as addition and multiplication of numbers, are commutative since the order does not matter. *See* anticommutative.

noncomputable: A problem for which there is no algorithm that can be used to solve it. The most famous example of noncomputability (or un-decidability) is the halting problem, the problem of determining, from a description of an arbitrary computer program and an input, whether the program will finish running, or continue to run forever. Roger Penrose believes that consciousness is also non-computable.

nondeterminism: An algorithm or process that, even for the same input, can exhibit different behaviors on different runs.

nonlocal: Not of, affecting, or confined to a limited region or part. Many aspects of quantum system appear to be nonlocal, especially entanglement. We believe this label is mistaken, since the universe is not really three dimensional at the quantum level.

nonlocality mechanisms: Some mechanism that causes the apparent nonlocality behavior to manifest, such as the hyperdimensional nature of reality.

nonmetric space: A mathematical space defined without spatial or temporal metrics of any kind. This space acts like pure information and topology without space, time, matter, or energy.

nontheist: Not having or involving a belief in a god or gods.

NOR logic: The joint denial; the NOR of a set of operands is true if, and only if, none of its operands are true. NOR gates (and NAND gates) are so-called "universal gates" since they can mimic all other logic gates.

Nostradamus: A French astrologer, physician, and reputed seer, who is best known for his book *Les Prophéties,* a collection of 942 poetic quatrains allegedly predicting future events.

OBEs: *See* out-of-body experiences.

observer frames: In special relativity, an observer is a frame of reference from which a set of objects or events are being measured. Usually this is an inertial reference frame or "inertial observer" or "observer frame."

Occam's razor: The principle (attributed to William of Occam) that in explaining a thing the minimum assumptions should be made as necessary. The principle is often invoked to defend reductionism or nominalism.

oneness: The fact or state of being unified or whole, though comprised of two or more parts.

OR logic: The logical disjunction; the OR of a set of operands is true if, and only if, one or more of its operands is true.

orbs: Free-floating aura balls that occasionally show up on photographs.

orthogonal: When two (or more) vectors are all ninety degrees apart from each other.

orthogonal vectors: *See* orthogonal.

orthonormal: When two (or more) vectors are all orthogonal to each other and of unit length.

out-of-body experiences (OBEs): An awareness and sensation of being outside one's own body, typically floating and being able to observe oneself from a distance.

panpsychism: The doctrine or belief that everything material, however small, has an element of individual consciousness.

paradigm: A distinct set of concepts or thought patterns, including theories, research methods, postulates, and standards for what constitutes legitimate contributions to a field. A prevailing worldview of how science interprets causal behavior of nature. The relativity and quantum advances in physics both required an expansion of the previous physics paradigm.

parallel programming: A manner of writing programs in which many computations or the execution of processes are carried out simultaneously. Large problems can often be divided into smaller ones, which can then be solved in parallel at the same time, and the results are combined.

Parseval's identity: A fundamental result on the summability of the Fourier series of a function. Geometrically, it is the Pythagorean theorem for inner-product spaces.

periodic table of elements: A tabular display of the chemical elements, which are arranged by atomic number, electron configuration, and recurring chemical properties, which shows the periodic trends.

phase: Both circles and sinusoidal wave are related based on the angle (0 to 360 degrees) from some starting point. The angle is the phase or phase difference.

photon: A type of elementary particle and the quantum of the electromagnetic field, including electromagnetic radiation such as light and radio waves. It is the force carrier for the electromagnetic force.

Physio-Kundalini Syndrome Index: A nineteen-item dichotomous questionnaire, in order to study Kundalini and its effects. The index includes four major categories: motor symptoms, somatosensory symptoms, audiovisual symptoms, and mental symptoms.

PK: *See* psychokinesis.

PK device: Any device that can be affected by thought and intention by psychokinesis.

Planck area: A natural unit of area defined by Planck length on a side. This is approximately equivalent to the minimum change of one bit to the surface area of a black hole.

Planck charge: A natural unit of charge where $q_p = e/\sqrt{\alpha}$, where e = elementary charge and α = fine structure constant.

Planck constant: A physical constant h that is the quantum of electromagnetic action, which relates the energy carried by a photon to its frequency.

Planck frequency: A repeating event that occurs once every Planck time and is considered the fastest possible frequency.

Planck length: A natural unit of length where $\left(l_p = \sqrt{\hbar G / c^3}\right) = 1.62 \times 10^{-35}$ m and is considered the smallest possible length.

Planck mass: A natural unit of mass equivalent to approximately 21.7647 micrograms.

Planck scale: Planck scale was invented as a set of universal or natural units, so it was a shock when those limits also turned out to be the limits where the known laws of physics applied. For example, a distance smaller than the Planck length just does not make sense—the physics breaks down.

Planck temperature: A natural unit of temperature $\left(T_p = \sqrt{\hbar c^5 / G k_B^2}\right)$ thought to be the upper limit of temperature.

Planck time: A natural unit of time $\left(t_p = \sqrt{\hbar G / c^5}\right)$, defined as the interval that light travels a distance of one Planck length in a vacuum.

Planck units: The natural units of length, mass, temperature, time, and charge that are derived from just five constants in nature including the speed of light and the gravitational constant.

point electrical force: *See* Coulomb's law.

point magnetic force: The attraction or repulsion that arises between electrically charged particles because of their motion. The force between two moving charges may be described as the effect exerted on either charge by a magnetic field created by the other.

Pramāṇa: From Buddhism, Hinduism, and Jainism, means "proof" or "means of knowledge." It is a theory of knowledge, and encompasses one or more reliable and valid means by which human beings gain accurate, true knowledge.

prana: In Hindu philosophy including yoga, Indian medicine, and Indian martial arts, prana permeates reality on all levels, including inanimate objects. Also known as the "life force."

prana flow: The flow of prana in the astral bodies, medians, and chakras.

pranayama: The regulation of the breath through certain techniques and exercises.

precognition: The ability of a human to cognitively be aware of an information event that has not yet occurred in spacetime. This term is generally applied to precognitive dreams or precognitive remote viewing. If the person is unconsciously influenced, it is call presentiment.

presentiment: The ability for the unconscious to tap into future feelings to make decisions in the now. Presentiment "pre-feeling" is defined as an unconscious form of precognition (or "pre-knowing").

presponse: When a response is influenced by something in the future, as is the case with retrocausation or presentiment.

primitive: In science, a primitive is a fundamental item that cannot be broken down into a more basic item.

primitive components: The Standard Model of physics is composed of the accepted seventeen primitive particles/bosons and the twelve antiparticles.

prism: A glass or other transparent object in prism form, especially one that is triangular with refracting surfaces at an acute angle with each other and that separates white light into a spectrum of colors.

probabilistic geometry ball and stick model: When probabilistic distances are represented using sticks and balls (like Tinker Toys) to visualize the geometric structure of those relationships.

probability: The extent to which an event is likely to occur, measured by the ratio of the favorable cases to the total number of possible cases. For example, when producing a pair in a dice throw, this represents 6/36 or probability of 1/6 or 16.66 percent of the throws.

probability amplitudes: The format of complex prefixes for quantum dimensions, that when squared represents a probability.

projection: A mapping of a set (or other structure) into a subset (or substructure). An example of a projection is the casting of shadows of 3D objects onto a flat sheet of paper.

proto: Means more primitive than or preceding the proper beginning of something.

protodimensions: We coined the term to indicate that bits are really primitive dimensions when represented in geometric algebra, thereby preceding the normal 3D dimensions.

protofrequency: We coined the term to indicate that change precedes time; represents preceding any notion of frequency.

protophobic X17 boson: A hypothetical subatomic particle proposed by Attila Krasznahorkay and his Hungarian colleagues to explain certain anomalous measurement results. This may represent a new "fifth" force for the Standard Model. It is called protophobic, since it does not interact with protons.

protophysics: "Proto" means preceding the proper beginning of something, so "protophysics" means preceding physics. We use this term to talk about the quantum states that preceded the Big Bang.

protospace: We coined the term to indicate that something is more primitive than or precedes space, hence protospace. *See* protodimensions.

prototime: We coined the term to indicate that something is more primitive than or precedes time, hence prototime. We believe change is more primitive than time.

psi: Term for supposed parapsychological or psychic faculties or phenomena.

psychoenergetics: The study of the links between the human psyche and mystical forms of energy.

psychokinesis: The ability of a human to move objects without physically touching them.

psychoneuroimmunology: The study of the interaction between psychological processes and the nervous and immune systems of the human body.

Pythagorean metric: In mathematics, the Euclidean distance or Euclidean metric is the "ordinary" straight-line distance between two points in Euclidean space. Older literature refers to the metric as the Pythagorean metric.

Python: A popular, interpreted, high-level, general-purpose programming language created by Guido van Rossum (released in 1991), and whose name was derived from British surreal comedy group.

quantization: The experimental observation by Planck that energy changes occur in discrete steps, as an integer multiple of some minimum size, rather than continuously. This concept has been expanded to embrace all fundamental variables, such as charge, space, time, mass, etc.

quantum bits: *See* qubits.

quantum computing-complete: The quantum version of von Neumann architecture that includes the quantum Turing machine. This term mimics the nomenclature of Turing-complete.

quantum dimensions: To put it simply, dimension is a minimal number of parameters needed to describe the object or space in question. In quantum mechanics, those dimensions are represented as orthogonal vector sets using matrix mathematics or geometric algebra.

quantum entanglement: Where two or more particles in a quantum state continue to be mutually dependent, even when separated by a large distance. Measurements of physical properties, such as position, momentum, spin, and polarization, performed on entangled particles are found to be correlated. *Also see* Bell States,

quantum field theory (QFT): Assumes that all of spacetime is constructed of twenty-five (depending how you count) overlapping quantum fields, one to support each of the primitive particles, including quarks, electrons, neutrinos, and bosons. These fields are described as a grid of little coupled spring oscillators, where simple quantized excitations of each field cause a wave to propagate in that field. For example, a photon is a quantized excitation of the quantum electromagnetic field.

quantum foam: The fluctuation of spacetime on very small scales due to quantum mechanics and uncertainty principle.

quantum gravity: A field of theoretical physics that seeks to describe gravity according to the principles of quantum mechanics, and where quantum effects cannot be ignored.

quantum interferometer device: Any device that exposes the wave nature of the quantum world, such as the double-slit experiment, or the Mach–Zehnder interferometer, which is a device used to determine the relative phase shift variations between two collimated beams derived by splitting light from a single source.

quantum mechanics (QM): The mathematical formalism and paradigm that superseded classical mechanics paradigm to describe the inner working processes of nature but based on quantization rules.

quantum mind: A model that posits that quantum superposition and entanglement may play an important part in the brain's function and could form the basis for an explanation of thought and consciousness. In this book, we distinguish quantum mind with space-like properties as required for real intelligence and are distinct from more traditional quantum brain models.

Quantum Oracle: In modern usage, any good source of information can be called an oracle. The word "oracle" can also be used to describe the utterances of a seer or anyone else who is pretty darn good at predicting the future. Our use of a quantum oracle in this book is that using quantum states outside time, then any answer is knowable.

quantum perspective: A view of the very small at the subatomic/atomic particle size scale where all entities are discrete (quantized) packets and all states look probabilistic and potentially entangled.

quantum probability amplitudes: In quantum mechanics, a probability amplitude is a complex number used in describing the behavior of systems. *Also see* probability amplitudes.

quantum register: A system comprising of multiple qubits. It is the quantum analog of the classical processor register. Quantum computers perform calculations by manipulating qubits within a quantum register.

quantum spin: An intrinsic form of angular momentum carried by elementary particles, composite particles, and atomic nuclei and can be visualized like spinning top. Spin is one of two types of angular momentum in quantum mechanics, the other being orbital angular momentum.

quantum state: The state of an isolated quantum system. A quantum state provides a probability distribution for the value of each observable, i.e. for the outcome of each possible measurement on the system.

quantum superposition: A fundamental property of spin ½ quantum states that can be represented as a phase angle between two orthogonal states. This phase computing gives rise to fundamental probabilistic nature of quantum measurements. Superposition and orthonormal states are the mechanism through which quantum algorithms can outperform classical algorithms.

quantum supremacy: The goal of demonstrating that a programmable quantum device can solve a problem that no classical computer can feasibly solve, which occurs when q>50.

Quantum Turing Machine (QTM): A universal quantum computer that is an abstract machine used to model the effects of a quantum computer. It provides a simple model that captures all of the power of quantum computation—that is, any quantum algorithm can be expressed formally as a particular Quantum Turing Machine.

quarks: A type of elementary particle (fermion) and a fundamental constituent of matter. Quarks combine to form composite particles called hadrons, the most stable of which are protons and neutrons, the main components of atomic nuclei.

quaternions: A number system that extends the complex numbers that was first described by Irish mathematician William Rowan Hamilton in 1843. A feature of quaternions is that multiplication of two quaternions is noncommutative and can be applied to rotational mechanics in 3D space. In GALG, quaternions can be easily expressed with three bivectors.

qubit: A quantum-bit (qubit) is the smallest discrete example of spin ½ quantum superposition due to two orthonormal state vectors.

qutrits: A unit of quantum information that is realized by a quantum system described by a superposition of three mutually orthogonal quantum states. We believe this is the main topology of a photon because this is nilpotent.

R-space: The inverse of spacetime according to Tiller's psychoenergetic science. *See* reciprocal space.

random event generators (REGs): Electronic apparatus that generates random numbers, used as targets in a psi test. A basic form of REG is an electronic coin-tossing machine, generating a series of "heads and tails" outputs.

random mechanical cascade (RMC): Robert Jahn and Brenda Dunne built this apparatus that yielded anomalous results correlated with pre-stated intentions of human operators. Based on a common statistical demonstration device, this machine allows 9,000 polystyrene balls to drop through a matrix of 330 pegs, scattering them into 19 collecting bins with a population distribution that is approximately Gaussian. As the balls enter the bins, exact counts are accumulated photo-electrically, displayed as feedback for the operator, and recorded online.

real intelligence (RI): The terminology used in this book to differentiate the real mechanisms behind human intelligence compared to the current models (neurological and mathematical) used to build artificial intelligence (AI) in machines.

reciprocal frequency: The period or duration of time of a cycle of a wave is the reciprocal (1 divided by) of the frequency. This is one of the coordinate mappings of Tiller's R-space.

reciprocal space (R-space): Defined by Tiller as the reciprocal of all the spacetime coordinates (1/x, 1/y, 1/z, 1/t), thereby defining a frequency domain space.

reference frame (RF): A coordinate system that an observer uses for both qualitatively and quantitatively describing an internally self-consistent explanation for all the manifold expressions of nature. In both the classical mechanics (CM) and present-day quantum mechanics (QM) paradigms, this has been three perpendicular coordinates of distance and one perpendicular coordinate of time (3D+1T) to comprise a 4D coordinate called "spacetime."

REG PK devices: *See* random event generators (REGs).

reiki: A healing technique based on the principle that the therapist can channel energy into the patient by means of touch, to activate the natural healing processes of the patient's body and restore physical and emotional well-being.

relativity: A view of relative motions of objects where the speed of the object is sufficiently high that space and time cannot be treated as independent variables but are intimately coupled, thus forming a spacetime continuum. Several unintuitive consequences include: constant speed of light in all reference frames, different measurements of simultaneity based on velocity, time dilation/space contraction when near light speed, gravitation mass is equivalent to acceleration, rest mass warps spacetime, and mass has an energy equivalence.

religion: A set of beliefs concerning the cause, nature, and purpose of the universe, especially when considered as the creation of a superhuman agency or agencies, usually involving devotional and ritual observances, and often containing a moral code governing the conduct of human affairs.

remote viewing: The ability of a human to cognitively access detailed information concerning a very distant site that may be hundreds to thousands of miles away (or in the future) via other than our visual sensory system. Usually, remote viewing is a formal process for testing the clairvoyant ability using blind targets and blind judging protocols.

retrocausation: The ability to tap into future knowing to change your current decisions.

reverse-order spectrum: When a prism splits light, this is called a Newtonian spectrum, that bends down based on frequency. Using auric vision, some people are also able to see another reverse-order spectrum that bends upward.

reversible: Capable of being reversed so that the previous state or situation is restored. In quantum computing, this is accomplished with the reverse operator of the original operator, all without looking or knowing the original quantum state.

rotes: A term coined by Robert Monroe for the packet of mental impressions received during remote viewing sessions. Rote packets essentially contain submodalities about the target site that must be unpacked without projecting unwanted information about the target rote. This term is synonymous with "thought balls."

sacred science: Our term that states that sacred topics can be studied as a science. We used this term as synonymous with source science.

sages: Someone who has attained wisdom. The term has also been used interchangeably with a "good person" and a "virtuous person."

saints: Persons who are recognized as having an exceptional degree of holiness or likeness or closeness to God.

savant intelligence: The kind of extraordinary intelligence needed to support savant behaviors.

savant syndrome: A condition in which someone with significant mental disabilities demonstrates certain abilities far in excess of average. The skills at which savants excel are generally related to memory.

scalar: A physical quantity that only has magnitude, possibly a sign, and no other characteristics. It does not have a direction, i.e., not a vector.

scalar state: A state that can only be defined using scalars. For a quanta state to be scalar, it has to be a quanta of a scalar field, such as the Higgs field.

scanning: A technique used by healers to scan the energy field of a patient with their hands to find areas of decoherence.

Schrodinger wave equation: A linear partial differential equation that describes the wave function or state function of a quantum-mechanical system. It is a key result in quantum mechanics, and its discovery was a significant landmark in the development of the subject. It uses the concept of energy conservation (Kinetic Energy + Potential Energy = Total Energy) to obtain information about the behavior of states.

scientific method: An empirical method of acquiring knowledge that has characterized the development of science that involves careful observation, applying rigorous skepticism about what is observed, given that cognitive assumptions can distort how one interprets the observation.

scientism: The premise that the promotion of science as the best or only objective means by which society should determine normative and epistemological values. The term "scientism" is generally used critically, implying a cosmetic application of science in unwarranted situations, so is often interpreted as science applied "in excess."

seers: A person who is supposed to be able, through supernatural insight, to see what the future holds.

self-healing: The process of recovery, motivated by and directed by the patient, guided often only by instinct. In fact, all living things have the ability to heal themselves naturally. The placebo effect may be due to the self-healing process. There are documented cases where people have spontaneously healed from stage-four cancer.

self-introspection: The examination of one's own conscious thoughts and feelings. In psychology, the process of introspection relies exclusively on observation of one's mental and emotional states, while in a spiritual context it may refer to the examination of one's soul.

Shannon bits: More commonly known as just a bit with two mutually exclusive states, which is also the entropy of a system with two equally probable states. The information content of either state occurring has the probability of ½.

Shannon information content: A basic quantity derived from the probability of a particular event or state occurring from a random variable.

shared dreams: The experience of having the same dream at the same time as another person. Usually this occurs between people who are emotionally close, such as siblings, close friends, family members, or romantic partners. Shared dreams are also known as "mutual dreams."

Shor-complete: New term for the requirement to support quantum speedup associated with Shor's (or other) quantum algorithm(s).

Shor's algorithm: The first quantum algorithm defined by Peter Shor in 1994 that demonstrated a new quantum complexity class beyond what is possible with any classical computer.

Siddha: A person who has achieved spiritual realization and supernatural powers.

siddhi: Material, paranormal, supernatural, or otherwise magical powers, abilities, and attainments that are the products of yogic advancement through such practices as meditation and yoga.

simulator: A programmable system designed to simulate the particular set of motions or events that reproduce a particular experience or result. An example is a flight simulator.

singular: An expression **X** is singular when is does not have a multiplicative inverse ($\mathbf{X}^{-1}$ does not exist). This occurs for irreversible **X** expressions, since the inverse would reverse the original operator $\mathbf{X}*\mathbf{X}^{-1} = 1$. In matrix expressions, the determinant is 0. *Also see* irreversible.

soul: In many religious, philosophical, and mythological traditions, the soul is the incorporeal essence of a living being. The soul or psyche comprises the mental abilities of a living being: reason, character, feeling, consciousness, memory, perception, thinking, etc.

source: The origin, beginning, or primitive mechanism behind some other set of behaviors or objects.

source science: Our label associated with the study of how humans are special that includes physics, relativity, neural computing, quantum physics, quantum computing, hyperdimensional mathematics, Law of Attraction, real intelligence, prana, and metaphysics. This model assumes hyperdimensional quantum bit protophysics is the source of all "things" and "no-things" in the universe, including space, time, matter, energy, and the meaning in our human minds.

source science age: In a similar analogy to the current "information age," this term applies to the next age when the source science of quantum consciousness is the norm.

source-complete: We define this term as the aggregate of these four types of informational completeness: Turing, quantum computing, Shor, and ebit.

source-like: New term that combines the properties of: space-like, verbnoun-balanced, Turing-complete, Shor-complete, and is ebit-complete.

space conditioning: Here, the meaning extends beyond adjustment of outer thermodynamic intensive variables of space, such as temperature, pressure, chemical concentration, etc., to include inner variables, such as electromagnetic gauge symmetry state, specific intention tuning (a matrix element) of that state, etc.

space-like: Description of region of spacetime that is outside the cone connected by traveling at the speed of light. Essentially these are non-causally connected regions of spacetime. An example is entangled systems.

spacetime: Spacetime is any mathematical model that fuses the three dimensions of space and the one dimension of time into a single 4D manifold. Spacetime diagrams can be used to visualize relativistic effects, such as why different observers perceive where and when events occur differently.

sparse distributed coding: A term associated with Pentti Kanerva's model of neural networks that describes how the random data points in a hyperdimensional model appears to be very far away from other data points.

sparse invariants: GALG expressions $I^{\pm}$ where half the states are 0 and other half are all + or all – so they mimic the mathematical behaviors of $(\pm 1)^2 = 1$, where $(I^{\pm})^2 = I^{+}$. Some examples include $I^{-} = +1 \pm$ **a0^a1^b0^b1** and $I^{+} = -1 \pm$ **a0^a1^b0^b1**, which represent two out-of-phase versions for Bell and Magic operators raised to even powers. These behaviors represent operators that form rings of states, such as $B^2 = I_b^{-}$, $M^2 = I_m^{-}$, $B^4 = I_b^{+}$, and $M^4 = I_m^{+}$, for $B^2 + M^2 = -1$ and $B^4 + M^4 = +1$.

spatial anchoring: A term from NLP, where position or location in space acts like an anchor, in contrast to anchors of visual, auditory, touch, or smell.

special relativity: Einstein's generally accepted and experimentally confirmed physical theory regarding the relationship between space and time, where the Galilean transformations of Newtonian mechanics are replaced with the Lorentz transformations.

spectrum: In optics, description of the rainbow of colors in visible light after passing through a prism.

speed of light: The speed of light in vacuum, commonly denoted as *c*, is a universal physical constant important in many areas of physics. Its exact value is defined as 299,792,458 meters per second. According to Einstein, the speed of light has the same value for all reference frames. This is sometimes called the "speed of causality," since both light and gravity waves propagate at this rate.

spin ½: An intrinsic property of all elementary particles known as fermions. A spin ½ of means that a particle must be fully rotated twice (through 720°) before it has the same configuration as when it started. Spin ½ is related to spinor geometry.

spinorgeometry: Any geometry where an object is invariant under rotations. For example, a qubit is invariant under phase rotations, which is a kind of spin. Generally, a spinor can be visualized as a spinning top or a plane with orientation.

spinors: Elements of a complex vector space that can be associated with Euclidean space. Like geometric vectors and more general tensors, spinors transform linearly when the Euclidean space is subjected to a slight rotation. In geometric algebra, a spinor is a bivector.

spirit: The nonphysical part of a person or animal that is the seat of emotions and character; the soul.

spirited science: An alternative name for source science, where science can be applied to spiritual concepts and behaviors.

standard distance: The average distance measure between any two random points in a high-dimensional space for $N \gg 20$. For a unit cube of N dimensions, the standard distance is $\sqrt{N/6}$. *Also see* standard radius.

Standard Model: In particle physics, a mathematical description of the elementary particles of matter and the electromagnetic, weak, and strong forces by which they interact.

standard radius: The average distance measure between the midpoint and any random point in a high-dimensional space for $N \gg 20$. For a unit cube of N dimensions, the standard radius is $\sqrt{N/12}$. *Also see* standard distance.

state: A particular condition of something at a specific time, even though that state might not be observable, knowable, or describable in some domains.

state count ratios: In our geometric algebra analysis, compute the row-state vector values (–1, 0, or 1), then count the number of each value, and place in sorted list. This list (or tuple) will be the same for all algebraic expressions with the same expressive power.

state of being: The mental state of a being and a quality of your present experience that exists independently of the body; can have an effect locally and nonlocally based on the size and coherence of a person or persons.

state of FSMs: Finite state machines (FSMs) come from a branch of computer science called "automata theory" and describes how the state changes based on inputs, providing the resulting output for the particular FSM algorithm.

state of grace: A feel-good condition of being perceivably connected to grace or God, which is the state described during NDEs. Most of the standard definitions of grace describe a negative, Old Testament perspective but we prefer this positive description.

sterile neutrino: Sterile neutrinos are hypothetical particles that interact only via gravity and do not interact through any of the fundamental interactions of the Standard Model. The term "sterile neutrino" is used to distinguish them from the three known active neutrinos in the Standard Model, which are charged under the weak interaction.

string correlithms: The term used to describe correlithm states that define sequences of events, so are much nearer than standard distance from other states. This is similar to the analogy of stepping stones in a pond.

SU(*n*): In mathematics, the special unitary group of degree n, denoted SU(n), is the group of $n \times n$ unitary matrices with determinant 1. The group operation is that of matrix multiplication. The special unitary group is a subgroup of the unitary group

U(n), consisting of all $n \times n$ unitary matrices. The SU(n) groups find wide application in the Standard Model of particle physics, especially SU(2) in the electroweak interaction and SU(3) in QCD. Also, SU(2) is isomorphic to the unit quaternions and Pauli matrices.

submodalities: A term used by the NLP community that breaks the main four modalities (visual, auditory, kinesthetic, and auditory-digital) into larger sets of specific subattributes (i.e., brightness, loudness, etc.). There are more than one hundred different submodalities in NLP.

subtle domains: Potential cognitive domains of the universe beyond the domain of physical cognition by humans or present physical instruments. Some humans presently sense these domains, most do not. Here, they have been labeled etheric, astral, emotional, mind, spirit, and divine.

subtle energies: All vibrations existing in the universe beyond the four known to and accepted by present-day science. There may be more to be discovered at the physical level and there are certainly be many more to be discovered in the subtle domain levels beyond the physical band of consciousness.

succussion: The action of strongly shaking or jolting a fluid. This step is required when preparing homeopathic remedies.

sudden savants: *See* instant savants.

super-operator: A term we use here for composition of two or more reversible operators into a single operator that has the same effect as the sequence of the other operators, but in one step.

superconductivity: The set of physical properties observed in certain materials wherein electrical resistance vanishes and from which magnetic flux fields are expelled.

superheart: The state of expanded heart chakras and positive emotions that switches the person to a zone state. *Also see* supermind.

superluminal states: A state wherein moieties (consistency mechanism) appear to travel faster than light in a physical vacuum. This term has been applied to apparent faster-than-light state exchange associated with entangled states.

supermind: This term applies to the state where the person has stepped outside time and appears much smarter and more intuitive than when inside time. Specifically, supermind is the result of dialing in and accessing any amount of computing resources just by letting go of spacetime, thereby switching from sequential computing to arbitrary amounts of concurrent meaning, space-like awareness, and quantum computing.

superposition: In quantum computing, a system may be in one of many configurations—arrangements of particles or fields. The most general state is a combination of all of these possibilities, where the amount in each configuration is specified by a complex number. A qubit contains the superposition of two states, which can be expressed as a phase angle.

superposition of states: *See* superposition.

superposition properties: *See* superposition.

supersymmetry properties: The observed properties that are accessed when a conditioned space is created with unusual properties and nonlocal effects.

symmetry: An operation that one can perform (at least conceptually) on a system that leaves the system invariant. For example, rotating a ball is a symmetric operation.

synaptic gap: When a nerve impulse reaches the synapse at the end of a neuron, it cannot pass directly to the next one. Instead, it triggers the neuron to release a chemical neurotransmitter. The neurotransmitter drifts across this synaptic gap between the two neurons.

synesthesia: A perceptual phenomenon in which stimulation of one sensory or cognitive pathway leads to involuntary experiences in a second sensory or cognitive pathway. For example, some people may see colors when listening to music, or view numbers as colored objects.

tau neutrino: The third generation of the neutrino and the last of the leptons to be discovered, and the second most recent particle of the Standard Model to be discovered (in 2000).

tauquernions: Term invented by Mike Manthey that represents a 4D version of the quaternions, with exactly the same 3D group properties. Tauquernions are the sum of three Bell states (sum of six bivectors), so represent an entangled version of the quaternions. *Also see* tauquinions.

tauquinions: Term invented by Mike Manthey that represents a 5D version of the quaternions, with exactly the same 3D group properties. Tauquinions are the sum of three pairs (a bivector and trivector), so represent an entangled version of the quaternions. *Also see* tauquernions.

telekinesis: A psychic ability allowing a person to influence a physical system without physical interaction. *See also* Descartes assumption.

teleological thinking: The historical perspective where a reason or explanation for something as a function of its end, purpose, or goal.

telepathy: Transmission of thought-based meaning from one person to another without using any known human sensory channels or physical interaction. Telepathy is real and is used as part of the business models of several companies.

Ten Commandments: A set of biblical principles relating to ethics and worship, which play a fundamental role in the Abrahamic and Christian religions.

tetrahedron: Also known as a triangular pyramid, a polyhedron composed of four triangular faces, six straight edges, and four vertex corners. The tetrahedron is the simplest of all the ordinary convex polyhedra and the only one that has fewer than five faces.

The Creation: The term used by many cultures to describe the beginning of the universe. *Also see* Big Bang.

"the singularity": Use to describe a discontinuity that started something. For example, many people presume there existed a singularity that started the Big Bang. Also used in computer science as a theoretical future point of unprecedented technological progress, caused in part by the ability of machines to rapidly learn using artificial intelligence. For example, Skynet in the Terminator movies was a technological singularity.

thermistor: An electrical device for measuring temperature via the accurate measurement of electrical resistance of a particular material (e.g., silicon).

thermodynamic free energy: A quality of substance that defines its potential for doing work. This quality includes both energy and entropy contributions and their dependence on the thermodynamic intensive variables of temperature, pressure, concentration of chemical species, etc.

thinkism: A belief that using current computer technology and design it is possible to build an AI that is "smarter than humans," and then all of sudden the new AI thinks hard and invents another AI "smarter than itself," which thinks harder and invents one even smarter, until it explodes in AI power, becoming almost godlike. We have no evidence that merely thinking about intelligence is enough to create new levels of intelligence. Kevin Kelly defined this term.

thought balls: *See* rotes.

thought vectors: A collection of orthonormal bit-vectors that represent a point (or correlithm) in a hyperdimensional space synonymous with the meaning of that thought. This representation is isotropic and can grow to any complexity, since it is formed by protodimensional bits that are embedded in spacetime and do not use energy.

time crystals: A structure that repeats in time, as well as in space. Normal 3D crystals have a repeating pattern in space, but remain unchanged as time passes. Time crystals repeat themselves in time as well, leading the crystal to change from moment to moment without using energy.

time-like: Description of region of spacetime that is inside the cone connected by traveling at the speed of light. Essentially, these are regions that are casually connected by particles traveling slower than the speed of light. An example of this is all classical computations.

timeline therapy: A set of techniques (from NLP and Hawaiian Huna) that assist individuals and business people to release unresolved emotions and limiting decisions from the past, as well as all types of phobias, anxieties, and depression. *Also see* Inspec.

Toffoli gates: A universal quantum logic gate that is reversible, invented by Tom Toffoli in 1980. Also known as the "controlled-controlled-not" gate, and has 3-bit inputs and outputs, where if the first two bits are both set to 1, it inverts the third bit, otherwise all bits stay the same.

Topsy system: A programming environment created by Mike Manthey using a distributed computational model of distributed systems called the "phase web" that represents a model that explicitly connects computation to a discrete geometric algebra, wherein the recursive nature of objects and boundaries becomes apparent and itself subject to hierarchical recursion.

Totemic Spirit Beings: Aboriginal spirituality where their totems are believed to be the descendants of the Dreamtime heroes, or totemic beings. Dreamtime heroes are linked to space and place and knowledge through time.

transcendable: To transcend is exceed or to go past defined limits, so means can transcend some previous set of limits (like OBEs and NDEs), or beyond presumed laws (like telepathy and PK).

transcendent: Existing apart from and not subject to the limitations of the material universe, so is beyond the range of normal human experience.

Transcendental Meditation (TM): A form of silent mantra meditation, developed by Maharishi Mahesh Yogi. The meditation practice involves the use of a mantra and is practiced for twenty minutes twice per day while sitting with one's eyes closed.

transitory: Something that is not permanent.

trivector: A 3D volumetric object with right-hand orientation formed by taking the outer product of three orthonormal vectors. *See* vector and bivector.

truth tables: A mathematical table used in logic—specifically in connection with Boolean algebra, Boolean functions, and propositional calculus—which produces the functional output values of logical expressions on each of their functional arguments, that is, for each combination of values taken by their logical input variables.

tuple: A finite ordered list of elements usually denoted inside parenthesizes. An *n*-tuple is a sequence of *n* elements, where *n* is a non-negative integer.

Turing machine: A mathematical model of computation that defines an abstract machine, which manipulates symbols on a strip of tape according to a table of rules. Despite the model's simplicity, given any computer algorithm, a Turing machine capable of simulating that algorithm's logic can be constructed.

Turing test: A test proposed by Alan Turing in 1950, of a machine's ability to exhibit intelligent behavior equivalent to, or indistinguishable from, that of a human.

Turing-complete: In computability theory, signifies that an abstract computing system is able to run any algorithm and is called a "universal computer." All modern computer systems are Turing-complete, and quantum computers can perform universal logic gates and so are also Turing-complete. It is not clear whether there exists (except the universe itself) a universal quantum computer that can run any quantum algorithm.

U(1): The group U(1) corresponds to the circle group of radius 1, consisting of all complex numbers with absolute value 1 under multiplication. All the unitary groups contain copies of this group.

unanswerables: Buddhism applied this term to represent questions that we should not expect to find answers, so Buddha refused to attempt to answer them.

uncertainty: Refers to epistemic situations involving imperfect or unknown information. It applies to predictions of future events, to physical measurements that are already made, or to the unknown. Shannon proposed that information reduces uncertainty and therefore reduces entropy.

unified field theory: A type of field theory that allows all that is usually thought of as fundamental forces and elementary particles to be written in terms of physical and virtual fields.

unitary: For some operators, there exists an inverse operator (or conjugate transpose) such that their product is 1 (or the unitary matrix *I* with 1s along the diagonal). This is true for Hilbert spaces and geometric algebras. In geometric algebra, expressions represent particles, where the square is unitary or (**P*P** = 1) and also for sparse invariants $(I^{\pm})^2 = I^{+}$.

Universal Laws: According to Tania Kotsos, there are seven Universal Laws by which everything in the universe is governed, which he derived from two sources: The 1923 book *The Science of Being* and the 1908 Hermetics book *The Kybalion*. Abraham also states that the Law of Attraction is a Universal Law. The Standard Model of physics is considered a Universal Law.

universal logic: Any logic operation that can mimic any other logic gate by combining multiple copies of that element. For example, NAND, NOR, and XNOR are universal logic operators, and Toffoli and Fredkin gates are also universal quantum logic gates.

universal mind: A metaphysical concept suggesting that consciousness is an underlying essence of all being and becoming in the universe.

Universal Turing Machine: A Turing machine that simulates an arbitrary Turing machine on arbitrary input. The universal machine essentially achieves this by reading both the description of the machine to be simulated as well as the input to that machine from its own tape. *See* Turing machine.

utopian: An imagined community or society that possesses highly desirable or nearly perfect qualities for its citizens.

vector: A 1D line object with up/down orientation formed by a coefficient and single orthonormal vector. *See* bivector and trivector.

verbnoun: A compound word that describes something with both verb (i.e. actions) and noun (i.e. things) properties. Examples include geometric algebra expressions and correlithms since they can represent both an operator (verby) and a state (nouny). *See* verbnoun balanced.

verbnoun-balanced: Describes the balance of "things" (i.e., nouns) and "actions" (i.e., verbs) as applied to quantum and neural computing to mimic the von Neumann architecture. Geometric algebra and correlithms both have verbnoun balanced representations because they can be used are as both states and actions. This convention is independent of reversible vs. irreversible operators.

vibrational complexity of being: The terminology used to describe how our spiritual selves are vibrational beings and our ability to interact with world is based on the complexity of that form. Building our personal complexity allows us to deal with our life in a coherent manner.

vibrations: This term is preferred over the term "frequency," when talking about a nonmetric space.

vibratory modes: When talking about the complexity and structure of non-metric bits, the term modes represents the loops, knots, and nodes without relying on frequency concepts. Similar to terminology used in knot theory and string theory.

virtual-reality: A simulated experience that can be similar to or completely different from the real world. Applications of virtual reality can include entertainment and educational purposes. Other, distinct types of VR style technology include augmented reality and mixed reality.

von Neumann architecture: An architecture proposed by John von Neumann, where a computer memory can store both data and programs, so it is possible to write programs that can modify themselves. Most modern computers utilize a von Neumann architecture.

vortex: A spiral pattern of dynamics usually associated with fluids (tornado and whirlpools). The LOA community uses this term regarding chakras and thought forms due to spinning dynamics.

walk-ins: A New Age concept of a person whose original soul has departed his or her body and has been voluntarily replaced with a new, generally more advanced, soul.

wave: A disturbance of one or more fields such that the field values oscillate repeatedly about a stable equilibrium value (usually 0). A sine wave is the simplest single-frequency wave.

wave-particle duality: The concept in quantum mechanics that every particle or quantum entity may be partly described in terms not only of particles, but also of waves. It expresses the inability of the classical concepts "particle" or "wave" to fully describe the behavior of quantum-scale objects.

wavelength: The spatial period of a periodic wave—the distance over which the wave's shape repeats.

X17 boson: The term used by recent announcement about new boson (i.e., fifth force and dubbed as X17 for 17 mega-electron-volts) detected by Hungarian scientists.

XNOR dominated: Any logic that is oriented around sameness or changes is dominated by XNOR-style logic.

XNOR logic: The exclusive-NOR implements logical equality; the XNOR of a set of two operands is true if, and only if, the inputs are the same.

yogis: A practitioner of yoga, including a practitioner of meditation in Indian religions. The feminine form, sometimes used in English, is yogini.

zero-point energy (ZPE): The difference between the lowest possible energy that a quantum mechanical system may have, and the classical minimum energy of the system. Quantum systems constantly fluctuate in their lowest energy state due to the Heisenberg uncertainty principle, and the empty space of the vacuum has these properties.

zone: "In the zone" is a mental state of focused concentration on the performance of an activity, in which one dissociates oneself from distracting or irrelevant aspects of one's environment.

Similar to the “flow state,” this is a state of heightened focus and blissful immersion.

Z/W bosons: Together known as the weak or as the intermediate vector bosons. These elementary particles mediate the weak interaction.

Endnotes

Section 1

Chapter 1

1 Center for Consciousness Studies (S. Hameroff, Center for Consciousness Studies Mission Statement 1994-2019)
2 Psychoenergetic Science website (W. A. Tiller, Tiller Institute for Psychoenergetic Science 2017-2019)
3 Overview (Wikipedia, New Age 2001-2019)
4 (Matzke, Proto-physics the link between Quantum Physics and Metaphysics 2011)
5 Tucson I (Hameroff, Kaszniak and Scott 1992)
6 First use of term "bit" for "binary digit" (Shannon 1948)
7 (Wikipedia, Simulation Hypothesis 2007-2019)
8 Information Is Physical (Landauer 1961)
9 Landauer Limit Demonstrated (S. K. Moore 2012)
10 Black Holes and Entropy (Bekenstein 1973)
11 It from Bit (Wheeler 1989) and see online http://cqi.inf.usi.ch/qic/wheeler.pdf
12 Discussion on "It from Bit" (Thomas 2015)
13 Original $E=mc^2$ paper (A. Einstein 1905), and also see the English translation.
14 Information Is Physical (Landauer 1961)
15 First use of term "qubit" (Schumacher 1995)
16 Original EPR paper (Einstein, Podolsky and Rosen 1935)
17 PhD dissertation (Matzke, Quantum Computation using Geometric Algebra 2002) and link Quantum Computation using Geometric Algebra
18 Universe Is Simulator (Lloyd 2006). Also Simulation Hypothesis at (Wikipedia, Simulation Hypothesis 2007-2019) and another modern paper here on Universe as Quantum Computer (Churikova 2015)

19 Shor's Algorithm (Shor 1994)
20 (Matzke, Proto-physics the link between Quantum Physics and Metaphysics 2011)
21 PhysComp96 paper (Matzke, Information is Protophysical 1996) in proceedings (Toffoli, Biafore and Leao 1996)
22 Consciousness and the double-slit experiments (Radin, Michel, et al. 2013)
23 Thoughts are Things (Mulford 1989)
24 Law of Attraction Talk (Matzke, Thoughts are Quantum Things 2011)
25 Why Quarks are Unobservable (Fox 2009)
26 Double-slit experiments (Radin, Michel, et al. 2013)
27 Definition (Wikipedia, Scientism 2002-2019)
28 Definition (Wikipedia, Scientific Method 2001-2019)

Chapter 2

1 (Wikipedia, Artificial general intelligence 2004-2019)
2 Book (Radin, Supernormal 2013)
3 Rene Descartes (Descartes 1600) summary found here http://www.iep.utm.edu/desc-sci/
4 Descartes assumption (W. A. Tiller, White Paper #XXIX 2015)
5 Descartes assumption (W. A. Tiller, White Paper #XXIX 2015)
6 Early engineering influence by (R. G. Jahn, The persistent paradox of psychic phenomena 1982)
7 SMU Technical Report (Matzke and Howard, A Review of Psychical Reasearch 1985)
8 SMU Technical Report (Matzke and Howard, Computational Resources for the Human Abstraction 1986)
9 Tucson I Consciousness paper (Matzke, Tucson I 1994)
10 Intention Host Device (Tiller and Dibble, New experimental evidence revealing an unexpected dimension to material science and engineering? 2001) plus books (Tiller, Dibble and Kohane, Conscious Acts of Creation: The Emergence of a New Physics 2001), (Tiller, Dibble and Fandel, Some Science Adventures with Real Magic 2005), (W. A. Tiller, Psychoenergetic Science: A Second Copernican-Scale Revolution 2007) and (W. A. Tiller, Science and Human Transformation: Subtle Energies, Intentionality and Consciousness 2007)
11 Physics behind random numbers (Wikipedia, Random Number Generation 2005-2019)
12 Radioactive decay PK (Schmidt 1987) and pages 64-67 (Braude 1979, 2002)

13 Pear Mechanical Cascade, see other machines at (Jahn, Dunne and Nelson, Princeton Engineering Anomalies Research (PEAR) 1979-2007)
14 Pear REG, see random Event Generator at (Jahn, Dunne and Nelson, Princeton Engineering Anomalies Research (PEAR) 1979-2007)
15 Pear Field REG, see FieldREG at (Jahn, Dunne and Nelson, Princeton Engineering Anomalies Research (PEAR) 1979-2007)
16 Psyleron PK Company (Pear Labs 2005)
17 Random Number Generator study (Radin, Mason and Petterson, Exploratory Study: The Random Number Generator and Group Meditation 2007)
18 Consciousness and the double-slit experiments (Radin, Michel, et al. 2013)
19 Gas Discharge Paper (W. A. Tiller, Gas Discharge 1990)
20 Intention Host Device (Tiller and Dibble, Intention Host Device with Water pH 1999)
21 Heart Math DNA (McCraty, Atkinson and Tomasino 2003)
22 Remote Staring (Sheldrake, Remote Staring 2001)
23 ISSSEEM Copper Wall (Green, et al. 1991)
24 Psychoneuroimmunology (Hodgson 1987-2019)
25 Intercessory Prayer (Dossey 1997)
26 Maharishi Effect (Orme-Johnson 2003)
27 Tucson II paper (Matzke, Prediction: Future electronic systems will be disrupted due to consciousness 1996)
28 (McTaggart, The Intention Experiment 2007)
29 Double-slit (Radin, Michel, et al. 2013)
30 Double-slit history (Davisson and Germer 1928) and (Wikipedia, Double-slit Experiment 2001-2019)
31 Doug Matzke built a custom semiconductor to test resonant tunneling diode current influence by mind (unpublished)
32 Neural Quantum proposals (Georgiev 2006)
33 Microtubules (S. Hameroff, Quantum coherence in microtubules: A neural basis for emergent consciousness? 1994)
34 Pyramidal Cells (Wikipedia, Pyramidal cell 2004-2019)
35 (Wikipedia, Mind-body dualism 2001-2019)
36 Myth of AI (Natale and Ballatore 2017)
37 Doug worked on Lisp Chip at Texas Instruments (Bosshart, et al. 1987)
38 (Wikipedia, Lisp machines 2001-2019)
39 Moore's Law (G. E. Moore 1965)

40 Thinkism: The Myth of a Superhuman AI (Kelly 2017)
41 IBM Deep Blue (Wikipedia, Deep Blue versus Garry Kasparov 1997)
42 AlphaGo (Wikipedia, AlphaGo 2016)
43 Google Translate Overview (Sommerlad 2018)
44 Watson wins Jeopardy (Gabbatt 2011)
45 (Wikipedia, Deep Learning 2001-2019)
46 Critique of General Artificial Intelligence (Dreyfus 1965-2003)
47 Singularity (Kurweil 1999)
48 End of Moore's Law (Fritze, et al. 2016); Next after End of Moore's Law (Bentley 2018)
49 IEEE CS Presentation (Matzke, Update on Physical Scalability Sabotaging Performance Gains! 2011)
50 Google Tensor Processing Unit announcement (Lynley 2018)
51 Quantum Computing replacing classical computing (Matzke, Is Quantum Computing a Solution for Semiconductor Scaling? 2007)
52 Biological Quantum Computers (Matzke, Premise: Humans are Biological Quantum Computers 2005)
53 Interview with Suzy Miller (Miller and Sedgbeer, Suzy Miller – The Truth About Telepathy, Autism, & Evolution 2019)
54 Mind Reach (Targ and Puthoff 1977)
55 (Wikipedia, Stargate Project 2003-2019)
56 Precognitive Dreams (Ketler 2019) and (Wikipedia, Stanley Krippner 2006-2019)
57 Precognitive Remote Viewing (Jahn and Dunne 1995) and (Jahn, Dunne and Nelson, Engineering Anomalies Research 1987)
58 Presentiment (Radin, Presentiment 2004)
59 Global Consciousness Project (Jahn, Dunne and Nelson, Global Consciousness Project 1998-2014)
60 Retrocognition (Bem 2011)
61 Occam's razor (Wikipedia, Occam's razor 2001-2019)
62 Bit Bang (Manthey and Matzke, Information, Entropy, and the Combinatorial Hierarchy: Calculations 2014)
63 Quantum Mechanics (Wikipedia, History of quantum mechanics 2007-2019)
64 Turing Complete (Wikipedia, Turing completeness 2001-2019)
65 Quantum Computing is Turing Complete (Matzke, Quantum Computation using Geometric Algebra 2002)
66 Quantum Polynomial Time Algorithms (Shor 1994)
67 Time-like, light-like and space-like (Wikipedia, Spacetime Light Cone 2001-2019)

68 Holography (Wikipedia, Holography (2001-2019)) and Living in a Hologram? (Sutter 2018)
69 (Wikipedia, Projection (mathematics) 2001-2019)
70 (Wikipedia, von Neumann Architecture 2001-2019)
71 The Field (McTaggart, The Field: The Quest for the Secret Force of the Universe 2002,2008)
72 (Wikipedia, Fields (physics) 2001-2019)
73 Acceleration effects on Entanglement (Martin-Martinez, Garay and Leon 2010) and (Dragonfall and atyy 2015)
74 (Wikipedia, Prana 2001-2019)
75 Prana detected after moving. Personal communication with Doug and Gareth
76 Phantom DNA (HeartMath, Phantom DNA 1993)
77 (Targ and Puthoff 1977)
78 LIGO Press Release (LIGO 2016)
79 QFT (Wikipedia, QFT 2001-2019)
80 (Wikipedia, Measurement in quantum mechanics 2001-2019)
81 (Wikipedia, Quantum decoherence 2001-2019)
82 (Wikipedia, Quantum nonlocality 2001-2019)
83 (Wikipedia, Faster than light 2001-2019)
84 Bill coined the term "Subtle Energy" (W. A. Tiller, What Are Subtle Energies? 1993)
85 Reciprocal Spaces (W. A. Tiller, White Paper XX 2009)
86 (W. A. Tiller, Science and Human Transformation: Subtle Energies, Intentionality and Consciousness 2007)
87 (W. A. Tiller, Towards a Quantitative Science and Technology thtat includes Human Consciousness 2003)
88 (Wikipedia, Prism 2001-2019)
89 (Manthey and Matzke, TauQuernions: 3+1 Dissipative Space out of Quantum Mechanics 2013)
90 Video on GALG of Standard Model (Matzke, The Higgs and the Pervasive Nature of Quantum Entanglement (Video) 2013)
91 (Manthey and Matzke, TauQuernions: 3+1 Dissipative Space out of Quantum Mechanics 2013)
92 (Wikipedia, Mathematical formulation of the Standard Model 2001-2019)
93 Correlithms (P. N. Lawrence 2004)
94 Sparse Distributed Memory (Kanerva 1988)
95 Correlithms (P. N. Lawrence 2004)

96 (Hawkins and el, Biological and Machine Intelligence (BAMI) 2016) and video (J. Hawkins, What is Intelligence, that a Machine Might have Some? 2016)
97 HTM (J. Hawkins, Hierarchical Temporal Memory: Overview 2016-2019)
98 (J. Hawkins, Sparse Distributed Representation 2016-2019)
99 Co-Exclusion (Manthey, Distributed Computation, the Twisted Isomorphism, and Auto-Poiesis 1998)
100 (Matzke, Manthey and Cantrell, Quantum Geometric Algebra 2002)
101 (Wikipedia, Gravitational time dilation 2001-2019)
102 Co-occurrence (Manthey, Distributed Computation, the Twisted Isomorphism, and Auto-Poiesis 1998)
103 Where the attention goes the prana flows (Seppala 2014)
104 Aka Cords (Waterman 2009)
105 Autistics as Orbs (Losey 2006)
106 (Miller, Awesomism 2014-2019)
107 Journeys Out of the Body book (Monroe, Journeys Out of the Body 1971)
108 (Wikipedia, Stuart Hameroff 2001-2019)
109 The Hidden Messages in Water (Emoto 2005)
110 Shared Dreams (Shafton 1995)
111 Rotes and remote viewing (McMoneagle 1993)
112 Orbs (Losey 2006)
113 (Monroe, Far Journeys 1992) and (Monroe, Ultimate Journey 1994)
114 Proof of Heaven (Alexander 2012) and Dying to be Me (Moorjani 2014)
115 Animal Telepathy (Spagna 2016)
116 (Hicks and Hicks, Ask and It is Given 2004)
117 Life Before Life (Tucker 2005)
118 Retrocausation (Graff and Cyrus 2017)
119 Stargate project (Wikipedia, Stargate Project 2003-2019)
120 Remote Viewing Conferences (IRVA 2019)
121 Light Language (Miller, The Journey Back to Love 2019)
122 Personal Communications from Doug
123 Personal Communications from Doug
124 (Ziesenis 2019)
125 Personal Story with Randy
126 ANPA 24 (Matzke, Chi Generators Exist 2002)
127 (Wikipedia, Homeopathic Dilutions 2001-2019)
128 Next Information Age (Matzke, Quantum Doug 2004)

Chapter 3

1 Four PhysComp Workshops (Fredkin, Landauer and Toffoli 1981), (Matzke, PhysComp 92 1992) and (Matzke, PhysComp 94 1994) and (Toffoli, Biafore and Leao 1996)
2 Page 163 in Vol 21, Nos 3/4 (Fredkin, Landauer and Toffoli 1981),
3 (Wikipedia, Universe 2001-2019)
4 (Wikipedia, Penrose–Hawking singularity theorems 2001-2019)
5 Matzke attended this lecture but do not have exact date or year.
6 Short version of Ph.D. Dissertation (Matzke, Manthey and Cantrell, Quantum Geometric Algebra 2002)
7 PhD dissertation (Matzke, Quantum Computation using Geometric Algebra 2002)
8 (Wikipedia, Complex number 2001-2019)
9 Geometric Algebra (Doran 2003)
10 The Python GALG package is available on request from Matzke.
11 Related to ANPA philosophy (ANPA Proceedings 1979-2019)
12 Ph.D. (Matzke, Quantum Computation using Geometric Algebra 2002)
13 (Manthey and Matzke, TauQuernions: 3+1 Dissipative Space out of Quantum Mechanics 2013)
14 (Wikipedia, Mathematical formulation of the Standard Model 2001-2019)
15 (Wikipedia, Truly neutral particle 2001-2019)
16 Manthey and Matzke research (Matzke, The Higgs and the Pervasive Nature of Quantum Entanglement (Slides) 2013)
17 Video of IEEE-CS Talk (Matzke, The Higgs and the Pervasive Nature of Quantum Entanglement (Video) 2013)
18 Discovery of Protophobic X boson (Krasznahorkay, et al. 2016)
19 Sterile Neutrino (Chicago 2019)
20 Pentaquark (Wikipedia, Pentaquark 2015)
21 (Wikipedia, Physics beyond the Standard Model 2001-2019)
22 Periodic Table (Mendeleev 1869)
23 Occult Chemistry (Besant and Leadbeater 1919) is available for free download on web
24 (Wikipedia, History of subatomic physics 2001-2019)
25 Theosophical Society Founder (Wikipedia, Helena Blavatsky 2001-2019)
26 Gravitation and Planck Length (Mead 1964)
27 (Wikipedia, Planck time 2001-2019)
28 (Matzke, PhysComp 94 Paper 1994)

29 CAMs (Kanerva 1988)
30 Correlithms (P. N. Lawrence 2004)
31 (Wikipedia, Spacetime Light Cone 2001-2019)
32 (Wikipedia, Faster than light 2001-2019)
33 Coin Demo page 8 (Manthey, Distributed Computation, the Twisted Isomorphism, and Auto-Poiesis 1998)
34 ANPA 2018 Paper (Manthey, Awareness Lies Outside Turing's Box 2018)
35 Beyond Algorithms (Penrose 2011)
36 (Wikipedia, Karnaugh map 2001-2019)
37 Fourth Neutrino Oscillations (Kopp 2018)
38 ANPA 2018 Paper (Manthey, Awareness Lies Outside Turing's Box 2018)
39 Free Will Crash Course Video (H. Green 2016)
40 (Wikipedia, Turing machine 2001-2019)
41 (Manthey, Topsy 1998)
42 Time Crystals (Zhang, et al. 2017)
43 (Wikipedia, Fourier transform 2001-2019)
44 (Wikipedia, Parseval's identity 2001-2019)
45 (Wikipedia, Planck units 2001-2019)
46 Planck Length (Hologrammata 2017)
47 Relativity from Planck Units (J. Johnson 2017)
48 Entanglement and Spacetime (Houser 2018)
49 Bubble-up hierarchy (Manthey, Topsy 1998)
50 Bubble-up hierarchy (Manthey, Topsy 1998)
51 On the Experience of Time (Orstein 1969)

Chapter 4

1 (Hicks, The Law of Attraction 2006)
2 Think and Grow Rich (Hill 1937)
3 You Can Heal Your Life (Hayes 1984)
4 LOA Website (Hicks and Hicks, Law of attraction Books 1980-2019)
5 (Hicks, About Abraham 2019)
6 (Byrne, The Secret (film) 2006)
7 (Byrne, The Secret (book) 2006)
8 The Secret on Oprah (Byrne, Discovering the Secret 2006)
9 Correlithms (P. N. Lawrence 2004)
10 The Matrix Videos (Reeves, Fishburne and Moss 1999)
11 Spooky Action at a Distance (Musser 2015)
12 The Teachings of Don Juan (Castaneda 1968)

13 (Matzke and Lawrence, Quantum Correlithms 2005)
14 (Wikipedia, Neuro-linguistic programming 2001-2019)
15 NLP book (Bandler and Grinder 1979)
16 NLP Master Practitioner Dec 2010
17 Time Line Therapy (James and Woodsmall 1988)
18 Fast Phobia Cure Video (Beale, Fast Phobia Cure 2017)
19 (Beale, NLP Senses and Submodalities 2017)
20 String Correlithms (P. N. Lawrence 2004)
21 Born on a Blue Day (Tammet 2007)
22 (Wikipedia, Savant syndrome 2001-2019)
23 Instant Savant (D. A. Treffert 2018)
24 Sudden Savant (D. Treffert 2010-2019)
25 See with your Tongue (Kendrick 2009)
26 Phase Invariant Quantum Correlithms (Matzke and Lawrence, Quantum Correlithms 2005)
27 Quantum Correlithm Patent (Lawrence, et al. 2007)
28 See details of Quantum Correlithms (Matzke, Math Over Mind And Matter 2013)
29 Double Helix structure of DNA (Wikipedia, List of dreams 2001-2019)
30 (Wikipedia, Akashic records 2001-2019)
31 (Matzke, The Really Hard Problem of Meaning (abstract only) 2000)
32 The Seven Universal Laws Explained (Kotsos 2011)
33 (Matzke, Thoughts are Quantum Things 2011)

Chapter 5

1 Page 114 (Hicks and Hicks, Ask and It is Given 2004)
2 Feeling vs Emotions (Hampton 2015)
3 Anchoring (Dilts 2019)
4 Psychoneuroimmunology and cancer (Green McDonald, O'Connell and Lutgendorf 2013)
5 (Castaneda 1968)
6 Personal communication of Doug with attendee of ISSEEEM conference
7 (HeartMath, About HeartMath 2019)
8 (HeartMath, HeartMath Mission statement 2019)
9 (HeartMath, HeartMath Videos 2019)
10 Book on Forest Bathing (Li 2018)
11 Maharishi Effect (Wikipedia, Transcendental Meditation 2001-2019) and research (TM 2007-2010)

Chapter 6

1 Men and Intimacy (Smalley 2019)
2 The Real Matrix (Valerian 1988-2019)
3 (Wikipedia, Anima and animus 2001-2019)
4 (Wikipedia, Jungian archetypes 2001-2019)
5 New Science of Life (Sheldrake, Morphic Resonance 1981)
6 (Sheldrake, Morphic Resonance and Morphic Fields – an Introduction 2019)
7 (McCraty, Atkinson and Tomasino 2003)
8 (HeartMath, Phantom DNA 1993)

Chapter 7

1 (Wikipedia, Chakras 2001-2019)
2 (Earthing.com 2019)
3 (Wikipedia, Etheric body 2001-2019)
4 Alex Gray Art (Grey 2019)
5 Kundalini Awakening Resources (Aliff 2019)

Section II

Chapter 8

1 (Monroe, Journeys Out of the Body 1971)
2 See refs for Green 1968, Poynton 1975, Blackmore 1982, 1983, 1984, Irwin 1988, and Glicksohn 1989 in (LaBerge and Levitan, Out-Of-Body Experiences and Lucid Dreams 1991)
3 See section 'Non-Physical Experience is Statistically Common Place' (Valerian 1988-2019)
4 (LaBerge and Rhiengold, Exploring the World of Lucid Dreaming 1990)
5 Beyond Biofeedback (E. Green 1978)
6 HP Announces the Memristor in 2008 (Wikipedia, Memristor 2007-2019)
7 Memristor for Neuromorphic AI (Burt 2017)
8 (Matzke, Prediction: Future electronic systems will be disrupted due to consciousness 1996)
9 (Wikipedia, Ingo Swan (see link to Magnetometer psychokinesis tests) 1972)
10 Buddha Relics (Tiller, Tiller, et al. 2012)
11 Bridging Science and Spirit (Manek 2019)

12 Copper Wall (Green, et al. 1991)
13 Quantum Correlithms (Matzke and Lawrence, Quantum Correlithms 2005)
14 Doug implemented CSP in DROID (Kollaritsch, et al. 1989)
15 Real Magic (Radin, Real Magic 2018)

Chapter 9

1 Quantum Supremacy (Villalonga, et al. 2019)
2 (Wikipedia, Curse of dimensionality 2001-2019)
3 Vol I (Bardon, Initiation into Hermetics 1956), Vol II (Bardon, Practice Of Magical Evocation 1956) and Vol III (Bardon, The Key to the True Kabbalah 1996)
4 (Wikipedia, Akashic records 2001-2019)
5 Power vs Force (D. R. Hawkins 1995)
6 (Wikipedia, Deep Blue versus Garry Kasparov 1997)
7 Watson wins at Jeopardy (Gabbatt 2011)
8 (Wikipedia, AlphaGo 2016)
9 Shor's Algorithm (Shor 1994) and Grover's Algorithm (Grover 1996)
10 Google Map Reduce (Dean and Ghemawat 2004)
11 Google buys D-Wave (Google, Google Buys a Quantum Computer 2013)
12 (Google, Google Announces a 72 Qubit Superconducting Quantum Chip 2018)
13 "Intelligence" is Dumb (Worth 2016)
14 Counting Savant of Daniel Tammet (R. Johnson 2005)
15 Death of Moore's Law (Fritze, et al. 2016)
16 Proof of Heaven (Alexander 2012)
17 Dying to be Me (Moorjani 2014)
18 Mind Reach (Targ and Puthoff 1977)
19 The NDE Tunnel (Williams 2016)

Chapter 10

1 Now: the Physics of Time (Muller 2016)
2 Time is what keeps everything from happening at once (Cummings 1921)
3 Datomic Introduction (Hunger 2012)
4 HTM (J. Hawkins, Hierarchical Temporal Memory: Overview 2016-2019)
5 Datomic (Wikipedia, Datomic 2017)
6 Mind Reach (Targ and Puthoff 1977)
7 Inspec (Monroe, Ultimate Journey 1994)

8 Conversing with the Future (Catherine 1998)
9 (Wikipedia, The Magical Number Seven, Plus or Minus Two 1956)
10 Flow (Csikszentmihalyi 2008)
11 Power of Now (Tolle 2004)
12 Legend of Bagger Vance (Damon and Lemmon 2001)
13 Hyperesthesia (R. A. Bandler 1993)
14 Yoga of Time Travel (Wolf 2004)
15 Experiences extended across time (Varey and Kahneman 1992)
16 Levitation pages 171-173 (Radin, Real Magic 2018)
17 Thermophoresis (Fung, et al. 2017)
18 Personal Communication as ISSSEEM Conference
19 (Wikipedia, Dreamtime 2002-2019)
20 Aboriginal Spirituality (Dreamtime 2019)
21 Life review experience (Donnelly 2017)

Chapter 11

1 Personal log of events of Matzke from Week trip at Monroe Institute
2 Time for a Change (R. A. Bandler 1993)
3 (Wikipedia, Kundalini 2001-2019)
4 Kundalini 101 (Whitfield 1995)
5 Kundalini Syndrome (chakras 2019)
6 KRN (Edwards 1990-2019)
7 Physio-Kundalini Syndrome (Greyson 1993)
8 Omega Project (Ring 1993)
9 (Wikipedia, Kundalini 2001-2019)
10 (Wikipedia, Breathwork (New Age) 2005-2019)
11 (Wikipedia, Pranayama 2004-2019)

Section III

Chapter 12

1 The Age of Spiritual Machines (Kurweil 1999)
2 Flash Crash on Wall Street (Salmon and Stokes 2010)
3 (D. R. Hawkins 1995)
4 Suzy Miller website (Miller, how-the-story-of-autism-positively-impacts-everyone 2017)
5 (Matzke, Supercomputer Suggest Supermind 2000)
6 (Wikipedia, Siddhi 2003-2019)
7 Larry Dossey Interview in NY Times (Steinfels 1993)

8 Larry Dossey quote (Dossey 1997)
9 Information Medicine (Manek 2019)
10 (Matzke, Wires stop Scaling 1997)

Chapter 13

1 (Wikipedia, Buddhist logico-epistemology 2001-2019)
2 (Wikipedia, The Secret Doctrine 2001-2019)
3 (Monroe, Ultimate Journey 1994)
4 Existence of Guardian Angels (Jovanovic 1995)
5 Gallup Poll on Existence of God (Newport 2016)
6 14 of the Greatest Religious Leaders in History (Marks 2019); Top 10 Religious Figures and Religious Founders (Danelek 2011)
7 Belief in Power of Prayer (Bohon 2011)
8 Are you a walk in? (Shapiro 2016)
9 Americans and the Afterlife (Weldon 2017)
10 25 percent of US Christians believe in reincarnation (Ryan 2015)
11 Focus 24-26 (Monroe, Journeys Out of the Body 1971)
12 Twelve LOA Principles (Hicks, A Synopsis of Twelve Abraham-Hicks' Teachings 2019)
13 Dying to be Me (Moorjani 2014)

Chapter 14

1 (Wikipedia, Drake equation 2001-2019)
2 (Wikipedia, Fermi paradox 2001-2019)
3 (Larkins, Talking to Extraterrestrials 2002), (Larkins, Calling on Extraterrestrials 2003) (Larkins, Listening to Extraterrestrials 2004),
4 Personal communications with Matzke
5 Quote from Ultimate Journey (Valerian 1988-2019)
6 (Wikipedia, Nostradamus 2001-2019)
7 (Catherine 1998)
8 Matzke's personal conversation
9 Conversing with the Future, see page X (Catherine 1998)
10 Utopia or Dystopia (Searle 2011-2019)
11 Spiritual Beings quote from (de Chardin 1927)

Chapter 15

1 (Palson 2017)

Bibliography

Arrival. DVD. Directed by Denis Villeneuve. Los Angeles: Paramount Pictures, 2016.

Alexander, Eben. *Proof of Heaven: A Neurosurgeon's Journey into the Afterlife.* New York: Simon & Schuster, 2012.

Aliff, Ashey. "Kundalini Awakening Resource." *The Awakened State.* 2019. See https://theawakenedstate.net

ANPA. *Proceedings of the Alternative Natural Philosophy Association.* 1979–2019. http://pub.anpa.onl/index.php/procs/about

Bandler, Richard A. *Time for a Change.* Capitola: Meta-Publications, 1993.

Bandler, Richard, and John Grinder. *Frogs into Princes.* Boulder, CO: Real People Press, 1979.

Bardon, Franz. *Initiation into Hermetics.* Vol. I. 3 vols. Salt Lake City: Merkur Publishing, 1956.

—. *Practice Of Magical Evocation.* Vol. II. 3 vols. Salt Lake City: Merkur Publishing, 1956.

—. *The Key to the True Kabbalah.* Vol. III . 3 vols. Salt Lake City: Merkur Publishing, 1996.

Beale, Michael. "NLP Fast Phobia Cure." May 2017. Accessed at https://www.youtube.com/watch?v=HfYt4s7_64E

—. "NLP Senses and Submodalities." May 2017. Accessed at www.youtube.com/watch?v=Le8Z0gnmgpI

Bekenstein, J. D. "Black Holes and Entropy." *Physical Review Journal* D7 (1973): 2333–2346.

Bem, Daryl. "Feeling the Future: Experimental Evidence for Anomalous Retroactive Influences on Cognition and Affect."

Journal of Personality and Social Psychology 100, no. 3 (2011): 407–425.

Bentley, Peter. "The End of Moore's Law: What Happens Next?" *Science Focus,* 2018. Accessed at www.sciencefocus.com/author/peterbentley/

Besant, Annie, and Charles W. Leadbeater. *Occult Chemistry Clairvoyant Observations on the Chemical Elements.* Edited by A. P. Sinnett. Wheaton, IL: Theosophical Publishing House, 1919.

Bohon, Dave. "Survey Confirms: Americans Believe in Power of Prayer." *thenewamerican.* 2011. Accessed at www.thenewamerican.com/culture/faith-and-morals/item/994-survey-confirms-americans-believe-in-power-of-prayer

Bosshart, Patrick, C. R. Hewes, D. Matzke et el. "A 553K-Transistor LISP Processor Chip." *1987 IEEE International Solid-State Circuits Conference. Digest of Technical Papers,* 202–203. New York: IEEE, 1987.

Braude, Stephen. *ESP and Psychokinesis: A Philosophical Examination.* Irvine, CA: Brown Walker Press, 1979, 2002.

Burt, Jeffrey. "Memristor Research Highlights Neuromorphic Device Future ." *nextplatform.* February 15, 2017. Accessed at www.nextplatform.com/2017/02/15/memristor-research-highlights-neuromorphic-device-future/

Byrne, Rhonda, interview by Oprah. *Discovering the Secret* (2006).

—. *The Secret* (book). 2006.

Castaneda, Carlos. *The Teachings of Don Juan: A Yaqui Way of Knowledge.* New York: Simon & Schuster, 1968.

Catherine, Jenna. *Conversing with the Future: Visions of the Year 2020.* Mill Spring, NC: Wild Flower Press, 1998.

Chicago, University of. "Fermilab Scientists Lead Quest to Find Elusive Fourth Kind of Neutrino." *phys.org.* University of Chicago. January 7, 2019. Accessed at https://phys.org/news/2019-01-fermilab-scientists-quest-elusive-fourth.html

Churikova, Alexandra "Sasha." "Is the Universe Actually a Giant Quantum Computer?" *MIT Creative Writing Website.* 2015.

Accessed at http://cmsw.mit.edu/angles/2015/is-the-universe-actually-a-giant-quantum-computer/

Csikszentmihalyi, Mihaly. *Flow: The Psychology of Optimal Experience.* New York: Harper & Row, 2008.

Cummings, Ray. "The Time Professor." *Argosy All-Story Weekly* 129, no. 3 (January 8, 1921): 371–378.

Danelek, Jeff. "Top 10 Religious Figures and Religious Founders in History ." *toptenz.* October 13, 2011. Accessed at www.toptenz.net/top-10-religious-figures-and-religious-founders-in-history.php

Davisson, Clinton J., and Lester H. Germer. "Reflection of Electrons by a Crystal of Nickel." *Proceedings of the National Academy of Sciences of the United States of America,* 317–322. Washington, DC: National Academy of Sciences, 1928.

de Chardin, Pierre Teilhard. "Quotes of Pierre Teilhard de Chardin." *goodreads.* 1927. Accessed at www.goodreads.com/author/quotes/5387.Pierre_Teilhard_de_Chardin

Dean, Jeffrey, and Sanjay Ghemawat. "MapReduce: Simplified Data Processing on Large Clusters." *Google User Content.* 2004. Accessed at https://static.googleusercontent.com/media/research.google.com/en//archive/mapreduce-osdi04.pdf

Descartes, René. *René Descartes: Scientific Method.* 1600. Accessed at www.iep.utm.edu/desc-sci/

Diamond, John M. *Behavioral Kinesiology.* New York: Harper and Row, 1979.

Dilts, Robert. "Anchoring." *NLP University.* 2019. Accessed at www.nlpu.com/Articles/artic28.htm

Dirac, Paul Adrien Maurice. "Paul Dirac—Discoverer of Antimatter." *awesomestories.* 1928. Accessed at www.awesomestories.com/asset/view/Paul-Dirac-Discoverer-of-Antimatter

Donnelly, Laura. "Your Life Really Does Flash before Your Eyes before You Die, Study Suggests." *The Telegraph.* January 29, 2017. Accessed at www.telegraph.co.uk/news/2017/01/29/life-really-does-flash-eyes-die-study-suggests

Doran, Chris. *Geometric Algebra for Physicists.* Cambridge, UK: Cambridge University Press, 2003.

Dossey, Larry. *Healing Words.* New York: Harper Collins Publishers, 1997.

"Dragonfall" and "atyy". "Effect of Acceleration on Entanglement." *Physics Forums.* 2015. Accessed at www.physicsforums.com/threads/effect-of-acceleration-on-entanglement.829066/

Dreamtime. "Aboriginal Spirituality." *The Eight Aspects of Religion.* Edited by Weebly. 2019. Accessed at http://religioneightaspects.weebly.com/aboriginal-spirituality.html

Dreyfus, Hubert. "Hubert Dreyfus's Views on Artificial Intelligence." *Wikipedia.* 1965–2003. Accessed at https://en.wikipedia.org/wiki/Hubert_Dreyfus%27s_views_on_artificial_intelligence

Eagleman, David. *The Mind Science Foundation Mission.* 1958–2019. Accessed at www.mindscience.org/the-foundation/ (accessed 2019).

Earthing. *What Is Earthing?* Earthing.com. 2019. Accessed at www.earthing.com/what-is-earthing/

Edwards, Lawrence. *Kundalini Research Network.* 1990–2019. Accessed at www.Kundalininet.org/

Einstein, A. "Does the Inertia of the Body Depend upon Its Energy Content." *Annalen der Physik 18* (1905): 639–643.

Einstein, A., B. Podolsky, and N. Rosen. "Can Quantum-Mechanical Description of Physical Reality Be Considered Complete?" *Physical Review* 47, no. 10 (1935): 777–780.

Emoto, Masaru. *The Hidden Messages in Water.* New York: Ataria Books, Beyond Words Publishing, 2005.

Fox, Tobias. *Why Quarks Are Unobservable.* 2009. Accessed at https://philpapers.org/rec/FOXWQA

Fredkin, Ed, Rolf Landauer, and Tom Toffoli. "Workshop on Physics of Computation." *Workshop on Physics of Computation.* Boston: International Journal of Theoretical Physics, 1981.

Fritze, Mike, Patrick Cheetham, Jennifer Lato, and Paul Syers. "The Death of Moore's Law." *The Death of Moore's Law.* Arlington, VA: Potomac Institute for Policy Studies, 2016.

Fung, Frankie, Mykhaylo Usatyuk, B. J. DeSalvo, and Cheng Chin. "Stable Thermophoretic Trapping of Generic Particles at Low Pressures." *Appl. Phys. Lett. 110* (University of Chicago), January 2017.

Gabbatt, Adam. "IBM Computer Watson Wins Jeopardy Clash." *The Guardian*, February 17, 2011. Accessed at www.theguardian.com/technology/2011/feb/17/ibm-computer-watson-wins-jeopardy

Georgiev, Danko D. "The β-Neurexin–Neuroligin Link Is Essential for Quantum Brain Dynamics." *arXiv.org.* Cornell University. August 8, 2006. Accessed at https://arxiv.org/vc/quant-ph/papers/0207/0207093v2.pdf

Golden, Carl. "The 12 Common Archetypes." *Soul Craft Website.* 2019. Accessed at www.soulcraft.co/essays/the_12_common_archetypes.html

Google. "Google Announces a 72-Qubit Superconducting Quantum Chip." Quantum Computing Report, 2018. Accessed at https://quantumcomputingreport.com/news/news-archive-2018/google-announces-a-72-qubit-superconducting-quantum-chip/

—. "Google Buys a Quantum Computer." *New York Times.* May 16, 2013. Accessed at www.dwavesys.com/press/new-york-times-google-buys-quantum-computer

Graff, Dale E., and Patricia S. Cyrus. "Perceiving the Future News: Evidence for Retrocausation." Edited by American Institute of Physics. *AIP Conference Proceedings,* 1–10. Melville, NY: AIP Publishing, 2017.

Green McDonald, Paige, Mary O'Connell, and Susan K. Lutgendorf. "Psychoneuroimmunology and Cancer: A Decade of Discovery, Paradigm Shifts, and Methodological Innovations." *Brain, Behavior, and Immunity* (2013). DOI:10.1016/j.bbi.2013.01.003. Green, Elmer. *Beyond Biofeedback.* New York: A Delta Book, 1978.

Green, Elmer E., Peter A. Parks, Paul M. Guyer, and Steven L. Fahrion, and Lolafaye Coyne. "Anomalous Electrostatic Phenomena in Exceptional Subjects." *Subtle Energies* (ISSSEEM) 2, no. 3 (1991): 244–267.

Green, Hank. "Determinism vs Free Will: Free-Will Crash Course." Crash Course, YouTube Channel, August 15, 2016. Accessed at www.youtube.com/watch?v=vCGtkDzELAI

Grey, Alex. "Alex Grey Art." *alex grey*. 2019. Accessed at www.alexgrey.com/art

Greyson, Bruce. "Near-Death Experiences and the Physio-Kundalini Syndrome." *Journal of Religion and Health* 32, no. 4 (Winter 1993): 277–290.

Grover, Lov K. "A Fast Quantum Mechanical Algorithm for Database Search." *arXiv.or.* May 29, 1996. Accessed at https://arxiv.org/abs/quant-ph/9605043

Hameroff, Stuart. "Center for Consciousness Studies Mission Statement." *Center for Consciousness Studies.* 1994–2019. Accessed at www.consciousness.arizona.edu/mission.htm

—. "Quantum Coherence in Microtubules: A Neural Basis for Emergent Consciousness?" *Journal of Consciousness Studies* 1, no. 1 (1994): 91–118.

Hameroff, Stuart R., Alfred W. Kaszniak, and Alwyn C. Scott. *Toward a Science of Consciousness: The First Tucson Discussions and Debates.* Cambridge, MA: MIT Press, 1992.

Hampton, Debbie. *What's the Difference between Feelings and Emotions?* thebestbrainpossible.com. January 13, 2015. Accessed at www.thebestbrainpossible.com/whats-the-difference-between-feelings-and-emotions/

Hawkins, David R. *Power vs. Force.* Sedona, AZ: Hay House, 1995.

Hawkins, Jeff. "Hierarchical Temporal Memory: Overview." In *Biological and Machine Intelligence (BAMI)*, edited by Jeff Hawkins. Berkeley, CA: Numenta, 2016–2019.

—. "Sparse Distributed Representation." In *Biological and Machine Intelligence (BAMI)*, Living book edited by Jeff Hawkins. Berkeley, CA: Numenta, 2016–2019.

—. "What Is Intelligence, That a Machine Might Have Some?" *UC Berkeley Events.* Berkeley, CA: UC Berkeley Events and Numenta, 2016.

Hawkins, Jeff, and Sandra Blakeslee. *On Intelligence.* Berkeley, CA: Times Books, 2004.

Hawkins, Jeff, et el. *Biological and Machine Intelligence (BAMI).* Berkeley, CA, 2016.

Hayes, Louise. *You Can Heal Your Life.* Sedona, AZ: Hay House, 1984.

HeartMath. *About HeartMath.* 2019. Accessed at www.huffingtonpost.com/heartmath-llc/heart-wisdom_b_2615857.html

—. *HeartMath Mission statement.* 2019. Accessed at www.heartmath.org/about-us/videos/heartmaths-mexico-adventure-heart/

—. *HeartMath Videos.* 2019. Accessed at www.heartmath.org/resources/videos/

—. "Phantom DNA." *bibliotecapleyades.* 1993. Accessed at www.bibliotecapleyades.net/ciencia/ciencia_genetica04.htm

Hicks, Esther. "A Synopsis of Twelve Abraham-Hicks' Teachings." *abraham-hicks.* 2019. Accessed at www.abraham-hicks.com/lawofattractionsource/about_hicks.php

—. "About Abraham." *abraham-hicks.com.* 2019. Accessed at www.abraham-hicks.com/about/

—. *The Law of Attraction.* Sedona, AZ: Hay House, 2006.

Hicks, Esther, and Jerry Hicks. *Ask and It is Given.* Sedona, AZ: Hay House, 2004.

—. *Law of Attraction Books.* Sedona, AZ: Hay House, 1980–2019. Accessed at www.abraham-hickslawofattraction.com/books.html

Hill, Napoleon. *Think and Grow Rich.* Wise, VA: Napoleon Hill Foundation, 1937.

Hoare, C.A.R. "Communicating Sequential Processes." *Communications of the ACM* (Association of Computing Machines) 21, no. 8 (1978): 666–677.

Hodgson, Deborah. *PsychoNeuroImmunology Journal.* 1987–2019. Accessed at www.pnirs.org/society/society_journal.cfm

Hologrammata. "Is the Planck Length the Minimum Possible Length?" *Hologrammata on Github.* February 20, 2017. Accessed at http://rantonels.github.io/is-the-planck-length-the-minimum-possible-length

Houser, Kristin. "Rethinking Space Time Nature." *Futurism.* January 6, 2018. Accessed at https://futurism.com/rethinking-space-time-nature

Hunger, Michael. "Rich Hickey's Datomic Embraces Cloud, Intelligent Applications and Consistency." *InfoQ News.* April 3, 2012. Accessed at www.infoq.com/news/2012/04/datomic

Interstellar. (Video). Directed by Christopher Nolan. Los Angeles: Paramount Pictures, 2014.

IRVA. *IRVA Remote Viewing Conferences.* Irva.org. 2019. Accessed at www.irva.org/conferences/

Jahn, Robert G. "The Persistent Paradox of Psychic Phenomena: An Engineering Perspective." *Proceeding of the IEEE* (IEEE) 70, no. 2 (1982): 136–170.

Jahn, Robert G., Brenda Dunne, and Roger Nelson. *Global Consciousness Project.* Princeton University. 1998–2014. Accessed at http://noosphere.princeton.edu/

—. "Princeton Engineering Anomalies Research (PEAR)." *PSI Encyclopedia.* 1979–2007. Accessed at https://psi-encyclopedia.spr.ac.uk/articles/princeton-engineering-anomalies-research-pear

Jahn, Robert, and Brenda Dunne. *Consciousness and Anomalous Physical Phenomena.* Technical Note PEAR 95004, Engineering, Princeton University. Princeton, NJ: Princeton University, 1995.

Jahn, Robert G., Brenda J. Dunne, and Roger D. Nelson. "Engineering Anomalies Research." *Scientific Exploration* 1, no. 1 (1987): 21–50.

James, Tad, and Wyatt Woodsmall. *Time Line Therapy and the Basis of Personality.* Capitola, CA: Meta-Publications, 1988.

Johnson, Jeremiah. "Special Relativity Using Two Dimensions and Planck Units." *Quora.* November 25, 2017. Accessed at https://gravity-blog.quora.com/Special-Relativity-Using-Two-Dimensions-and-Planck-Units

Johnson, Richard. "A Genius Explains." *The Guardian.* February 11, 2005. Accessed at www.theguardian.com/theguardian/2005/feb/12/weekend7.weekend2

Jovanovic, Pierre. *An Inquiry into the Existence of Guardian Angels: A Journalist's Investigative Report* 1995. New York: M. Evans and Company, Inc.

Kanerva, Pentti. *Sparse Distributed Memory*. Cambridge, MA: A Bradford Book, MIT Press, 1988.

Kelly, Kevin. "The Myth of a Superhuman AI." *Wired*. April 25, 2017. Accessed at www.wired.com/2017/04/the-myth-of-a-superhuman-ai/

Kendrick, Mandy. "Tasting the Light: Device Lets the Blind 'See' with Their Tongues." *Scientific American*. August 2009. Accessed at www.scientificamerican.com/article/device-lets-blind-see-with-tongues/

Ketler, Alanna. "Scientist Demonstrates Fascinating Evidence of Precognitive Dreaming." *Collective Evolution*. January 2019. Accessed at www.collective-evolution.com/2019/01/14/scientist-demonstrates-evidence-of-precognitive-dreaming/

Kollaritsch, Paul, Steve Lusky, Douglas Matzke, Derek Smith, and Paul Stanford. "A Unified Design Representation Can Work." *26th ACM/IEEE Design Automation Conference*. 1989, 811–813.

Kopp, Joachim. "Viewpoint: The Plot Thickens for a Fourth Neutrino." *Physics of APS* 11, no. 122 (November 2018).

Kotsos, Tania. "The Seven Universal Laws Explained." *mind-your-reality*. 2011. Accessed at www.mind-your-reality.com/seven_universal_laws.html

Krasznahorkay, A.J., et al. "Observation of Anomalous Internal Pair Creation in ^{8}Be a Possible Indication of a Light, Neutral Boson." *Physical Review Letters* 116 (January 2016). Accessed at https://journals.aps.org/prl/abstract/10.1103/PhysRevLett.116.042501

"Kundalini Syndrome." *chakras.info*. 2019. Accessed at www.chakras.info/Kundalini-syndrome/

Kurweil, Ray. *The Age of Spiritual Machines: When Computers Exceed Human Intelligence*. New York: Penguin Books, 1999.

LaBerge, Stephen, and Howard Rhiengold. *Exploring the World of Lucid Dreaming*. New York: Ballantine Books, 1990.

LaBerge, Stephen, and Lynne Levitan. "Out-Of-Body Experiences and Lucid Dreams." *Lucidity Institute.* Nightlight Newsletter. 1991. Accessed at www.lucidity.com/NL32.OBEandLD.pdf

Landauer, Rolf. "Irreversibility and Heat Generation in the Computing Process." *IBM Journal of Research and Development* 5, no. 3 (1961): 183–191.

Larkins, Lisette. *Calling on Extraterrestrials.* Newburyport, MA: Hampton Roads, 2003.

—. *Listening to Extraterrestrials.* Newburyport, MA: Hampton Roads, 2004.

—. *Talking to Extraterrestrials.* Newburyport, MA: Hampton Roads, 2002.

Lawrence, P. Nick. *Correlithm Object Technology.* Dallas, TX: Correlithm Publications, 2004.

Lawrence, P. Nick, Matzke, Douglas J., Burgess, and Chandler L. "Representing and Manipulating Correlithm Objects Using Quantum Objects." Patent Number 7,310,622. Dallas, TX, December 18, 2007.

Li, Qing. *Forest Bathing: How Trees Can Help You Find Health and Happiness.* New York: Penguin House, 2018.

LIGO. "LIGO website." *Caltech.* February 2016. Accessed at www.ligo.caltech.edu/news/ligo20160211

Lloyd, Seth. *Programming the Universe: A Quantum Computer Scientist Takes on the Cosmos.* New York: First Vintage Books/Random House, 2006.

Losey, Meg Blackburn. *The Children of Now.* Newburyport, MA: New Page Books, 2006.

Lynley, Matthew. "Google Announces a New Generation for Its TPU Machine Learning Hardware." *Tech Crunch* (Tech Crunch), May 8, 2018. Accessed at https://techcrunch.com/2018/05/08/google-announces-a-new-generation-for-its-tpu-machine-learning-hardware/

Manek, Nisha. *Bridging Science and Spirit: The Genius of William A. Tiller's Physics and the Promise of Information Medicine.* Sedona, AZ: Tom Bird Publisher, 2019.

Manthey, Michael. "Awareness Lies outside Turing's Box." Edited by John C. Amson, 339–368. ANPA Proceedings, Cambridge, UK: ANPA, 2018.

—. "Co-exclusion." *Tauquernions.* 2013. Accessed at www.tauquernions.org/tag/co-exclusion/

—. "Distributed Computation as Hierarchy." *arXiv.org.* September 14, 1998. Accessed at https://arxiv.org/abs/cs/9809019

—. "Distributed Computation, the Twisted Isomorphism, and Auto-Poiesis." *arXiv.org.* 1998. Accessed at https://arxiv.org/pdf/cs/9809125.pdf

Manthey, Michael, and Douglas J. Matzke. *Information, Entropy, and the Combinatorial Hierarchy: Calculations.* In *Scientific Essays in Honor of H. Pierre Noyes on the Occasion of His 90th Birthday,* edited by John C. Amson and Louis H. Kauffman, vol. 54, chap. 15. Singapore: World Scientific, 2014.

—. "TauQuernions: 3+1 Dissipative Space out of Quantum Mechanics." *Tauquernions.* April 2013. Accessed at www.tauquernions.org/wp-content/uploads/2013/04/TauQuernions.pdf

Marks, Kelley. "14 of the Greatest Religious Leaders in History." *owlcation.* January 13, 2019. Accessed at https://owlcation.com/humanities/10-Greatest-Religious-Leaders-in-History

Martin-Martinez, E., L.J. Garay, and J. Leon. "Unveiling Quantum Entanglement Degradation Near a Schwarzschild Black Hole." *arXiv.org.* 2010. Accessed at www.physicsforums.com/threads/effect-of-acceleration-on-entanglement.829066

What the Bleep Do We Know!? (video). Directed by William Arntz and Betty Chasse. Nashua, NH: Captured Light, 2004.

Matzke, Douglas J. "Chi Generators Exist." Edited by ANPA. *Proceedings of ANPA 24.* Cambridge, UK: ANPA, 2002.

—. "Consciousness: A New Computational Paradigm." In *Toward a Science of Consciousness,* edited by Stuart R Hameroff, Alfred W. Kaszniak, and Alwyn C. Scott. 541–542, 569–578. Cambridge: MIT Press, 1994.

—. "Impact of Locality and Dimensionality Limits on Architectural Trends." In *Proceedings of the Workshop on Physics and Computing,* edited by Douglas J. Matzke, 30–35. Richardson, TX: IEEE Computer Society Press, 1994.

—. "Information is Protophysical." In *PhysComp 96 Proceedings, New England Complex Systems Institute*, 223–225 Cambridge, MA: New England Complex Systems Institute, North-Holland: Elsevier, 1996.

—. "Is Quantum Computing a Solution for Semiconductor Scaling?" In *Dallas IEEE Computer Society*. Richardson, TX: Dallas IEEE, 2007.

—. "Math over Mind and Matter." *Quantum Mind II Conference*. Tucson, AZ, 2013.

—. "Prediction: Future Electronic Systems Will Be Disrupted Due to Consciousness." In *Towards a Science of Consciousness, Tucson II*, edited by Stuart R. Hameroff, A. W. Kaszniak, and A. C. Scott, 161–162. Cambridge: MIT Press, 1996.

—. "Premise: Humans Are Biological Quantum Computers." *Annual Mensa Regional Gatherings*. Dallas, TX: North Texas Mensa, 2005.

—. "Proto-physics the Link between Quantum Physics and Metaphysics." *Presented at Cafe MetaPhysics*. Dallas, TX: Quantum Doug, November 17, 2011.

—. *Quantum Computation using Geometric Algebra*. Richardson, TX: University of Texas at Dallas, 2002.

—. "Quantum Doug." *Originally an Article for Prodigy*. 2004. Accessed at www.matzkefamily.net/doug/papers/prodigy.html

—. "Supercomputer Suggests Supermind." *ISSSEEM Bridges* (ISSSEEM 2000 Conference Paper and ISSSEEM Winter 2000 Bridges Paper), Winter 2000.

—. "The Higgs and the Pervasive Nature of Quantum Entanglement (Slides)." *IEEE Computer Society Meeting Presentation*. Richardson, TX: Quantum Doug, March 8, 2013.

—. "The Higgs and the Pervasive Nature of Quantum Entanglement." Video. *Presented at IEEE Computer Society Meeting*. Richardson, TX: Quantum Doug on YouTube, March 8, 2013.

—. "The Higgs and the Pervasive Nature of Quantum Entanglement." Richardson, TX: Dallas IEEE, March 2013.

—. "The Really Hard Problem of Meaning" (abstract only). *Consciousness Conference Paper Tucson 2000.* 2000. Accessed at www.matzkefamily.net/doug/papers/tucson2000.html

—. "Thoughts Are Quantum Things." *Law of Attraction Talk.* Austin, TX, April 12, 2011.

—. "Update on Physical Scalability Sabotaging Performance Gains!" *Dallas IEEE Computer Society Presentation.* Richardson, TX: Dallas IEEE, 2011.

—. "Will Physical Scalability Sabotage Performance Gains?" *IEEE Computer Magazine* 30, no. 9 (September 1997): 37–39.

—.*Workshop on Physics and Computation.* Dallas: IEEE Computer Society Press, 1992.

—.*Workshop on Physics and Computation.* Dallas: IEEE Computer Society Press, 1994.

Matzke, Douglas J., and Lorn L. Howard. *A Model for Providing Computational Resources for the Human Abstraction Process.* Technical Report, Electrical Engineering, Southern Methodist University. Dallas: SMU EE Technical Report, 1986, 1–66.

—. *A Review of Psychical Research at SRI and Princeton University.* Technical Report, Electrical Engineering, Southern Methodist University. Dallas: EE Technical Report Department, 1985, 1–46.

Matzke, Douglas J., Michael Manthey, and Cy D. Cantrell. "Quantum Geometric Algebra." In *Proceedings of ANPA 24,* edited by Keith G. Bowden, 48–72. Cambridge, UK: ANPA, 2002.

Matzke, Douglas J., and P. Nick Lawrence. "Invariant Quantum Ensemble Metrics." In *SPIE Defense and Security Symposium.* Orlando, FL: SPIE Defense and Security Symposium, 2005.

McCraty, Rollin, Mike Atkinson, and Dana Tomasino. "Modulation of DNA Conformation by Heart-Focused Intention." *Heart Math Research Center.* Boulder Creek, CA, 2003.

McMoneagle, Joseph W. *Mind Trek.* Norfolk, VA: Hampton Roads, 1993.

McTaggart, Lynne. *The Field: The Quest for the Secret Force of the Universe.* New York: HarperCollins, 2002, 2008.

—. *The Intention Experiment.* New York: Free Press, 2007.

Mead, C. Alden. "Possible Connection between Gravitation and Fundamental Length." *Phys. Rev.* 135, no. 3B (August 1964): B849–B862.

Mendeleev, Dmitri. "The Dependence between the Properties of the Atomic Weights of the Elements." *Zeitschrift für Chemie,* 1869.

Miller, Suzy. *Awesomism.* 2014–2019. Suzymiller.com. Accessed at https://suzymiller.com/awesomism-i-program/

—. *The Journey Back to Love.* 2019. Suzymiller.com. Accessed at https://suzymiller.com/thejourneybacktolove/

Miller, Suzy, and Sandie Sedgbeer. "Suzy Miller–The Truth About Telepathy, Autism, & Evolution." *What's Going OM.* OMTimes Radio, April 2019. Accessed at www.youtube.com/watch?v=7TghCfAngzQ

Miller, Suzy, Cindy Reed, Fan Tang, Nisha Manek, and William A. Tiller. "Impact of Broadcast Intention on Autism Spectrum Behaviors." *Journal of Alternative and Complementary Medicine* 20, no. 5 (2014): A146.

Monroe, Robert A. *Far Journeys.* 1992.

—. *Journeys Out of the Body.* New York: Doubleday, 1971.

—. *Ultimate Journey.* New York: Random House, 1994.

Moore, Gordon E. "Cramming More components onto Integrated Circuits." *Electronics Magazine* 38, no. 8 (1965): 4.

Moore, Samuel K. "Landauer Limit Demonstrated." *IEEE Spectrum at Spectrum.ieee.org,* 2012. Accessed at https://spectrum.ieee.org/computing/hardware/landauer-limit-demonstrated

Moorjani, Anita. *Dying to Be Me: My Journey from Cancer, to Near Death, to True Healing.* Carlsbad, CA: Hay House, 2014.

Mulford, Prentice. *Thoughts Are Things.* New York: Barnes and Noble, 1989.

Muller, Richard A. "NOW: The Physics of Time." New York: W.W. Norton & Company, 2016.

Musser, George. *Spooky Action at a Distance.* New York: Scientific American, 2015.

Natale, Simone, and Andrea Ballatore. "Imagining the Thinking Machine: Technological Myths and the Rise of Artificial Intelligence." *Convergence,* 2017. https://doi.org/10.1177/1354856517715164

Newport, Frank. "Most Americans Still Believe in God." *Gallup Poll Website.* 2016. Accessed at https://news.gallup.com/poll/193271/americans-believe-god.aspx

Orme-Johnson, David W. "Preventing Crime through the Maharishi Effect." *Journal of Offender Rehabilitation* 36, no. 1–4 (2003): 257–282.

Orstein, Robert E. *On the Experience of Time.* New York: Penguin Books, 1969.

Paulson, Steve. "Roger Penrose on Why Consciousness Does Not Compute." *Nautilus,* May 2017. Accessed at http://nautil.us/issue/47/consciousness/roger-penrose-on-why-consciousness-does-not-compute

Pear Labs, Friends. *Psyleron.* 2005. Accessed at www.psyleron.com

Penrose, Roger. "Roger Penrose – Beyond Algorithms." *Conscious Entities.* 2011. Accessed at www.consciousentities.com/roger-penrose/.

Radin, Dean I. "Electrodermal Presentiments of Future Emotions." *Journal of Scientific Exploration* 18, no. 2 (2004): 253–273.

—. *Real Magic.* New York: Harmony Books, 2018.

—. *Supernormal.* New York: Deepak Chopra Books, 2013.

Radin, Dean I., Leena Michel, Karla Galdamez, Paul Wendland, and Robert Rickenbach. "Consciousness and the Double-Slit Interference Pattern: Six Experiments." *Physics Essays* 25, no. 2 (2013): 157–171.

Radin, Dean I., Lynne I. Mason, and Robert P. Petterson. "Exploratory Study: The Random Number Generator and Group Meditation." *Journal of Scientific Exploration* 21, no. 2 (2007): 295–317.

Ring, Kenneth. *The Omega Project: Near-Death Experiences, UFO Encounters, and Mind at Large* . New York: William Morrow, 1993.

Ryan, Thomas. "25 Percent of US Christians Believe in Reincarnation. What's Wrong with This Picture?" *America Magazine.* October 21, 2015. Accessed at www.americamagazine.org/faith/2015/10/21/25-percent-us-christians-believe-reincarnation-whats-wrong-picture

Salmon, Felix, and Jon Stokes. "Algorithms Take Control of Wall Street." *Wired.com.* December 27, 2010. Accessed at www.wired.com/2010/12/ff-ai-flashtrading/

Schmidt, Helmut. "The Strange Properties of Psychokinesis." *Journal of Scientific Exploration* 1, no. 2 (1987): 103–118.

Schumacher, Benjamin. "Quantum Coding." *Physical Review* A. 51, no. 4 (1995): 2738–2747.

Searle, Rick. *Utopia or Dystopia.* 2011–2019. Accessed at https://utopiaordystopia.com/

Seppala, Emma. "Where the Attention Goes, the Prana Flows." *yogaofrecovery.com.* 2014. Accessed at http://yogaofrecovery.com/2014/03/where-the-attention-goes-the-prana-flows/

Shafton, Anthony. *Dream Reader.* New York: SUNY Press, 1995.

Shannon, Claude. "A Mathematical Theory of Communication." *Bell Labs Technical Journal* 27 (1948): 379–423, 623–656.

Shapiro, Robert. *Are You A Walk-In?* Flagstaff, AZ: Light Technology Publishing, 2016.

Sheldrake, Rupert. *A New Science of Life: The Hypothesis of Morphic Resonance.* New Orleans, LA: Park Street Press, 1981.

—. "Experiments on the Sense of Being Stared At: The Elimination of Possible Artefacts." *Journal of the Society for Psychical Research* 65 (2001): 122–137.

—. "Morphic Resonance and Morphic Fields – An Introduction." *sheldrake.org.* 2019. Accessed at www.sheldrake.org/research/morphic-resonance/introduction

Shor, Peter W. "Algorithms for Quantum Computation: Discrete Logarithms and Factoring." *Proceedings 35th Annual Symposium on Foundations of Computer Science.* Santa Fe: IEEE, 1994, 124-134.

Smalley, Greg. "Men and Intimacy." *iMom Website.* 2019. Accessed at www.imom.com/men-and-intimacy

Sommerlad, Joe. "Google Translate: How Does the Search Giant's Multilingual Interpreter Actually Work?" *Independent.* 2018. Accessed at www.independent.co.uk/life-style/gadgets-and-tech/news/google-translate-how-work-foreign-languages-interpreter-app-search-engine-a8406131.html

Spagna, Lori. *Learn Animal Communication and Telepathy Workbook: Communicate with Your Pets and Any Animal Workbook.* lorispagna.com, 2016.

Steinfels, Peter. "Conversations: Larry Dossey, M.D.: A Doctor Looks to Science for Proof of a Spiritual Realm." *NY Times.* December 19, 1993. Accessed at www.nytimes.com/1993/12/19/weekinreview/conversations-larry-dossey-md-doctor-looks-science-for-proof-spiritual-realm.html

Sutter, Paul. "Are We Living in a Hologram?" *Space.com.* January 2018. Accessed at www.space.com/39510-are-we-living-in-a-hologram.html

Tammet, Daniel. *Born on A Blue Day: Inside the Extraordinary Mind of an Autistic Savant.* New York: Free Press, 2007.

Targ, Russell, and Harold E. Puthoff. *Mind Reach.* Charlottesville, VA: Hampton Roads, 1977.

The Legend of Bagger Vance. Directed by Robert Redford. Los Angeles: Twentieth Century Fox, 2001.

The Matrix. Directed by Lana and Lilly Wachowski. Los Angeles: Warner Bros., 1999.

The Secret (film). Directed by Drew Heriot. Performed by Rhonda Byrne. 2006.

Thomas, Rachel. "It from Bit?" *Plus Magazine,* December 18, 2015. Accessed at https://plus.maths.org/content/it-bit

Tiller, William A. "A Gas Discharge Device for Investigating Focused Human Attention." *Journal of Scientific Explorations* 4, no. 2 (1990): 255–271.

—. *Application of Psychoenergetic Science to 'The Placebo Effect.'* White Paper, Phoenix: Tiller Institute, 2009, 1–14.

—. *Psychoenergetic Science: A Second Copernican-Scale Revolution.* Walnut Creek, CA: Pavior, 2007.

—. *Science and Human Transformation: Subtle Energies, Intentionality, and Consciousness.* Walnut Creek, CA: Pavior, 2007.

—. *Tiller Institute for Psychoenergetic Science.* 2017–2019. Accessed at www.tillerinstitute.com/

—. "Towards a Predictive Model of Subtle Domain Connections to the Physical Domain Aspect of Reality: The Origins of Wave-Particle Duality, Electric-Magnetic Monopoles, and the Mirror Principle." *J. Sci. Expl.* 13, no. 41 (1999).

—. "Towards a Quantitative Science and Technology That Includes Human Consciousness." *The Journal of New Thinking for New Action* 1, no. 4 (2003): 1–35.

—. "Towards an Orthodox Science that Meaningfully Integrates with Psychotherapy & the Healing Arts." *Tiller Institute.* 2015. Accessed at www.tillerinstitute.com/pdf/White%20Paper%20XXIX.pdf

—. "What Are Subtle Energies?" *Journal of Scientific Exploration* 7, no. 3 (1993): 293–304.

Tiller, William A., and Walter E. Dibble. "Electronic Device-Mediated pH Changes in Water." *Journal of Scientific Exploration* 13, no. 2 (1999): 155–176.

—. "New Experimental Evidence Revealing an Unexpected Dimension to Material Science and Engineering?" *Mat. Res. Innov.* 5 (2001): 21–34.

—. "Towards General Experimentation and Discovery in Conditioned Laboratory and Complementary and Alternative Medicine Spaces: Part V, Data on 10 Different Sites Using a Robust New Type of Subtle Energy Detector." *JACM* 13, no. 1 (2007): 133–149.

Tiller, William A., Jean E. Tiller, Walter E. Dibble, Raj Manek, and Nisha Manek. "The Buddha Relics and Evidence of Physical Space Conditioning with Unimprinted Intention Host Devices." *Journal of Alternative and Complementary Medicine* 18, no. 4 (April 2012): 379–381.

Tiller, William A., Walter E. Dibble, and J. Gregory Fandel. *Some Science Adventures with Real Magic.* Walnut Creek, CA: Pavior, 2005.

Tiller, William A., Walter E. Dibble, and M. J. Kohane. *Conscious Acts of Creation: The Emergence of a New Physics.* Walnut Creek, CA: Pavior, 2001.

TM. "Study on the Maharishi Effect: Can group meditation lower crime rate and violence?" *Transcendental Meditation.* 2007–2010. Accessed at https://tmhome.com/benefits/study-maharishi-effect-group-meditation-crime-rate/

Toffoli, Tommaso, Michael Biafore, and Joao Leao. "Fourth Workshop on Physics and Computation." *Proceedings of the Fourth Workshop on Physics and Computation: Boston, November 22–24,* 223–225. Amsterdam: Elsevier, 1998.

Tolle, Eckhart. *The Power of Now: A Guide to Spiritual Enlightenment.* 2004.

Treffert, Darold A. "Brain Gain: A Person Can Instantly Blossom into a Savant—and No One Knows Why." *Scientific American.* July 2018. Accessed at https://blogs.scientificamerican.com/observations/brain-gain-a-person-can-instantly-blossom-into-a-savant-and-no-one-knows-why/

—. "The Case of the 'Sudden' Savant." *wisconsin medical society.* 2010–2019. Accessed at www.wisconsinmedicalsociety.org/professional/savant-syndrome/resources/articles/the-case-of-the-sudden-savant/

Tucker, Jim B. *Life before Life: A Scientific Investigation of Children's Memories of Previous Lives.* New York: St. Martin's Press, 2005.

Valerian, Val. "The Real Matrix — Above and Below." *Leading Edge International Research Group.* 1988–2019. Accessed at http://tru-fax.org/matrix5/segments/intro1.htm

Varey, Carol, and Daniel Kahneman. "Experiences Extended across Time: Evaluation of Moments and Episodes." *Journal of Behavioral Decision Making* (Wiley Online) 5, no. 3 (July/Sept 1992): 169–185.

Villalonga, Benjamin, et al. "Establishing the Quantum Supremacy Frontier with a 281 Pflop/s Simulation." *arXiv.org.* May 1, 2019. Accessed at https://arxiv.org/abs/1905.00444

Vrba, Anton, ed. "Proceedings of Alternate Natural Philosophy Association." *Alternate Natural Philosophy Association.* 1979–2019. Accessed at http://pub.anpa.onl/index.php/procs/index

Waterman, Robert D. *Eyes Made of Soul: The Theory and Practice of Noetic Balancing.* n.p.: Xlibris, 2009.

Weldon, Kathleen. "Paradise Polled: Americans and the Afterlife." *Huffington Post,* December 6, 2017. Accessed at www.huffingtonpost.com/kathleen-weldon/paradise-polled-americans_b_7587538.html

Wheeler, John A. "Information, Physics, Quantum: The Search for Links." In *Complexity, Entropy, and the Physics of Information,* edited by Wojciech Hubert Zurek, 300–336. Boston, MA: Addison-Wesley, 1989.

Whitfield, Barbara Harris. "Kundalini 101: The Energy and How It Works." *Kundalini Research Network.* 1995. Accessed at http://krnweb.blogspot.com/2011/06/Kundalini-101-energy-and-how-it-works.html

Wikipedia. "Akashic Records." *Wikipedia.* 2001–2019. Accessed at https://en.wikipedia.org/wiki/Akashic_records

—. "AlphaGo." *Wikipedia.* 2016. Accessed at https://en.wikipedia.org/wiki/AlphaGo

—. "Anima and animus." *Wikipedia.* 2001–2019. Accessed at https://en.wikipedia.org/wiki/Anima_and_animus

—. "Artificial general intelligence." *Wikipedia.* 2004–2019. Accessed at https://en.wikipedia.org/wiki/Artificial_general_intelligence

—. "Breathwork (New Age)." *Wikipedia.* 2005–2019. Accessed at https://en.wikipedia.org/wiki/Breathwork_(New_Age)

—. "Buddhist logico-epistemology." *Wikipedia.* 2001–2019. Accessed at https://en.wikipedia.org/wiki/Buddhist_logico-epistemology

—. "Chakras." *Wikipedia.* 2001–2019. Accessed at https://en.wikipedia.org/wiki/Chakra

—. "Code Division Multiple Access (CDMA)." *Wikipedia.* 2001–2019. Accessed at https://en.wikipedia.org/wiki/Code-division_multiple_access

—. "Communicating Sequential Processes." *Wikipedia.* 2001–2019. Accessed at https://en.wikipedia.org/wiki/Communicating_sequential_processes

—. "Complex number." *Wikipedia.* 2001–2019. Accessed at https://en.wikipedia.org/wiki/Complex_number

—. "Curse of dimensionality." *Wikipedia.* 2001–2019. Accessed at https://en.wikipedia.org/wiki/Curse_of_dimensionality

—. "Datomic." *Wikipedia.* 2017. Accessed at https://en.wikipedia.org/wiki/Datomic

—. "Deep Blue versus Garry Kasparov." *Wikipedia.* 1997. Accessed at https://en.wikipedia.org/wiki/Deep_Blue_versus_Garry_Kasparov

—. "Deep Learning." *Wikipedia.* 2001–2019. Accessed at https://en.wikipedia.org/wiki/Deep_learning

—. "Double-Slit Experiment." *Wikipedia.* 2001–2019. Accessed at https://en.wikipedia.org/wiki/Double-slit_experiment

—. "Drake Equation." *Wikipedia.* 2001–2019. Accessed at https://en.wikipedia.org/wiki/Drake_equation

—. "Dreamtime." *Wikipedia.* 2002–2019. Accessed at https://en.wikipedia.org/wiki/Dreamtime

—. "Etheric Body." *Wikipedia.* 2001–2019. Accessed at https://en.wikipedia.org/wiki/Etheric_body

—. "Faster than Light." *Wikipedia.* 2001–2019. Accessed at https://en.wikipedia.org/wiki/Faster-than-light

—. "Fermi Paradox." *Wikipedia.* 2001–2019. Accessed at https://en.wikipedia.org/wiki/Fermi_paradox

—. "Fields (Physics)." *Wikipedia.* 2001–2019. Accessed at https://en.wikipedia.org/wiki/Field_(physics)

—. "Flow (Psychology)." *Wikipedia.* 2004–2019. Accessed at https://en.wikipedia.org/wiki/Flow_(psychology)

—. "Fourier Transform." *Wikipedia.* 2001–2019. Accessed at https://en.wikipedia.org/wiki/Fourier_transform

—. "Gravitational Time Dilation." *Wikipedia.* 2001–2019. Accessed at https://en.wikipedia.org/wiki/Gravitational_time_dilation

—. "Helena Blavatsky ." *Wikipedia.* 2001–2019. Accessed at https://en.wikipedia.org/wiki/Helena_Blavatsky

—. "History of Quantum Mechanics." *Wikipedia.* 2007–2019. Accessed at https://en.wikipedia.org/wiki/History_of_quantum_mechanics

—. "History of Subatomic Physics." *Wikipedia.* 2001–2019. Accessed at https://en.wikipedia.org/wiki/History_of_subatomic_physics

—. "Holography." *Wikipedia.* 2001–2019. Accessed at https://en.wikipedia.org/wiki/Holography

—. "Homeopathic Dilutions." *Wikipedia.* 2001–2019. Accessed at https://en.wikipedia.org/wiki/Homeopathic_dilutions

—. "Ingo Swan (see link to Magnetometer psychokinesis tests)." *Wikipedia.* 1972. Accessed at https://en.wikipedia.org/wiki/Ingo_Swann#Magnetometer_psychokinesis_tests

—. "Jungian Archetypes." *Wikipedia.* 2001–2019. Accessed at https://en.wikipedia.org/wiki/Jungian_archetypes

—. "Karnaugh Map." *Wikipedia.* 2001–2019. Accessed at https://en.wikipedia.org/wiki/Karnaugh_map

—. "Kundalini." *Wikipedia.* 2001–2019. Accessed at https://en.wikipedia.org/wiki/Kundalini

—. "Lisp Machines." *Wikipedia.* 2001–2019. Accessed at https://en.wikipedia.org/wiki/Lisp_machine

—. "List of Dreams." *Wikipedia.* 2001–2019. Accessed at https://en.wikipedia.org/wiki/List_of_dreams#Double_Helix_structure_of_DNA

—. "List of Particles." *Wikipedia.* 2001–2019. Accessed at https://en.wikipedia.org/wiki/List_of_particles

—. "Mathematical Formulation of the Standard Model." *Wikipedia.* 2001–2019. Accessed at https://en.wikipedia.org/wiki/Mathematical_formulation_of_the_Standard_Model

—. "Measurement in Quantum Mechanics." *Wikipedia.* 2001–2019. Accessed at https://en.wikipedia.org/wiki/Measurement_in_quantum_mechanics

—. "Memristor." *Wikipedia.* 2007–2019. Accessed at https://en.wikipedia.org/wiki/Memristor

—. "Mind-Body Dualism." *Wikipedia.* 2001–2019. Accessed at https://en.wikipedia.org/wiki/Mind%E2%80%93body_dualism

—. "Neuro-Linguistic Programming." *Wikipedia.* 2001–2019. Accessed at https://en.wikipedia.org/wiki/Neuro-linguistic_programming

—. "New Age." *Wikipedia.* 2001–2019. Accessed at https://en.wikipedia.org/wiki/New_Age

—. "Nostradamus." *Wikipedia.* 2001–2019. Accessed at https://en.wikipedia.org/wiki/Nostradamus

—. "Occam's Razor." *Wikipedia.* 2001–2019. Accessed at https://en.wikipedia.org/wiki/Occam%27s_razor

—. "Parseval's Identity." *Wikipedia.* 2001–2019. Accessed at https://en.wikipedia.org/wiki/Parseval%27s_identity

—. "Penrose–Hawking Singularity Theorems." *Wikipedia.* 2001–2019. Accessed at https://en.wikipedia.org/wiki/Penrose%E2%80%93Hawking_singularity_theorems

—. "Pentaquark." *Wikipedia.* 2015. Accessed at https://en.wikipedia.org/wiki/Pentaquark

—. "Physics beyond the Standard Model." *Wikipedia.* 2001–2019. Accessed at https://en.wikipedia.org/wiki/Physics_beyond_the_Standard_Model

—. "Planck Time." *Wikipedia.* 2001–2019. Accessed at https://en.wikipedia.org/wiki/Planck_time

—. "Planck Units." *Wikipedia.* 2001–2019. Accessed at https://en.wikipedia.org/wiki/Planck_units

—. "Prana." *Wikipedia.* 2001–2019. Accessed at https://en.wikipedia.org/wiki/Prana

—. "Pranayama." *Wikipedia.* 2004–2019. Accessed at https://en.wikipedia.org/wiki/Pranayama

—. "Prism." *Wikipedia.* 2001–2019. Accessed at https://en.wikipedia.org/wiki/Prism

—. "Probability Amplitude." *Wikipedia.* 2001–2019. Accessed at https://en.wikipedia.org/wiki/Probability_amplitude

—. "Projection (Mathematics)." *Wikipedia.* 2001–2019. Accessed at https://en.wikipedia.org/wiki/Projection_(mathematics)

—. “Pyramidal Cell.” *Wikipedia.* 2004–2019. Accessed at https://en.wikipedia.org/wiki/Pyramidal_cell

—. “QFT.” *Wikipedia.* 2001–2019. Accessed at https://en.wikipedia.org/wiki/Quantum_field_theory

—. “Quantum Decoherence.” *Wikipedia.* 2001–2019. Accessed at https://en.wikipedia.org/wiki/Quantum_decoherence

—. “Quantum Nonlocality.” *Wikipedia.* 2001–2019. Accessed at https://en.wikipedia.org/wiki/Quantum_nonlocality

—. “Random Number Generation.” *Wikipedia.* 2005–2019. Accessed at https://en.wikipedia.org/wiki/Random_number_generation

—. “Savant Syndrome.” *Wikipedia.* 2001–2019. Accessed at https://en.wikipedia.org/wiki/Savant_syndrome

—. “Schrödinger Equation.” *Wikipedia.* 2001–2019. Accessed at https://en.wikipedia.org/wiki/Schr%C3%B6dinger_equation

—. “Scientific Method.” *Wikipedia.* 2001–2019. Accessed at https://en.wikipedia.org/wiki/Scientific_method

—. “Scientism.” *Wikipedia.* 2002–2019. Accessed at https://en.wikipedia.org/wiki/Scientism

—. “Siddhi.” *Wikipedia.* 2003–2019. Accessed at https://en.wikipedia.org/wiki/Siddhi

—. “Simulation Hypothesis.” *Wikipedia.* 2007–2019. Accessed at https://en.wikipedia.org/wiki/Simulation_hypothesis

—. “Spacetime Light Cone.” *Wikipedia.* 2001–2019. Accessed at https://en.wikipedia.org/wiki/Spacetime#Light_cone

—. “Stanley Krippner.” *Wikipedia.* 2006–2019. Accessed at https://en.wikipedia.org/wiki/Stanley_Krippner

—. “Stargate Project.” *Wikipedia.* 2003–2019. Accessed at https://en.wikipedia.org/wiki/Stargate_Project

—. “Stuart Hameroff.” *Wikipedia.* 2001–2019. Accessed at https://en.wikipedia.org/wiki/Stuart_Hameroff

—. “The Magical Number Seven, Plus or Minus Two.” *Wikipedia.* 1956. Accessed at https://en.wikipedia.org/wiki/The_Magical_Number_Seven,_Plus_or_Minus_Two

—. “The Secret Doctrine.” *Wikipedia.* 2001–2019. Accessed at https://en.wikipedia.org/wiki/The_Secret_Doctrine

—. "Transcendental Meditation." *Wikipedia.* 2001–2019. Accessed at https://en.wikipedia.org/wiki/Transcendental_Meditation

—. "Truly Neutral Particle." *Wikipedia.* 2001–2019. Accessed at https://en.wikipedia.org/wiki/Truly_neutral_particle

—. "Turing Completeness." *Wikipedia.* 2001–2019. Accessed at https://en.wikipedia.org/wiki/Turing_completeness

—. "Turing Machine." *Wikipedia.* 2001–2019. Accessed at https://en.wikipedia.org/wiki/Turing_machine

—. "Universe." *Wikipedia.* 2001–2019. Accessed at https://en.wikipedia.org/wiki/Universe

—. "von Neumann Architecture." *Wikipedia.* 2001–2019. Accessed at https://en.wikipedia.org/wiki/Von_Neumann_architecture

Williams, Kevin R. "The Tunnel and the Near-Death Experience." *near-death.com.* 2016. Accessed at www.near-death.com/science/research/tunnel.html

Wolf, Fred Alan. *The Yoga of Time Travel.* Wheaton, IL: Quest Books, 2004.

Worth, Josh. "Stop Calling It Artificial Intelligence." *josh-worth.* February 10, 2016. Accessed at www.joshworth.com/stop-calling-in-artificial-intelligence/

Zhang, J., et al. "Observation of a Discrete Time Crystal." *Nature.* March 8, 2017. Accessed at www.nature.com/articles/nature21413

Ziesenis, Randy. *About Me Randy Ziesenis.* 2019. Accessed at https://about.me/rziesenis

About the Authors

William A. Tiller, PhD, born September 18, 1929, in Toronto, Canada, received his doctorate in physical metallurgy at the University of Toronto in 1955. He then worked as a research scientist and advisory physicist at Westinghouse Research Laboratories. In 1964, Dr. Tiller accepted a professorship at Stanford University in the Department of Material Science, becoming chairman of that department in 1966.

At Stanford, Dr. Tiller began personal investigations of human consciousness and the potential for inner enlightenment through meditation. While on sabbatical a few years later, Dr. Tiller realized that future science needed a competent US investigator to seriously commit long-term to both experimental and theoretical investigations of psychoenergetic phenomena, an area then anathema to the conventions of science. Dr. Tiller's subsequent scientific experiments led him to the conclusion that human consciousness and intention can significantly influence physical reality. He also came across fragmentary experimental data from psychoenergetic studies conducted at various locations around the world over the past two centuries, which combined to further substantiate his theory.

Unwilling to entrust his accumulating data to another researcher, Dr. Tiller returned to Stanford but gave up the chairmanship of his department, as well as most of his committee work, in order to pursue formal research of psychoenergetics that would be complement his traditional research at Stanford. Although Jean—his wife and meditation partner for fifty years—solidly supported his work on psychoenergetics, most of his Stanford colleagues staunchly opposed it.

Dr. Tiller spent thirty-four years in academia: taught graduate-level classes in thermodynamics, kinetics, phase transformation, and semiconductor processing; supervised more than fifty doctoral theses; was either principle investigator or co-principle investigator on $10 million-budget DOD and NASA contracts; served on numerous professional and government committees; consulted with many industrial corporations; and published more than two hundred conventional scientific papers and three books. In 1992, Stanford University named Dr. Tiller professor emeritus of the Department of Materials Science and Engineering.

For more than fifty years, Dr. Tiller has pursued serious experimental and theoretical study of the field of psychoenergetics, publishing more than 150 scientific papers and four seminal books in this area. Dr. William A. Tiller is a fellow of the American Academy for the Advancement of Science and was a founding director of the Academy of Parapsychology and Medicine and the Institute of Noetic Science. In 2015, he founded the WAT Foundation for Human Intention Applications to show that intention affects the familiar world in ways that can solve today's problems.

For more information on Dr. Tiller's work or to participate in his research, please visit Dr. Tiller's nonprofit research foundation: www.tillerfoundation.org/

Douglas J. Matzke, PhD, was born April 29, 1953, in Green Bay, Wisconsin. Dr. Matzke entered computer engineering and computer science more than fifty years ago, when he started programming in high school in 1968. In college, Dr. Matzke started researching the engineering aspects of metaphysics, because if psi exists, then physics must be expanded to comprehend it. He earned a bachelor's degree from the University of Wisconsin in 1975 and a master's degree from the University of Texas in 1980, both in electrical engineering, before earning a doctorate in quantum computing from the University of Texas in 2002. His master's and doctorate theses were, respectively, *Biofeedback Using Home Computers* and *Quantum Computing Using Geometric Algebra.*

From 1976 through 2001, Dr. Matzke worked at Texas Instruments, where he worked on design tools for semiconductor-based computers and helped create the "Lisp Chip," a DARPA-funded chip that won the prestigious 1987 ISSCC Best Paper award for best chip of the year. After being promoted to TI Senior Member of the Technical Staff in 1990, he was chairman of PhysComp '92 and PhysComp '94, two Dallas workshops on physics and computation. He has published more than fifty papers and presentations throughout his career, most notably the lead-off article entitled "Will Physical Scalability Sabotage Performance Gains?" for the 1997 *Computer Magazine* special issue on Billion Transistor Processors.

Starting in 2001, Dr. Matzke worked at Lawrence Technologies as principle investigator for $1 million SBIR contracts on quantum and neural computing. Overall, he received eight issued patents, including some on high-dimensional math-based neural networks and the intersection of quantum and correlithm neural computing. Since 2006, Dr. Matzke has been employed full-time creating advanced applications using the Python programming language.

On the personal side, Dr. Matzke spent the mid-1990s helping to market Dr. Yuri Kronos's "Vital Energy Tapes," which had been filled with prana. During the 2000s, he trained in multiple subtle energy modalities and graduated in 2010 with the certificate of Master Practitioner in Neural Linguistic Programming (NLP). Since 2010, in his personal time, he continued to research the use of geometric algebra for quantum computing as related to the Standard Model, entanglement, Higgs boson, dark energy, and dark matter. He regularly lectures at conferences on quantum computing, geometric algebra, hyperdimensional math, quantum mind, quantum thoughts, and metaphysics topics, while creating YouTube videos of some of those lectures. He meditates and has taken yoga classes for many years. He has been singing for twenty-five years with the thirteen-time international men's chorus champion of Dallas, The Vocal Majority Chorus.

For more information, see www.quantumdoug.com and www.DeepRealityBook.com.

Index

(**bold**=illustration/table; *italic*=Glossary)

Made in the USA
Las Vegas, NV
18 May 2022